Optimum and Equilibrium for Regional Economies
Collected Papers of Noboru Sakashita

Springer
Berlin
Heidelberg
New York
Barcelona
Budapest
Hong Kong
London
Milan
Paris
Santa Clara
Singapore
Tokyo

Komei Sasaki (Ed.)

Optimum and Equilibrium for Regional Economies

Collected Papers of Noboru Sakashita

Springer

Editor

Prof. Dr. Komei Sasaki
Tohoku University
Graduate School of Information Sciences
Katahira 2, Aoba-ku
Sendai 980, Japan

Author

Prof. Dr. Noboru Sakashita
University of Tsukuba
Institute of Socio-Economic Planning
Tsukuba, Ibaraki 305, Japan

Die Deutsche Bibliothek - CIP-Einheitsaufnahme

Sakashita, Nōbōru:
Optimum and equilibrium for regional economies : collected papers of Noboru Sakashita / Komei Sasaki (ed.). - Berlin ; Heidelberg ; New York ; Barcelona ; Budapest ; Hong Kong ; London ; Milan ; Paris ; Santa Clara ; Singapore ; Tokyo : Springer, 1996

NE: Sasaki, Kōmei [Hrsg.]; Sakashita, Nōbōru: [Sammlung <engl.>]

ISBN-13: 978-3-642-80137-2 e-ISBN-13: 978-3-642-80135-8
DOI: 10.1007/ 978-3-642-80135-8

Softcover reprint of the hardcover 1st edition 1996

SPIN 10532520 42/2202 - 5 4 3 2 1 0 – Printed on acid-free paper

Introduction

This volume reproduces some important contributions to regional and urban economics made by Noboru Sakashita – one of the leading scholars in this field. Since graduation from the University of Tokyo, Noboru Sakashita has been teaching and advancing the research at Hokkaido University, Tohoku University, Osaka University and the University of Tsukuba.

The career of Noboru Sakashita as a regional and urban economist started in 1965 when he visited the University of Pennsylvania's Regional Science Department as a Fulbright scholar. While staying there, he concentrated on research on regional science in a stimulative atmosphere surrounded by Walter Isard, the founder of Regional Science, and Isard's young colleagues, all of who were full of passion for this newborn research field. The first two papers in this volume were written during his stay at the University of Pennsylvania. Since returning to Japan, he has been carrying out his own research activities as well as fostering many promising disciplines in the field of regional and urban economics. Of course, Noboru Sakashita is a world renowned famous scholar, presenting many influential papers at World Congress, North American and European Meetings of the Regional Science Association, and other conferences, and publishing many articles in respected journals. He was elected president of the Regional Science Association International for 1987–88, and served as the first president of the Applied Regional Science Conference from 1987 to 1989.

The academic contribution of Noboru Sakashita is characterized by the following three distinguished features:

1. demonstrating rigorous theoretical analysis
2. modeling practical subjects
3. providing methodology for policy evaluation.

These are all important and indispensable features to regional science which intends to solve various real world regional problems scientifically. Noboru Sakashita is not a pure theorist, although he is an excellent theorist. His research has been strongly motivated by real problems of regional and urban economy. We are impressed to see that in his many papers, theoretical analysis is complemented by empirical or numerical simulation analysis so that the meaning of theoretical models can be fully understood.

We will introduce several articles which seem to reflect clearly Sakashita's characteristics. The paper – *Production Function, Demand Function and Location Theory of the Firm* – generalized the previous location-choice model by allowing the simultaneous choice of production technology and location under the substitutability among inputs. As one of the basic works in location theory, this paper still attracts many readers even though it was written twenty seven years ago. Two papers on *National Growth and Regional Income Inequality* are also types of rigorous theoretical analysis of regional economics: they showed that there is no trade-off relation between national economic growth and regional income equality under a proper measure of regional disparity. As for models of practical subjects, two papers can be cited: *Economics of Multi-habitation* and *Optimal Utilization of the Central Business District with Economy and Diseconomy of Agglomeration.* The former article was intended to explore the rationale of multi-habitation policy in Japan as a measure of population dispersion from the viewpoint of regional economic theory. Readers might be surprised that this topic is tackled from the standpoint of optimizing allocation of living time. The latter article is concerned with agglomeration economy and diseconomy of a CBD in a city, arguing the measure for utilizing the function of a CBD efficiently. Both *Distributional Biases in the Welfare Pricing of Public Transport Service* and *Evaluation of Regional Development Policy* are policy-oriented papers although they are theoretical analyses. In the first paper, public transport pricing is treated in an attempt to integrate welfare pricing theory and public investment decision theory. The second paper compares alternative regional development policies to attain a desired regional population distribution from the point of view of social costs as well as the amount of subsidy needed. The only empirical study in this volume, *Urban Growth Analysis in Postwar Japan* is an excerpt from the comprehensive analysis of urban dynamics in postwar Japan undertaken by Sakashita and his research group at Japan's Economic Planning Agency. In this paper, Hoover indices for Japanese cities for 1955–1975 are used intensively to show the tendency of population to concentrate in a few metropolitan areas despite the U-turn or J-turn population phenomenon during the period considered.

In 1996, Noboru Sakashita will retire from the University of Tsukuba. The publication of these collected papers was planned by his colleagues, students, and friends to commemorate his retirement. Even after retirement from the University of Tsukuba, Noboru Sakashita will continue research and education of regional and urban economics. We hope these collected papers will stimulate young scholars particularly so that they will further evolve regional and urban economics study.

Komei Sasaki

Contents

Papers of the Regional Science Association, Arizona, Vol. 19 (1967) 161–182

REGIONAL ALLOCATION OF PUBLIC INVESTMENT

NOBORU SAKASHITA, Tohoku University, Japan

In many countries, the allocation of public funds among regions to promote the social capital formation in each regional unit is becoming one of the most important decisions by the central government. In spite of the significance of this problem, however, there is scarcely any definite guiding principle for the efficient regional allocation of public investment even in a theoretical sense. The causes of this may be explained as follows.

On the one hand, those regions which have almost the same set of industries in each territory lack the complementarity to each other existing in a related system of many industries. So some simple optimizing criterion like the maximization of total national income may easily lead to a very extreme and unpractical (if not unrealistic) conclusion. We can observe this phenomenon in some of the Rahman-type models of investment allocation.[1]

On the other hand, the regional allocation of public funds may be typically a political rather than economic problem, especially in the presence of conflicting provincialism among the regions. In these cases, an efficiency criterion of the allocation will be powerless (if not useless) in persuading the interested participants to reach a rational conclusion.

Granting that these difficulties are extremely hard to overcome, we still need some guidepost capable of examining the desirability of particular regional allocation policies taken by the central government. Without such an efficiency guidepost, every decision on such matters will be made on the *ad hoc* basis and, in the long run, may bring a tremendous waste of resources.

In the present paper, a pair of models will be proposed to evaluate the effect of regional allocation of public investment on the growth pattern of a multiregion economy.[2] The difference between the two models comes from different presumptions on the productivity of the public investment.

In the first model, it is assumed that the public investment has no direct productivity, but it contributes to raising the productivity of the private capital

---

The author is a postdoctoral fellow with the University of Pennsylvania. The present paper is a product of his research on the basic theory of regional growth which has been supported by a grant from the Ford Foundation. This support is gratefully acknowledged. He is indebted to Professors W. Isard, B. H. Stevens, and J. Kissin for their valuable comments on the earlier draft of this paper. Of course, the author alone is responsible for any remaining errors.

[1] Rahman, Md. Anisur, "Regional Allocation of Investment," *Quarterly Journal of Economics*, LXXVII, No. 1, February, 1963, pp. 26-39.

———, "Regional Allocation of Investment: The Continuous Version," *Quarterly Journal of Economics*, LXXX, No. 1, February, 1966, pp. 159-60.

[2] Our analysis, however, will be concentrated on the cases of two-region economy for the sake of simplicity. The results obtained in a two-region model can be generalized into those of three or more regions without essential difficulty. 1

through its externality effect. We call this type the social overhead investment or the Hirschman-type public investment.[3]

In the second model, the public investment is assumed to possess a direct productivity effect as does the private investment, and we call this category the investment by public enterprises or the Musgrave-type public investment.[4]

Of course, we cannot suppose any clear-cut borderline between those two categories of public investment. But this distinction is useful, at least, for the analysis of the perturbation effect of public investment on the process of economic growth, because each presumption requires a different technique of analysis.

THE CASE OF SOCIAL OVERHEAD INVESTMENT

Growth Pattern in a Two-Region Economy

If we neglect the activity of the public sector in a two-region economy for a while, the supply of funds for investment in the economy will be limited to the sum of private savings in each region. In addition, if we take a neoclassical point of view, this sum will be divided into the realized investments in respective regions. The shares of the realized investment in each region, λ and $1-\lambda$, will be determined by some market mechanism that is far from being easily identified.

In theory, there is no reason to assume λ to be a constant over time. But, in practice, we may consider it as a relatively stable parameter for a certain length of time compared to other fluctuating economic variables. In other words, it will be permitted to apply a technique of piece-wise linearization as to the intertemporal change of the value of λ, and we wish to take advantage of this convenience.

The realized investment in each region will have an incremental productivity effect on the same region's aggregate income, and this effect will be measured by a certain output-capital ratio of the region. The increased income of the region will, in turn, determine the amount of the region's saving in the next period.

The preceding discussion may result in a following system of differential equations as a descriptive model of the two-region economy.

Parameters

$s_i =$ the saving ratio in region $i (i = 1, 2)$,

$\sigma_i =$ the incremental output-capital ratio in region $i (i = 1, 2)$, and

$\lambda =$ the proportion of private investment shared to the first region $(0 \leqq \lambda \leqq 1)$.

Variables

[3] Hirschman, Albert O., *The Strategy of Economic Development* (New Haven: Yale University Press, 1958), chap. 5.

[4] Musgrave, Richard A., *The Theory of Public Finance: A Study in Public Economy* (New York: McGraw-Hill, 1959), chap. 20, C.

$x, y =$ the regional incomes of the first and the second regions,
$z = x + y =$ the national income, and
$W = x - y =$ the regional income disparity.

$$\frac{dx}{dt} = \sigma_1\lambda(s_1x + s_2y) \tag{1}$$

$$\frac{dy}{dt} = \sigma_2(1-\lambda)(s_1x + s_2y) \,. \tag{2}$$

The above two equations are not independent of each other, so some special treatment is needed for the solution, see Mathematical Appendix A. The final solutions are

$$x = \frac{\sigma_1\lambda(s_1x_0 + s_2y_0)}{g} e^{gt} - \frac{s_2\{\sigma_1\lambda y_0 - \sigma_2(1-\lambda)x_0\}}{g} \tag{3}$$

$$y = \frac{\sigma_2(1-\lambda)(s_1x_0 + s_2y_0)}{g} e^{gt} + \frac{s_1\{\sigma_1\lambda y_0 - \sigma_2(1-\lambda)x_0\}}{g} \tag{4}$$

where x_0 and y_0 are the initial values of x and y, and

$$g = s_1\sigma_1\lambda + s_2\sigma_2(1-\lambda) \,. \tag{5}$$

The growth path of the aggregate income in this two-region economy will be expressed as

$$z = x + y = \alpha\beta(e^{gt} - 1) + (x_0 + y_0) \tag{6}$$

where

$$\alpha = (s_1x_0 + s_2y_0)$$

$$\beta = \frac{\sigma_1\lambda + \sigma_2(1-\lambda)}{s_1\sigma_1\lambda + s_2\sigma_2(1-\lambda)} \,.$$

On the other hand, the time behavior of the discrepancy between two regions' incomes will be given as

$$W = x - y = \alpha\gamma(e^{gt} - 1) + (x_0 - y_0) \tag{7}$$

where

$$\gamma = \frac{\sigma_1\lambda - \sigma_2(1-\lambda)}{s_1\sigma_1\lambda + s_2\sigma_2(1-\lambda)} \,.$$

If we assume that the labor force is immobile among regions, W can be taken as an approximation of the discrepancy in the regions' per capita incomes.

Disaggregation of σ_i and λ

There may be little vagueness about the implications of such parameters as s_1 and s_2 in the formulation of the preceding model. But further explanation will be needed as to the composition of σ_i and λ in the same model.

Suppose there are R industries in this two-region economy; each of which has incremental output-capital ratios of σ_{1j} and σ_{2j} in region 1 and 2 respectively, $(j = 1, \ldots, R)$. In addition, let r_j be the share of j-industry in the nationwide, 3 private capital formation ($\sum_{j=1}^{R} r_j \equiv 1$), and $\lambda_{1j} : (1 - \lambda_{1j})$ be the regional allocation ratio of the investment in j-industry.

Under the assumptions of over time constancy of σ_{1j}, σ_{2j}, r_j, and λ_{1j} $(j = 1, \ldots, R)$, constant aggregate parameters σ_1, σ_2 and λ will be given as

$$\sigma_1 = \frac{\sum_{j=1}^{R} r_j \lambda_{1j} \sigma_{1j}}{\sum_{j=1}^{R} r_j \lambda_{1j}} \tag{8}$$

$$\sigma_2 = \frac{\sum_{j=1}^{R} r_j (1 - \lambda_{1j}) \sigma_{2j}}{\sum_{j=1}^{R} r_j (1 - \lambda_{1j})} \tag{9}$$

$$\lambda = \sum_{j=1}^{R} r_j \lambda_{1j} \, . \tag{10}$$

Then, we have detailed expressions for $\sigma_1 \lambda$ and $\sigma_2(1 - \lambda)$ as

$$\sigma_1 \lambda = \sum_{j=1}^{R} r_j \lambda_{1j} \sigma_{1j} \tag{11}$$

$$\sigma_2 (1 - \lambda) = \sum_{j=1}^{R} r_j (1 - \lambda_{1j}) \sigma_{2j} \, . \tag{12}$$

It may not be so implausible to assume that r_j's are absolutely constant over time, i. e., they would not change even if such parameters as σ_{ij}'s have changed.[5]

[5] Here, we are thinking that the interindustry allocation of total investment fund depends only upon the industrial composition of the incremental final demand in a nation-wide setting that is assumed to be stable over time, and that the increase in capital productivities by the social overhead investment is uniform over different industries in the sense that even this increase does not change the values of r_z's.

In this context, it must be noticed that σ_{ij} is not the same thing as the marginal efficiency of investment in industry j in region i. σ_{ij} is nothing more than the ratio of the increase in value-added created by the new investment to the latter. Let c_{ij} be the incremental physical output-capital ratio and l_{ij} be the incremental physical labor-capital ratio corresponding to σ_{ij}. In addition, let p_{ij} be the price of the product of industry j in region i, k_{ij} be the intermediate unit cost of the same product excluding the labor cost, w_i be the wage rate in region i, and p_c be the uniform price of capital goods. Then σ_{ij} can be expressed as

$$\sigma_{ij} = \frac{(p_{ij} - k_{ij}) c_{ij}}{p_c} \, .$$

On the other hand, the profitability of investment, π_{ij}, will be given by an expression of

$$\pi_{ij} = \frac{(p_{ij} - k_{ij}) c_{ij} - w_i l_{ij}}{p_c} \, .$$

Such being the case, the equilibrium condition of the interregional and interindustrial flow of capital fund is the equality of π_{ij}'s for all i and all j, not that of σ_{ij}'s. This is the reason why we can have different values of σ_{ij} among i and j at an equilibrium compatible with nonzero values of all λ_{ij}'s.

But on the contrary, it may be more natural to assume certain dependency of λ_{1j} upon the relative size of σ_{1j} and σ_{2j}. If an industry (k) is producing very local commodities such as perishable foods or house repair services, the share parameter λ_{1k} may be almost insensitive to the change of σ_{1k} and σ_{2k}, because only the amounts of local demands for those commodities are relevant to the investment allocation. On the other hand, if the products of another industry (m) have a greater mobility, λ_{1m} should be regarded as a function of the relative sizes of σ_{1m} and σ_{2m}, and the simplest form of this function will be an all-or-nothing criterion, i.e., $\lambda_{1m}=1$ if $\sigma_{1m}>\sigma_{2m}$ and $\lambda_{1m}=0$ if $\sigma_{1m}<\sigma_{2m}$.[6]

In general, we can assume the following practical relationship between λ_{1j} and $(\sigma_{1j}-\sigma_{2j})$.

$$\lambda_{1j}=\begin{cases}1 & \text{if } \tilde{\lambda}_{1j}>1\\ \tilde{\lambda}_{1j}=\lambda_{1j}^{0}+\mu(\sigma_{1j}-\sigma_{2j}) & \text{if } 0\leqq\tilde{\lambda}_{1j}\leqq 1\\ 0 & \text{if } \tilde{\lambda}_{1j}<0\,.\end{cases} \tag{13}$$

where $0\leqq\lambda_{1j}^{0}\leqq 1$. The extreme case of perfectly local commodities may be explained by setting $\mu=0$, and the other extreme case of all-or-nothing criterion may also be included in this formula with a large positive value of μ.

Impact of Social Overhead Investment

Some realized projects of social overhead investment at the initial period in one or both of two regions will influence almost all items in the expression of (6) or (7).

First, they may raise the value of α, the national saving at the initial period, and that of (x_0+y_0), the national income at the initial period, through the improvement in the productivity of already installed private capital stock

[6] We can develop this functional relationship more precisely by the use of the expression for π_{ij} in the previous footnote. It is plausible to assume p_{1j} as a decreasing function of λ_{1j} and p_{2j} as an increasing function of the same variable under a given growth pattern of the demands for the product of the j-industry in each region.

By the simplest assumption of a linear relationship of p_{ij}'s on λ_{1j}, the equilibrium of the interregional condition capital flow in the j-industry is given as

$$\pi_{1j}=\frac{\{(p_{1j}^{0}-q_{1j}\lambda_{1j})-k_{1j}\}c_{1j}-w_1l_{1j}}{p_c}=\frac{\{(p_{2j}^{0}-q_{2j}(1-\lambda_{1j}))-k_{2j}\}c_{2j}-w_2l_{2j}}{p_c}=\pi_{2j}\,.$$

Then we have the following relation in the case of interior solution for λ_{1j},

$$\lambda_{1j}=\frac{1}{q_{1j}c_{1j}+q_{2j}c_{2j}}[(q_{2j}c_{2j}+w_2l_{2j}-w_1l_{1j})+\{(p_{1j}^{0}-k_{1j})c_{1j}-(p_{2j}^{0}-k_{2j})c_{2j}\}]$$

which can be well approximated by equation (13).

Large values of q_{1j} and q_{2j} should be assumed for the local industry, and smaller values of them should correspond to the industries with the products of greater mobility.

in each region.[7] Second, the value of β will be influenced through the changes of σ_1, σ_2 and λ, and the latter changes will also give a different value of g.

β is the reciprocal of a weighted average of s_1 and s_2, and its change is limited within an interval between the maximum and the minimum of $[1/s_1, 1/s_2]$. α and $(x_0 + y_0)$ may have more substantial changes compared to that of β, but the only outcomes of these changes (increases) are some upward shifts in the path of national income growth. This is not cumulative.

After all, the most important change which should be traced in our comparative dynamics study is that of the composite growth rate g, at least for the long run. If we adopt a criterion of national income maximization for the regional allocation of social overhead investment, g must be our long-run target of maximization.

The impact of social overhead investment on g is a complicated mixture of its impacts on σ_{ij} and λ_{ij}. Refraining from more general cases, we shall only consider a simple two-region, two-industry case where the following assumptions are met: $u =$ the proportion of social overhead investment which goes to the first region, $(0 \leqq u \leqq 1)$. It is assumed that all proposed projects of social overhead investment are realized at or before the initial period when

---

[7] We can visualize the effect of social overhead investment on the productivities of private industries by a model of input-output relation. An economy would enjoy the following bill of final commodities $\hat{y} = (\hat{y}_1, \hat{y}_2, \ldots, \hat{y}_n)'$ if all its industries could operate at the normal levels of production $\hat{x} = (\hat{x}_1, \hat{x}_2, \ldots, \hat{x}_n)'$, ("$'$" means the transposition of a vector), i. e, $\hat{y} = [I - A]\hat{X}$ where A is the matrix of input-output coefficients and I is an identity matrix of n-order. For each industry, there is a *normal* value of *gross* productivity coefficient which is equivalent to its output-capital ratio of

$c_i = \dfrac{\hat{x}_i}{k_i}$, $i = 1, \ldots, n$, where k_i is the amount of capital stock in i-industry.

However, if we have the shortage of some social overhead capital that serves as a primary factor-input for the industries with primary input coefficients of $v_i (i = 1, \ldots, n.)$, the levels of production must obey the constraint of $\sum_{i=1}^{n} v_i x_i \leqq V$ where V implies the available amount of the same social overhead capital. We are thinking a situation where $\sum_{i=1}^{n} v_i \hat{x}_i > V$.

One way to meet the above constraint is to cut down all production levels by a common rate of $h (0 < h < 1)$ to have an equation of

$\sum_{i=1}^{n} v_i (h\hat{x}_i) = V$. In this case, *actual* values of the gross productivity coefficients will be

$$c_i^* = \frac{h\hat{x}_i}{k_i} = hc_i, \; i = 1, \ldots, n.$$

Under these situations, a removal of the shortage of this social overhead capital by an additional investment in it will raise the values of the gross productivity coefficients from their suppressed levels of c_i^* to their normal levels of c_i. At the same time we shall see corresponding increases in the *actual* values of the *net* productivity coefficients (σ_i) for those industries, although we may need a dollar's-worth input-output table for the calculation of those *net* coefficients.

This is an explanation of the effect of social overhead investment on the productivity of private capital.

our tracing of growth paths begins.
The impacts on σ_{ij} ($i = 1, 2$: Region, $j = 1, 2$: Industry).

$$\sigma_{11} = \sigma_{11}^0(1 + \delta u), \ \sigma_{21} = \sigma_{21}^0(1 + \delta(1 - u)) \tag{14}$$

$$\sigma_{12} = \sigma_{12}^0(1 + \delta u), \ \sigma_{22} = \sigma_{22}^0(1 + \delta(1 - u)) \, . \tag{15}$$

The changes of λ_{1j} ($j = 1, 2$: Industry).

$$\lambda_{11} \equiv \text{constant} \tag{16}$$

$$\lambda_{12} = \lambda_{12}^0 + \mu(\sigma_{12} - \sigma_{22}) \tag{17}$$

where μ takes a small value so that we need not worry about the upper and lower limits of λ_{12} ($0 < \lambda_{12}^{'} < 1$).

We are assuming that industry 1 is a local one whose product has no mobility but industry 2 is a more nationwide industry with a certain degree of mobility of its products. Substitution of (15) into (17) will give λ_{12} as a function of u,

$$\lambda_{12} = p + qu \tag{17'}$$

where

$$p = \lambda_{12}^0 + \mu(\sigma_{12}^0 - \sigma_{22}^0 - \sigma_{22}^0\delta) \, ,$$
$$q = \mu(\sigma_{12}^0 + \sigma_{22}^0)\delta \, .$$

By (5), (11), and (12) we have an expression of g as

$$g = s_1(r_1\lambda_{11}\sigma_{11} + r_2\lambda_{12}\sigma_{12}) + s_2\{r_1(1 - \lambda_{11})\sigma_{21} + r_2(1 - \lambda_{12})\sigma_{22}\} \, . \tag{18}$$

After a troublesome computation, we can show g as a function of u,

$$g = A + Bu + Cu^2 \tag{19}$$

where

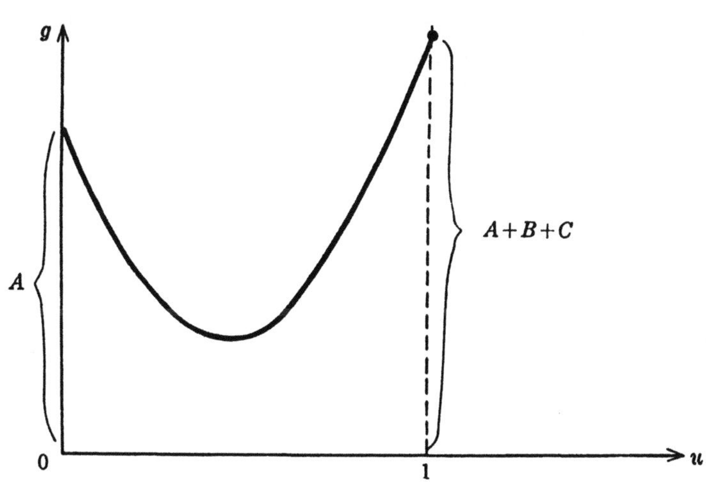

FIGURE 1

$$A = s_1(r_1\lambda_{11}\sigma_{11}^0 + r_2 p\sigma_{12}^0) + s_2\{r_1(1-\lambda_{11})(1+\delta)\sigma_{21}^0 + r_2(1-p)(1+\delta)\sigma_{22}^0\},$$
$$B = r_1\{s_1\sigma_{11}^0\lambda_{11} - s_2\sigma_{21}^0(1-\lambda_{11})\}\delta + r_2\{s_1\sigma_{12}^0(p\delta + q) - s_2\sigma_{22}^0((1-p)\delta + q(1+\delta))\},$$
$$C = r_2(s_1\sigma_{12}^0 + s_2\sigma_{22}^0)\delta q .$$

It is obvious that $A > 0$ and $C > 0$, and it is possible that $B < 0$, but $B + 2C > 0$ if s_2 is appropriately larger than s_1. Under the latter assumptions, the dependence of g on u is depicted as in Figure 1.[8]

For the maximization of g, u must take an extreme value of 0 or 1 in accordance with the sign of $B + C$,

$$\bar{u} = 0 \quad \text{if} \quad B + C < 0$$
$$\bar{u} = 1 \quad \text{if} \quad B + C > 0 .$$

This result means that the concentration of social overhead investment to one of the regions is more efficient than its dispersion over many regions, at least from the viewpoint of straightforward maximization of the national growth rate.

On the other hand, such an extreme policy will cause an expanding effect on income disparity among the regions. If we assume the interregional immobility of labor force and measure the degree of income disparity by a relative index of

$$w = \frac{x - y}{x + y}, \tag{20}$$

w will be given as follows by the use of (6) and (7).

$$w = \frac{\{\sigma_1\lambda - \sigma_2(1-\lambda)\} + \dfrac{(x_0 - y_0)g}{(s_1x_0 + s_2y_0)(e^{gt} - 1)}}{\{\sigma_1\lambda + \sigma_2(1-\lambda)\} + \dfrac{(x_0 - y_0)g}{(s_1x_0 + s_2y_0)(e^{gt} - 1)}}. \tag{21}$$

As time passes, the second parts in both numerator and denominator will become negligible. In addition, the first part of the denominator is a weighted average of two positive numbers, σ_1 and σ_2, and its variation in response to the change of u will be relatively small in comparison to that of the first part of the numerator, so we may concentrate our attention to the absolute value of the latter term.

---

[8] Notice that

$$g = A \text{ when } u = 0,$$
$$g = A + B + C \text{ when } u = 1,$$
$$\left(\frac{dg}{du}\right)_{u=0} = B < 0,$$
$$\left(\frac{dg}{du}\right)_{u=1} = B + 2C > 0, \text{ and}$$
$$\frac{d^2g}{du^2} = 2C > 0.$$

Under the same assumptions of (14)-(17), we have an expression for $w^* = \{\sigma_1\lambda - \sigma_2(1-\lambda)\}$ as

$$w^* = E + Fu + Gu^2 \tag{22}$$

where

$$E = (r_1\lambda_{11}\sigma_{11}^0 + r_2 p\sigma_{12}^0) - r_1(1-\lambda_{11})(1+\delta)\sigma_{21}^0 - r_2(1-p)(1+\delta)\sigma_{22}^0\,,$$
$$F = r_1\{\sigma_{11}^0\lambda_{11} + \sigma_{21}^0(1-\lambda_{11})\}\delta + r_2\{\sigma_{12}^0(p\delta+q) + \sigma_{22}^0((1-p)\delta + q(1+\delta))\},\text{ and}$$
$$G = r_2(\sigma_{12}^0 - \sigma_{22}^0)\delta q\,.$$

$F > 0$ and w^* is an monotonically increasing function of u for the range of $0 \leqq u \leqq 1$. Furthermore, if we assume that $E < 0$, $G > 0$, (i.e., $\sigma_{12}^0 > \sigma_{22}^0$) and $E + F + G > 0$, the behavior of w^* is depicted as on Figure 2.

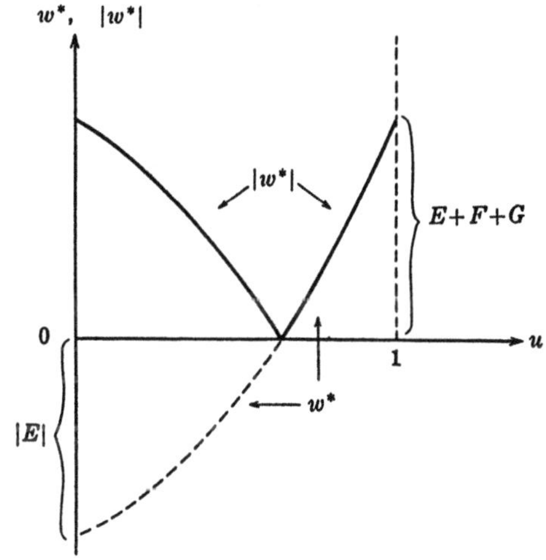

FIGURE 2

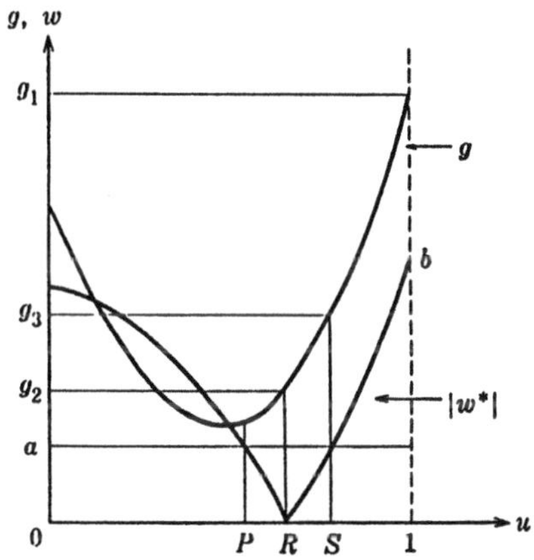

FIGURE 3

In this case, however, our concern is not the value of w^* itself but its absolute value $|w^*|$, and the latter corresponds to the solid curve on the same diagram.

Now we are in a position to contrast the conflicting effects of the regionally allocated social investment for the particular case of Figures 1 and 2. A superimposed diagram, Figure 3, will be convenient for that purpose.

From the viewpoint of the maximization of national growth rate, an extreme value of $u = 1$ that gives the growth rate, 'g_1', is most preferable. But this policy also gives a very high degree of disparity as 'b' between two regions' incomes. For the purpose of minimizing regional income disparity, an allocation policy with $u = R$ is the most desirable one, but it gives a considerably low growth rate of 'g_2'.

Some compromise must be found between these mutually contradicting targets. One of these compromises may be to get a relative maximum of g, keeping the value of $|w^*|$ at or below a certain permissible level. For instance, 9 if we impose a restriction of $|w^*| \leq a$, the admissible range of u is an interval between P and S. Then, we obtain a relative maximum of g at 'g_s' with $u = S$.

On the contrary, we can seek a relative minimum of $|w^*|$, keeping g at or beyond a certain permissible level, or some weighted sum of g and $(-|w^*|)$ can be selected as the target of maximization. In any case, the need for compromise among plural objects must be an essential feature of the regional allocation policy as far as the criterion of regional equality is considered one of the rational targets of an economic policy.

In order to measure definitely the effect of social overhead investment on the regional growth pattern, we must identify: (1) its effect on the productivity of each industry in each region, equations (14) and (15), and (2) the resultant changes in the flows of private investment fund, equations (16) and (17). Each of these problems is far from an easy task to the econometrician, and we may need another complete article to discuss them.[9]

Some Qualifications

As is intuitively clear from equations (14) and (15), the extremeness of the g-maximizing solution in the above example has come from an assumption of linear dependence of σ_{ij} upon u. If we revise σ_{1j} as strictly concave functions of u and σ_{2j} as similar functions of $(1-u)$, there would be some possibility of an interior g-maximizing solution for u.

However, the concentration of social overhead investment in one of the regions has a duplicate effect on the composite growth rate. First, it raises the productivity of private capital in this region. The latter effect, in turn, changes more favorably the flow of private investment fund to the same region, see (17). Because of this "accelerating" character of concentrated social overhead investment, the g-maximizing solution of u is apt to be an extreme one even in the case of "diminishing" return in such an investment. Only a sharp rate of diminishing return in the concave functions mentioned above may produce an interior solution of the u-variable.

In the models of this and subsequent Chapters, we are assuming that the produced income in each region is exactly equal to its distributed income. But, this is not the case in general. To a certain extent, there is the interregional flow of distributed incomes due to the previous capital flow from one region to the other regions. It is, however, formidably difficult to trace the historical pattern of interregional capital flow in order to identify the present pattern of income flow. Because, unlike the usual commodity flows, there is a possibility of crosshauling in the case of capital flow.

A practical solution to this problem is to assume fixed income-leakage rates, ρ_{ik}, from region i to region k. By this concept, the common term in the right-hand sides of equations (1) and (2) will be rewritten as

---

[9] As one of the recent contributions to the measurement of public investment benefits, see Dorfman, Robert, ed., *Measuring Benefits of Government Investments* (Washington, D. C.: The Brookings Institution, 1963).

$$s_1\{(1-\rho_{12})x+\rho_{21}y\}+s_2\{(1-\rho_{21})y+\rho_{12}x\}\ ,$$

and we can follow the same course of discussion as in previous Sections by redefining s_1^* and s_2^* as equal to $\{s_1(1-\rho_{12})+s_2\rho_{12}\}$ and $\{s_2(1-\rho_{21})+s_1\rho_{21}\}$.

THE CASE OF PRODUCTIVE GOVERNMENT EXPENDITURE

As the second part of our analysis on the regional allocation of public investment, we shall proceed to the study of a Musgrave-type model in which the government investment has the direct productivity effect by itself.[10]

In this case, we will concentrate our attention on discovering the optimal dynamic fiscal policy in the sense of national income maximization. Therefore, the problem of regional disparity will be put aside for a moment, although it is not difficult to take account of it in the analysis as an additional constraint on the range of our instrumental variables. The following analysis may be considered as a generalization of the Rahman-type model of investment allocation toward an economy of the free enterprise system with a public sector.[11]

Growth Pattern in a Two-Region Economy with Tax System

Consider a two-region economy in which the central government can impose current income taxes within a certain limit anytime it wishes. Before taxation, some part of the regional income, x or y, is withheld as the consumption allowance (including noninvestment expenditures by the government). The taxable incomes are given as $(1-c_1)x$ and $(1-c_2)y$ where c_1 and c_2 are the average propensities of consumption in each region.[12]

A variable but uniform tax rate r is applied every time to these taxable incomes by an equality principle of the tax burden up to an upper limit of $\theta(0<\theta<1)$, and the resultant tax revenues will be allocated among the regions to be used as the fund for productive public investment within each region. Under these circumstances, we shall have the following model of regional growth:

$$\frac{dx}{dt}=\sigma_1\lambda(1-r)(s_1x+s_2y)+\delta_1ur(s_1x+s_2y) \tag{23}$$

$$\frac{dy}{dt}=\sigma_2(1-\lambda)(1-r)(s_1x+s_2y)+\delta_2(1-u)r(s_1x+s_2y) \tag{24}$$

where

σ_i = the incremental output-capital ratio of the private investment in region $i(i=1, 2)$,

δ_i = the incremental output-capital ratio of the public investment in region $i(i=1, 2)$,

$s_i=1-c_i(i=1, 2)$,

---

[10] Musgrave, *op. cit.*, chap. 20, C, pp. 484-7.

[11] Rahman, *op. cit.* Also see Sakashita, N., "Regional Allocation of Investment: A Further Comment," mimeograph, April, 1965.

[12] Refer to the previous Chapter for the complete system of notation.

$\lambda =$ the proportion of private investment shared to the first region, and

$u =$ the proportion of public investment shared to the first region,

and

$$\begin{cases} 0 \leqq r \leqq \theta \\ 0 < \lambda < 1 . \\ 0 \leqq u \leqq 1 \end{cases} \tag{25}$$

We treat σ_i, δ_i, s_i and λ as constant coefficients and u and r as instrumental variables for the central government.[13]

By the adoption of new variables, $\theta_1 = ur$ and $\theta_2 = (1-u)r$, the system of equations (23) and (24) will be rewritten as

$$\frac{dx}{dt} = \{\sigma_1 \lambda (1 - \theta_1 - \theta_2) + \delta_1 \theta_1\}(s_1 x + s_2 y) , \tag{26}$$

$$\frac{dy}{dt} = \{\sigma_2 (1 - \lambda)(1 - \theta_1 - \theta_2) + \delta_2 \theta_2\}(s_1 x + s_2 y) , \tag{27}$$

where

$$0 \leqq \theta_1 , \ 0 \leqq \theta_2 , \ \theta_1 + \theta_2 \leqq \theta . \tag{28}$$

Optimum Path of Growth with a Finite Time Horizon

In this Section, our target is to maximize the national income at the final time period, $t = T$, starting with a set of initial conditions, x_0 and y_0 at $t = 0$ under the constraints of (26), (27), and (28). Our problem can be formulated as

(*) Maximize $\left[\{x(T) + y(T)\} = \int_0^T \left(\frac{dx}{dt} + \frac{dy}{dt} \right) dt + (x_0 + y_0) \right]$
with respect to $\theta_1(t)$ and $\theta_2(t)$, $0 \leqq t \leqq T$ subject to (26), (27), and (28).

This problem of dynamic programming should be solved by the use of the theory of optimal processes developed by L. S. Pontryagin and others.[14] Theorem 7 in Chapter 1 of their book is particularly applicable to our case.[15] First of all, a Hamiltonian function for the problem must be formulated as follows,

$$H = -\psi_0 \left(\frac{dx}{dt} + \frac{dy}{dt} \right) + \psi_1 \frac{dx}{dt} + \psi_2 \frac{dy}{dt} , \tag{29}$$

where

ψ_0, ψ_1, and ψ_2 are auxiliary variables whose behaviors are given by

[13] See the Section, Disaggregation of σ_i and λ, concerning the implications of σ_i, s_i, and λ.

[14] Pontryagin, L. S., and others, *The Mathematical Theory of Optimal Processes*, trans. by K. N. Trirogoff, (New York: John Wiley & Sons, Inc., 1962).

[15] *Ibid.*, pp. 68-9.

$$\begin{cases} \dfrac{d\psi_0}{dt} \equiv 0 \\ \dfrac{d\psi_1}{dt} = -\dfrac{\partial H}{\partial x} \\ \dfrac{d\psi_1}{dt} = -\dfrac{\partial H}{\partial y}\,. \end{cases} \tag{30}$$

At $t = T$, we see that $\psi_0(T) = -1$ (then $\psi_0(t) \equiv -1$) and $\psi_1(T) = \psi_2(T) = 0$ by the transversality conditions at the terminal point.[16] We can, therefore, rewrite (29) and (30) by the introduction of new auxiliary variables, $\phi_1 = 1 + \psi_1$ and $\phi_2 = 1 + \psi_2$.

$$\begin{aligned} H = [&\{\sigma_1\lambda\phi_1 + \sigma_2(1-\lambda)\phi_2\} \\ &+ \{(\delta_1 - \sigma_1\lambda)\phi_1 - \sigma_2(1-\lambda)\phi_2\}\theta_1 \\ &+ \{-\sigma_1\lambda\phi_1 + (\delta_2 - \sigma_2(1-\lambda))\phi_2\}\theta_2](s_1x + s_2y)\,. \end{aligned} \tag{31}$$

$$\begin{cases} \dfrac{d\phi_1}{dt} = -s_1[\{\sigma_1\lambda(1-\theta_1-\theta_2) + \delta_1\theta_1\}\phi_1 + \{\sigma_2(1-\lambda)(1-\theta_1-\theta_2) + \delta_2\theta_2\}\phi_2] \\ \dfrac{d\phi_2}{dt} = -s_2[\{\sigma_1\lambda(1-\theta_1-\theta_2) + \delta_1\theta_1\}\phi_1 + \{\sigma_2(1-\lambda)(1-\theta_1-\theta_2) + \delta_2\theta_2\}\phi_2]\,. \end{cases} \tag{32}$$

Here, we notice that two equations in (32) are mutually dependent, so that ϕ_1 and ϕ_2 are linearly dependent on each other.

Before applying the maximum principle of the theory of optimal processes[17] to the system of (31) and (32), we shall make the following assumptions on the relative sizes of parameters to get a concrete solution to the problem:

$$\delta_1 < \delta_2 < \sigma_2 < \sigma_1\,. \tag{33}$$

$$s_1\delta_1 < s_1\sigma_1 < s_2\delta_2 < s_2\sigma_2\,. \tag{34}$$

$$s_1\sigma_1\lambda + s_2\sigma_2(1-\lambda) < s_2\delta_2\,. \tag{35}$$

Of course, the above set of assumptions is only one of many possible sets, and the final solution may change drastically, depending upon what assumptions we make. Nevertheless, the combination of (33), (34), and (35) will produce a solution which is at least one of the most interesting cases.

Let the multiplicative factor to θ_i in (31) be $P_i (i = 1, 2)$. The maximum principle tells us that:

(I) $\theta_i = 0$ if $P_i < 0$, $(i = 1, 2)$

(II) $\theta_i = 0$ and $\theta_j \overline{\overline{\gtrless}}\, \theta$ if $P_i < 0 < P_j$ or $0 < P_i < P_j$
$(i = 1, 2,\ j = 1, 2$ and $i \neq j)$

where

$$P_1 = (\delta_1 - \sigma_1\lambda)\phi_1 - \sigma_2(1-\lambda)\phi_2\,,$$

and

$$P_2 = -\sigma_1\lambda\phi_1 + \{\delta_2 - \sigma_2(1-\lambda)\}\phi_2\,.$$

[16] *Ibid.*, p. 69.

[17] *Ibid.*, pp. 17–21, 66–9.

At $t = T$, we have

$$P_1(T) = \delta_1 - \{\sigma_1\lambda + \sigma_2(1-\lambda)\} < 0$$
$$P_2(T) = \delta_2 - \{\sigma_1\lambda + \sigma_2(1-\lambda)\} < 0$$

because of $\phi_1(T) = \phi_2(T) = 1$, then

$$\theta_1(T) = \theta_2(T) = 0$$

by (I). This gives us

$$\begin{cases} \dfrac{d\phi_1}{dt} = - s_1\sigma_1\lambda\phi_1 - s_1\sigma_2(1-\lambda)\phi_2 \\ \dfrac{d\phi_2}{dt} = - s_2\sigma_1\phi_1 - s_2\sigma_2(1-\lambda)\phi_2 \end{cases} \tag{36}$$

in the left-hand neighborhood of T. After solving (36) for $\phi_1(t)$ and $\phi_2(t)$, we obtain the following expressions for P_1 and P_2, see Mathematical Appendix B,

$$P_1 = \{\sigma_1\lambda + \sigma_2(1-\lambda)\}\left(\frac{s_1\delta_1}{g} - 1\right)\{e^{g(T-t)} - 1\}$$
$$+ [\delta_1 - \{\sigma_1\lambda + \sigma_2(1-\lambda)\}]\,, \quad \text{for} \quad t \leqq T\,, \tag{37}$$

$$P_2 = \{\sigma_1\lambda + \sigma_2(1-\lambda)\}\left(\frac{s_2\delta_2}{g} - 1\right)\{e^{g(T-t)} - 1\}$$
$$+ [\delta_2 - \{\sigma_1\lambda + \sigma_2(1-\lambda)\}]\,, \quad \text{for} \quad t \leqq T \tag{38}$$

where

$$g = s_1\sigma_1\lambda + s_2\sigma_2(1-\lambda)\,.^{18} \tag{39}$$

It is obvious by the assumptions of (34) and (35) that

$$\begin{cases} \dfrac{dP_1}{dt} > 0 \\ \dfrac{dP_2}{dt} < 0 \end{cases} \quad \text{for} \quad t \leqq T\,. \tag{40}$$

These qualitative statements tell us that P_1 is always negative for $0 \leqq t \leqq T$

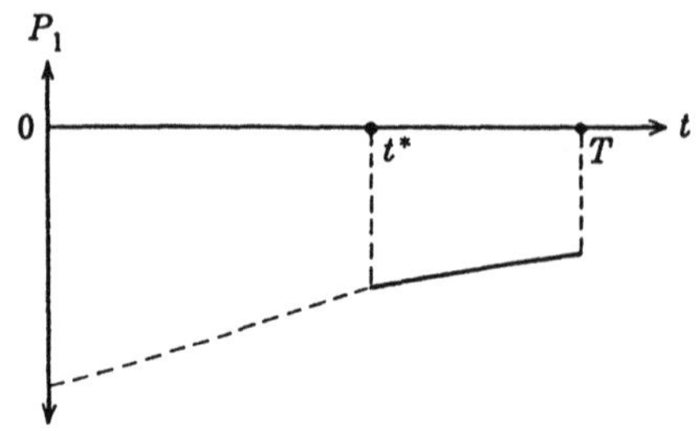

FIGURE 4

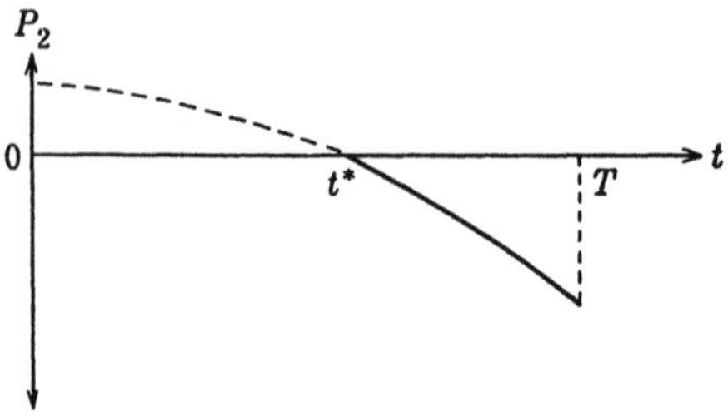

FIGURE 5

[18] See the next Section of this Chapter for the economic interpretation of (37) and (38).

as far as the system of (36) is concerned, but there is some possibility that P_2 *was* nonnegative if T is sufficiently large. We are tracing time *backward,* see Figures 4 and 5.

In fact P_2 becomes zero at $t = t^* > 0$ which is the solution of

$$g(T - t^*) = \log\left[1 + \frac{\{\sigma_1\lambda + \sigma_2(1-\lambda)\} - \delta_2}{\{\sigma_1\lambda + \sigma_2(1-\lambda)\}((s_2\delta_2/g) - 1)}\right], \tag{41}$$

and t^* is a switching time point from $\theta_2 = 0$ to $\theta_2 > 0$, proceeding backward with time. Then, we can say that

$$\begin{cases} \theta_1(t) = 0 \\ \theta_2(t) = 0 \end{cases} \quad \text{for} \quad t^* < t \leqq T \tag{42}$$

provided that $T > t^* > 0$.

At $t = t^*$, θ_1 is still zero because $P_1(t^*)$ is negative, but we can say nothing about the value of θ_2. However, we can show that

$$\left(\frac{dP_2}{dt}\right)^-_{t=t^*} < 0$$

regardless of the value of θ_2, see Mathematical Appendix C. Therefore, $P_2(t)$ is undoubtedly positive in the left-hand neighborhood of t^*, and we have $\theta_1 = 0$ and $\theta_2 = \theta$ during this phase.

In this case, the differential equations are such that

$$\begin{cases} \dfrac{d\phi_1}{dt} = -s_1\sigma_1\lambda(1-\theta)\phi_1 - s_1\{\sigma_2(1-\lambda)(1-\theta) + \delta_2\theta\}\phi_2 \\ \dfrac{d\phi_2}{dt} = -s_2\sigma_1\lambda(1-\theta)\phi_1 - s_2\{\sigma_2(1-\lambda)(1-\theta) + \delta_2\theta\}\phi_2 \end{cases} \tag{43}$$

for $t \leqq t^*$.

The solutions of (43) give us

$$P_1 = \frac{1}{s_1}(s_1\delta_1 - g)\left[\phi_1^* - \frac{(s_2 - s_1)\{\sigma_2(1-\lambda)(1-\theta) + \delta_2\theta\}}{g'}\right]\cdot\{e^{g'(t^*-t)} - 1\} + k_1 \tag{44}$$

$$P_2 = \frac{1}{s_1}(s_2\delta_2 - g)\left[\phi_1^* - \frac{(s_2 - s_1)\{\sigma_2(1-\lambda)(1-\theta) + \delta_2\theta\}}{g'}\right]\cdot\{e^{g'(t^*-t)} - 1\} + k_2 \tag{45}$$

where $g' = s_2\delta_2\theta + g(1-\theta)$, and k_1 and k_2 are some appropriate constant terms.

In addition, we can show that

$$\phi_1^* - \frac{(s_2 - s_1)\{\sigma_2(1-\lambda)(1-\theta) + \delta_2\theta\}}{g'} > 0\,. \tag{46}$$

See Mathematical Appendix D.

Therefore, we are sure that

$$\begin{cases} \dfrac{dP_1}{dt} > 0 \\ \dfrac{dP_2}{dt} < 0 \end{cases} \qquad \text{for} \quad 0 \leqq t \leqq t^* \tag{47}$$

so that

$$\begin{cases} \theta_1(t) = 0 \\ \theta_2(t) = \theta \end{cases} \qquad \text{for} \quad 0 \leqq t \leqq t^* . \tag{48}$$

See Figures 6 and 7 and recall (I) and (II).

Combining (42) and (48), we have reached the solution to a dynamic programming problem (*) under assumptions (33), (34), and (35) such that:

a) For the time interval of $0 \leqq t \leqq t^*$, where t^* is the solution to (41), impose a tax rate θ upon both regions and concentrate public investment to the second region where such investment produces a greater growth rate $s_2\delta_2$ than the combined growth rate of

$$g = s_1\sigma_1\lambda + s_2\sigma_2(1-\lambda) .$$

b) For the time interval of $t^* < t \leqq T$, there should be no tax and thus no public investment. The behaviors of the private sector exclusively determine the path of economic growth.

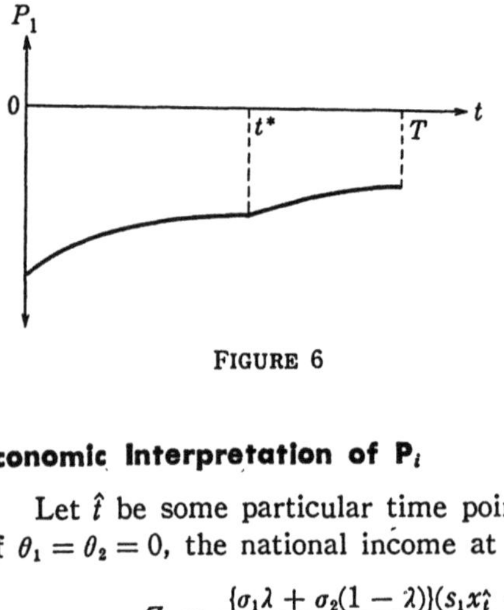

FIGURE 6

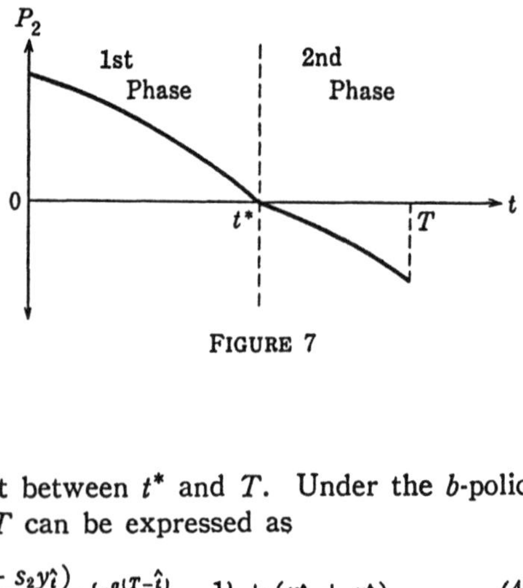

FIGURE 7

Economic Interpretation of P_i

Let $\hat{t}$ be some particular time point between t^* and T. Under the *b*-policy of $\theta_1 = \theta_2 = 0$, the national income at T can be expressed as

$$Z_T = \frac{\{\sigma_1\lambda + \sigma_2(1-\lambda)\}(s_1 x_{\hat{t}} + s_2 y_{\hat{t}})}{g}\{e^{g(T-\hat{t})} - 1\} + (x_{\hat{t}} + y_{\hat{t}}) \tag{49}$$

by (6) regarding $x_{\hat{t}} = x(\hat{t})$ and $y_{\hat{t}} = y(\hat{t})$ as truncated initial conditions. Changes in the values of $x_{\hat{t}}$ and $y_{\hat{t}}$ affect the value of final target as follows,

$$\Delta Z_T = \frac{\{\sigma_1\lambda + \sigma_2(1-\lambda)\}}{g}\{e^{g(T-\hat{t})} - 1\}(s_1\Delta x_{\hat{t}} + s_2\Delta y_{\hat{t}}) + (\Delta x_{\hat{t}} + \Delta y_{\hat{t}}) . \tag{50}$$

Now let τ be a very small time interval whose right-hand end is $\hat{t}$ and assume $\bar{x} = x(\hat{t} - \tau)$ and $\bar{y} = y(\hat{t} - \tau)$ are of some fixed values. By (5) and (6), it is shown that

$$x_{\hat{t}} - \bar{x} \doteqdot \left(\frac{dx}{dt}\right)_{x=\bar{x}} \cdot \tau = \{\sigma_1 \lambda(1 - \theta_1 - \theta_2) + \delta_1 \theta_1\}(s_1 \bar{x} + s_2 \bar{y}) \cdot \tau \,. \tag{51}$$

$$y_{\hat{t}} - \bar{y} \doteqdot \left(\frac{dy}{dt}\right)_{y=\bar{y}} \cdot \tau = \{\sigma_2(1 - \lambda)(1 - \theta_1 - \theta_2) + \delta_2 \theta_2\}(s_1 \bar{x} + s_2 \bar{y}) \cdot \tau \,. \tag{52}$$

Then the effect of a change in the value of θ_2 during the τ-period on $x_{\hat{t}}$ and $y_{\hat{t}}$ will be given as

$$\Delta x_{\hat{t}} \doteqdot \frac{\partial x_{\hat{t}}}{\partial \theta_2} \cdot \Delta\theta_2 = -\sigma_1 \lambda (s_1 \bar{x} + s_2 \bar{y}) \cdot \tau \cdot \Delta\theta_2 \,. \tag{53}$$

$$\Delta y_{\hat{t}} \doteqdot \frac{\partial y_{\hat{t}}}{\partial \theta_2} \cdot \Delta\theta_2 = \{-\sigma_2(1 - \lambda) + \delta_2\}(s_1 \bar{x} + s_2 \bar{y}) \cdot \tau \cdot \Delta\theta_2 \,. \tag{54}$$

Substituting (53) and (54) into (50), we see an approximate effect of the change in θ_2 during the τ-period on Z_T as follows,

$$\Delta Z_T(\Delta\theta_2) \doteqdot \left[(\sigma_1 \lambda + \sigma_2(1 - \lambda))\left(\frac{s_2 \delta_2}{g} - 1\right)\{e^{g(T-\hat{t})} - 1\} + \{\delta_2 - (\sigma_1 \lambda + \sigma_2(1 - \lambda))\}\right](s_1 \bar{x} + s_2 \bar{y}) \cdot \tau \cdot \Delta\theta_2 \,. \tag{55}$$

The right-hand side of (55) is exactly the same as that of (38), excepting some positive multiplicative terms in the former. Then, the sign of P_2 of (38) corresponds to that of $\Delta Z_T(\Delta\theta_2)$ of (55).

Now, we can give the following interpretation to P_2 at $\hat{t}$ where $t^* \leqq \hat{t} \leqq T$: $P_2(\hat{t})$ indicates the marginal change in the target value Z_T to be maximized, the national income at $t = T$, by a small increase of one of the instrumental variables θ_2, during the τ-period, a very small time interval which precedes $\hat{t}$, given the adoption of the $\theta_1 = \theta_2 = 0$ policy from $\hat{t}$ to T and also given $x(\hat{t} - \tau)$ and $y(\hat{t} - \tau)$ as $\bar{x}$ and $\bar{y}$.

Thus, if $P_2(\hat{t})$ is positive, θ_2 should be increased from its zero level to its upper limit (in this case, the upper limit is $\theta_2 = \theta$ provided that $P_1(\hat{t}) < 0$) at least for the very small time interval, $\hat{t} - \tau \leqq t \leqq t$, because the value of $P_2(\hat{t})$ is independent of θ_2. But if it is negative, θ_2 should be kept at zero level for the same τ-period.

Observation of (50) and (55) tells us that the above marginal change in Z_T consists of two parts: the first part is the change in the growth gradient from $t = \hat{t}$ to $t = T$, and the second part is the change in the values of truncated initial conditions, $x_{\hat{t}}$ and $y_{\hat{t}}$ at $t = \hat{t}$. In the case of the θ_2-variable, the first part is positive but the second is negative as is easily seen by (55), (33), and (35). As the distance of $\hat{t}$ from T becomes sufficienctly large, the first component dominates the second, and $P_2(\hat{t})$ turns to positive from negative, where we have a switching time point of $t = t^*$, see Figure 8 for an intuitive understanding.

Exactly the same argument is applicable to the interpretation of P_1 of (37)

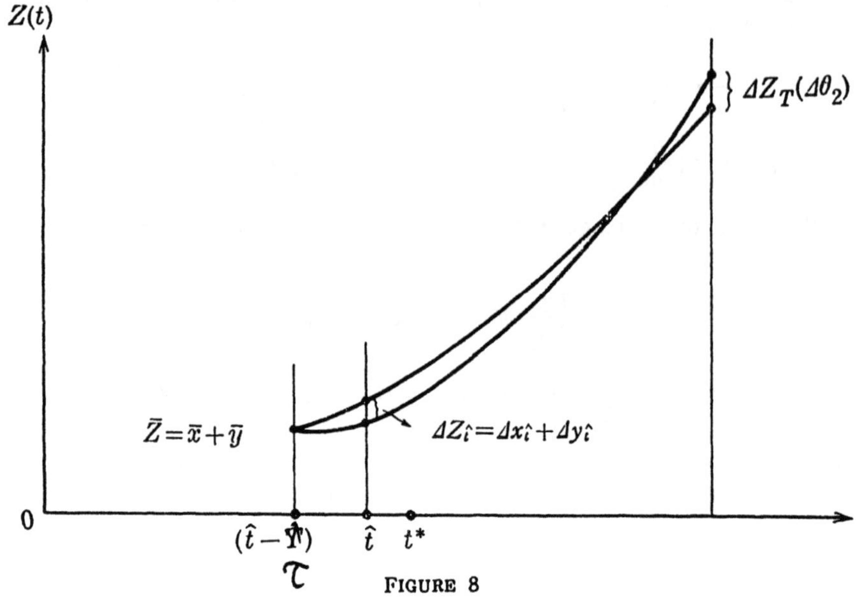

FIGURE 8

as an indicator of $\Delta Z_T(\Delta\theta_1)$. P_1 and P_2 of (44) and (45) can be explained in a similar fashion, although the interpretation will be very complicated in the latter cases.[19]

It is easily seen that the above argument has a close relationship to the so-called principle of optimality of dynamic programming which says that *any portion of an optimal process is also an optimal process.*[20]

CONCLUSION

In the previous Sections, we have observed the following interesting properties of the optimum solution to this regional allocation problem.

First, as indicated by assumptions (33), (34), and (35), public investment in one of the regions will be justified during some phase of the planning period, even if it is less productive than the private investment in the same region. The reason is that the central government can directly control the interregional flow of public funds *outside* the market mechanism and can concentrate its public investment on the region with greater growth potential.

Second, as seen by equation (41), the value of $(T - t^*)$, the length of the second phase of planning, is independent from the length of planning horizon T provided that $T > T - t^*$. Then, the relative significance of the second phase will be less and less as T becomes larger and larger. This is one of the

[19] For a similar interpretation in a discrete time case, see Dorfman, Robert, "Regional Allocation of Investment: Comment," *Quarterly Journal of Economics*, LXXVII, No. 1, February, 1963, pp. 162–5.

[20] Pontryagin, *op. cit.*, p. 16. Also see Bellman, R. E., *Dynamic Programming* (Princeton, New Jersey: Princeton University Press, 1957).

characteristics which have been observed in the dynamic programming problems with linear form.[21] Therefore, if T is very large, the public investment should be almost persistently concentrated to the second region, as far as there is no change in the values of relevant parameters.

Third, the resultant optimum solution is very sensitive to the relative sizes of such parameters as s_i, σ_i, $\delta_i (i = 1, 2)$, and λ. Then, if there is some slight change in them by means of social overhead investment, for instance, which was analyzed earlier in this paper, we may observe a drastic change of the optimum solution. Such being the case, it may be possible for us to utilize some combination of those two kinds of public investment policy in order to attain the *optimum optimorum* in the set of feasible growth paths.

MATHEMATICAL APPENDICES

A. Solution to Equations (1) and (2)

From (1) and (2), we have the following relation between (dx/dt) and (dy/dt),

$$\frac{dy}{dt} = \frac{\sigma_2}{\sigma_1} \frac{1-\lambda}{\lambda} \frac{dx}{dt} \tag{A1}$$

with the solution of

$$y - \frac{\sigma_2}{\sigma_1} \frac{1-\lambda}{\lambda} x + \frac{Q_0}{\sigma_1 \lambda} \tag{A2}$$

where

$$Q_0 = \sigma_1 \lambda y_0 - \sigma_2 (1-\lambda) x_0 \, .$$

Putting (A1) into (1) we get a single differential equation with respect to x as follows

$$\frac{dx}{dt} = gx + s_2 Q_0 \tag{A3}$$

where

$$g = s_1 \sigma_1 \lambda + s_2 \sigma_2 (1-\lambda) \, .$$

The solution of (A3) for x is given as

$$x = \left(x_0 + \frac{s_2 Q_0}{g} \right) e^{gt} - \frac{s_2 Q_0}{g} \, , \tag{A4}$$

and we also get the solution for y as

$$y = \frac{\sigma_2}{\sigma_1} \frac{1-\lambda}{\lambda} \left\{ \left(x_0 + \frac{s_2 Q_0}{g} \right) e^{gt} - \frac{s_2 Q_0}{g} \right\} + \frac{Q_0}{\sigma_1 \lambda} \tag{A5}$$

by the use of (A2).

A little calculation on (A4) and (A5) will lead to (3) and (4).

[21] Sakashita, *op. cit.*

B. Solution to Equation (36)

First, we have

$$\phi_2 = \frac{s_2}{s_1}\phi_1 + c \tag{B1}$$

where c is a constant because $(d\phi_2/dt) = (s_2/s_1)(d\phi_1/dt)$ by (36). $\phi_1 = \phi_2 = 1$ at $t = T$, then $c = (s_1 - s_2/s_1)$ and (B1) becomes

$$\phi_2 = \frac{1}{s_1}\{s_2\phi_1 + (s_1 - s_2)\} \quad \text{for} \quad t \leqq T\,. \tag{B2}$$

Putting (B2) into the first equation of (36) we have

$$\frac{d\phi_1}{dt} = -\, g\phi_1 - (s_1 - s_2)\sigma_2(1 - \lambda)\,, \tag{B3}$$

and its solution is

$$\phi_1 = \left\{1 - \frac{(s_2 - s_1)\sigma_2(1 - \lambda)}{g}\right\}\{e^{g(T-t)} - 1\} + 1 \tag{B4}$$

where

$$g = s_1\sigma_1\lambda + s_2\sigma_2(1 - \lambda)\,.$$

On the other hand,

$$\begin{aligned} P_1 &= (\delta_1 - \delta_1\lambda)\phi_1 - \sigma_2(1 - \lambda)\phi_2 \\ &= \frac{1}{s_1}\{(s_1\delta_1 - g)\phi_1 - (s_1 - s_2)\sigma_2(1 - \lambda)\}\,, \end{aligned} \tag{B5}$$

and inserting the right-hand side of (B4) into ϕ_1 of (B5) we get

$$P_1 = \{\sigma_1\lambda + \sigma_2(1 - \lambda)\}\left(\frac{s_1\delta_1}{g} - 1\right)\{e^{g(T-t)} - 1\} + [\delta_1 - \{\sigma_1\lambda + \sigma_2(1 - \lambda)\}]\,. \tag{B6}$$

By a similar argument, we have

$$P_2 = \{\sigma_1\lambda + \sigma_2(1 - \lambda)\}\left(\frac{s_2\delta_2}{g} - 1\right)\{e^{g(T-t)} - 1\} + [\delta_2 - \{\sigma_1\lambda + \sigma_2(1 - \lambda)\}]\,. \tag{B7}$$

C. Proof of $(dP_2/dt)^-_{t=t^*} < 0$

Let $\phi_1(t^*) = \phi_1^*$ and $\phi_2(t^*) = \phi_2^*$. We have

$$\phi_2^* = \frac{1}{s_1}\{s_2\phi_1^* + (s_1 - s_2)\}$$

$$P_2(t^*) = -\,\sigma_1\lambda\phi_1^* + \{\delta_2 - \sigma_2(1 - \lambda)\}\phi_2^* = 0$$

by (B2) and the definition of P_2. From these two equations, we have

$$\phi_1^* = \frac{(s_2 - s_1)\{\delta_2 - \sigma_2(1 - \lambda)\}}{s_2\delta_2 - g}\,. \tag{C1}$$

$$\phi_2^* = \frac{(s_2 - s_1)\sigma_1\lambda}{s_2\delta_2 - g}\,. \tag{C2}$$

On the other hand, at $t = t^*$

$$\left(\frac{dP_2}{dt}\right)^- = -\sigma_1\lambda\left(\frac{d\phi_1}{dt}\right)^- + \{\delta_2 - \sigma_2(1-\lambda)\}\left(\frac{d\phi_2}{dt}\right)^-$$
$$= \left[-\sigma_1\lambda + \frac{s_2}{s_1}\{\delta_2 - \sigma_2(1-\lambda)\}\right]\left(\frac{d\phi_1}{dt}\right)^-$$
$$= -(s_2\delta_2 - g)\cdot[\sigma_1\lambda(1-\theta_2)\phi_1^* + \{\sigma_2(1-\lambda)(1-\theta_2) + \delta_2\theta_2\}\phi_2^*] \qquad (C3)$$

where $(dP_2/dt)^-$, $(d\phi_1/dt)^-$, and $(d\phi_2/dt)^-$ mean the left-hand time derivative of P_2, ϕ_1 and ϕ_2.

Putting (C1) and (C2) into (C3), we have

$$\left(\frac{dP_2}{dt}\right)^-_{t=t^*} = -\sigma_1\lambda(s_2 - s_1)[(1-\theta_2)\{\delta_2 - \sigma_2(1-\lambda)\} + (1-\theta_2)\sigma_2(1-\lambda) + \delta_2\theta_2]$$
$$= -\sigma_1\lambda(s_2 - s_1)\delta_2 < 0$$

by assumptions (33) and (34).

D. Solution to Equation (43)

Again, we have

$$\phi_2 = \frac{1}{s_1}\{s_2\phi_1 + (s_1 - s_2)\} \quad \text{for} \quad t \leqq t^* \qquad (D1)$$

by the continuities of ϕ_1 and ϕ_2 at t^*. Then, the first equation of (43) becomes

$$\frac{d\phi_1}{dt} = -[s_1\sigma_1\lambda(1-\theta) + s_2\{\sigma_2(1-\lambda)(1-\theta) + \delta_2\theta\}]\phi_1$$
$$-(s_1 - s_2)\{\sigma_2(1-\lambda)(1-\theta) + \delta_2\theta\} \qquad (D2)$$

and its solution is

$$\phi_1 = \left[\phi_1^* - \frac{(s_2 - s_1)\{\sigma_2(1-\lambda)(1-\theta) + \delta_2\theta\}}{g'}\right]\{e^{g'(t^*-t)} - 1\} + \phi_1^* \qquad (D3)$$

where

$$g' = s_2\delta_2\theta + \{s_1\sigma_1\lambda + s_2\sigma_2(1-\lambda)\}(1-\theta).$$

P_1 is again expressed as:

$$P_1 = \frac{1}{s_1}\{(s_1\delta_1 - g)\phi_1 - (s_1 - s_2)\sigma_2(1-\lambda)\}, \qquad (D4)$$

and using (D3) it becomes

$$P_1 = \frac{1}{s_1}\left[(s_1\delta_1 - g)\left[\phi_1^* - \frac{(s_2 - s_1)\{\sigma_2(1-\lambda)(1-\theta) + \delta_2\theta\}}{g'}\right]\{e^{g'(t^*-t)} - 1\}\right.$$
$$\left. + \{(s_1\delta_1 - g)\phi_1^* - (s_1 - s_2)\sigma_2(1-\lambda)\}\right]. \qquad (D5)$$

Similarly

$$P_2 = \frac{1}{s_1}\Bigg[(s_2\delta_2 - g)\bigg[\phi_1^* - \frac{(s_2 - s_1)\{\sigma_2(1-\lambda)(1-\theta) + \delta_2\theta\}}{g'}\bigg]\{e^{g'(t^*-t)} - 1\}$$

$$+ \{(s_2\delta_2 - g)\phi_1^* + (s_1 - s_2)(\delta_2 - \sigma_2(1-\lambda))\}\Bigg]. \tag{D6}$$

Recalling (C1), we can show that

$$\phi_1^* - \frac{(s_2 - s_1)\{\sigma_2(1-\lambda)(1-\theta) + \delta_2\theta\}}{g'}$$

$$= (s_2 - s_1)\left\{\frac{\delta_2 - \sigma_2(1-\lambda)}{s_2\delta_2 - g} - \frac{\sigma_2(1-\lambda)(1-\theta) + \delta_2\theta}{s_2\delta_2\theta + g(1-\theta)}\right\}$$

$$= \frac{(s_2 - s_1)\delta_2 s_1\sigma_1\lambda}{(s_2\delta_2 - g)\{s_2\delta_2\theta + g(1-\theta)\}} > 0\,.$$

Papers of the Regional Science Association, Arizona, Vol. 20 (1967) 109-122

PRODUCTION FUNCTION, DEMAND FUNCTION AND LOCATION THEORY OF THE FIRM

by Noboru Sakashita*

"There is no need for much of the esoteric paraphernalia sometimes employed by location specialists."—Leon N. Moses.

1. INTRODUCTION

One of the conclusions of Moses' 1958 article on location theory of the firm was that: "... the optimum location is seen finally to depend on the following factors: base prices on inputs; transportation rates on inputs and on the final product; the geographic positions of materials and markets; the production function; the demand function."[1]

Although there is no doubt about the general validity of this statement, it appears to be too general for certain practical applications. In addition to this general statement, it is equally important to know under what conditions the various above-mentioned factors would become relevant or irrelevant to the firm's decision on the optimal location. Putting it another way, we wish to know the minimum requisite information for the firm's locational decision under alternative assumptions, particularly those assumptions concerning its production function.

In Moses' paper, it was specified that only under the assumption of fixed input coefficients, do all factors other than transportation rates and the geographic positions of materials and markets become irrelevant to the locational decision, and that with a production function, which allows input substitution and is not linear homogeneous, we have to take into account all of the aforementioned factors. But there has been no further investigation about an intermediate case of the input-substitutable *and* linear homogeneous production function which is probably the most familiar one in the economic analysis.[2]

---

* The author is associated with Tohoku University, Sendai, Japan. This article was written while the author held a postdoctoral fellowship at the University of Pennsylvania. The author is indebted to Professors Walter Isard, Benjamin H. Stevens, Thomas A. Reiner and Tony E. Smith of the University of Pennsylvania for their valuable comments on an earlier version of this article. Naturally, the author accepts full responsibility for any errors that may appear.

[1] Moses [5; p. 269].

[2] We must be careful to distinguish three types of the "linear" production function: linear with fixed input coefficients; linear with respect to the input-variables (without a constant term); linear homogeneous with respect to the input-variables. The first and the second types can be considered special cases of the third type. However, the first is quite different from the second, and the third type does include the case of diminishing rate of substitution between a pair of inputs, a case which is excluded in the other two types.

In the present paper, we would like to investigate several cases of the optimum location of the firm under the assumptions of a linear homogeneous production function of a general type and a demand function for the firm's final product which is appropriately price-elastic. It will be shown that an analytical technique is at least as useful as a diagrammatical one for deriving operationally meaningful propositions for certain locational problems.[3]

2. A SIMPLE CASE OF COST-MINIMIZATION

As a common assumption for this and the following two sections, we postulate that the firm's production function is linear homogeneous, continuously twice differentiable and includes only two input-variables. This function can be expressed as:

$$Q = F(V_1,\ V_2) \tag{1}$$

where

Q = amount of the final product;
V_1 = amount of the input of the first material;
V_2 = amount of the input of the second material.

It is also assumed that the productivity function,

$$f(v) = F(v,\ 1) \tag{2}$$

where

$$v = \frac{V_1}{V_2},$$

associated with this production function has the following characteristics;

$$\lim_{v\to 0} f(v) = 0\ ; \tag{3}$$

$$f'(v) > 0 \quad \text{for all} \quad v = 0, \qquad \lim_{v\to\infty} f'(v) = 0\ ; \tag{4}$$

$$f''(v) < 0 \quad \text{for all} \quad v \geqq 0\ . \tag{5}$$

Remember that we do not assume $\lim_{v\to\infty} f(v) = \infty$ nor $\lim_{v\to 0} f'(v) = \infty$ so that the general CES production function is included in our F-function. But, of course, the strictly linear production function is excluded here.[4]

Now let us specify the locational situation of our firm. Our firm is going to find its best location at some point on the straight line which links the site of the first raw material, M_1, and that of the second raw material, M_2. The following notation will be used:

s: distance between M_1 and M_2,
x: distance between M_2 and the firm's location point, $0 \leqq x \leqq s$,
r_1: price of the first raw material at its source,
r_2: price of the second raw material at its source,

[3] Isard is somewhat pessimistic about this point. See his preface to the Japanese edition of [3], 1964.

[4] The condition that: $f(v) - vf'(v) > 0$ for all $v > 0$, is deduced from expressions (3), (4) and (5) and need not be stated as an independent assumption.

m_1: transport rate on the first raw material,
m_2: transport rate on the second raw material.

In those symbols, all quantities other than x are to be considered as constants. See Figure 1.

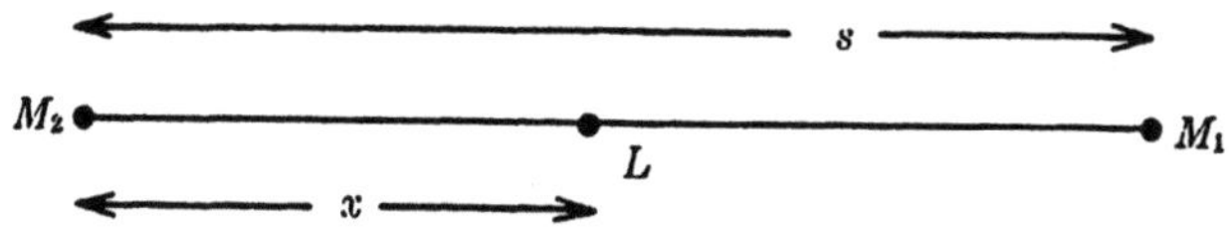

FIGURE 1. Locational Line.

The cost function of the firm associated with a fixed level of output $Q = \bar{Q}$ is shown as:

$$C = \{r_1 + m_1(s - x)\}V_1 + \{r_2 + m_2x\}V_2$$
$$= [\{r_1 + m_1(s - x)\}v + \{r_2 + m_2x\}]V_2 \,, \tag{6}$$

where

$$\bar{Q} = f(v)V_2 \,. \tag{7}$$

First, we wish to find the optimum input ratio, $v = v^*$, for the firm at a *given* value of x. The minimizing conditions of the C-function are:

$$\frac{f(v^*) - v^*f'(v^*)}{f'(v^*)} = \frac{r_2 + m_2x}{r_1 + m_1(s - x)} \tag{8}$$

$$\bar{Q} = f(v^*)V_2^* \,, \tag{9}$$

and we can obtain a unique optimum with respect to v (and also with respect to V_2) by these two conditions.[5]

[5] We cannot assume convexity of the cost function with respect to v and V_2. However, in this special case, it is very easy to show the uniqueness of the optimum solution. By equation (7), we can show that:

$$\frac{dV_2}{dv} = -\frac{f'}{f}V_2, \quad \text{then we have:}$$

$$\frac{dC}{dv} = \frac{V_2}{f}[\rho_1(f - vf') - \rho_2 f'] \quad \text{for all} \quad v \geqq 0$$

where

$$\rho_1 = r_1 + m_1(s - x) \quad \text{and} \quad \rho_2 = r_2 + m_2x \,.$$

Since

$$\frac{d}{dv}[\rho_1(f - vf') - \rho_2 f'] = -(v\rho_1 + \rho_2)f'' > 0 \quad \text{for all} \quad v \geqq 0 \,,$$

it is obvious from equation (8) that:

$$\frac{dC}{dv} < 0 \quad \text{for} \quad 0 \leqq v < v^*;$$

$$\frac{dC}{dv} = 0 \quad \text{for} \quad v = v^*;$$

$$\frac{dC}{dv} > 0 \quad \text{for} \quad v^* < v \,.$$

The uniqueness of the optimum solution, $v = v^*$, can be concluded from this well-behaved C-function.

Obviously v^* and the corresponding C^* are functions of x. So secondly, let us see the effect of the change of x upon them. By a well-known theorem of comparative statics,[6] we can see that:

$$\frac{dC^*}{dx} = \frac{\partial C^*}{\partial x} = (-m_1v^* + m_2)V_2^* \,, \tag{10}$$

and with further computation it can be shown that:[7]

$$\begin{aligned} \frac{d^2C^*}{dx^2} &= \left[-m_1 - (-m_1v^* + m_2)\frac{f'(v^*)}{f(v^*)}\right]V_2^*\frac{dv^*}{dx} \\ &= \frac{[-m(f(v^*) - v^*f'(v^*)) - m_2f'(v^*)]^2V_2^*}{[(r_2 + m_2x) + v^*\{r_1 + m_1(s - x)\}]f(v^*)f''(v^*)} \,. \end{aligned} \tag{11}$$

By equation (11), we can conclude that:

$$\frac{d^2C^*}{dx^2} < 0 \qquad \text{for all } x;\ \ 0 \leqq x \leqq s\,. \tag{12}$$

Relationship, (12), which says that the optimized cost function of the firm is strictly concave with respect to x, contains a very important implication. By this relationship, any intermediate locations between M_1 and M_2 are *stricly* excluded in our simple location problem.[8] Writing $\{-m_1v^*(x) + m_2\} = \phi(x)$, we have the following three cases of the optimum location in a sense of the *minimum minimoram* of the cost function, as shown in Table 1.

TABLE 1. Optimum Location Possibilities

$\phi(s)$ / $\phi(0)$	$-$	0 or +
$-$ or 0	$x^* = s$ (M_1)	impossible
+	?	$x^* = 0$ (M_2)

We are now in the position to define the procedure for determining the optimum location of the firm in this simple cost-minimizing problem for an arbitrarily fixed level of output.

R1. Obtain the values of $v^*(0)$ and $v^*(s)$ by equation (8). Then calculate $\phi(0)$ and $\phi(s)$ with them.

R2. If $\phi(0) \leqq 0$, then $M_1(x^* = s)$ is the optimum location.

---

[6] See Samuelson [6; p. 34].

[7] $\dfrac{dV_2^*}{dx} = \left(\dfrac{dV_2}{dv}\right)_{v=v^*}\cdot\dfrac{dv^*}{dx}$ and $\dfrac{dV_2}{dv} = -\dfrac{f'}{f}V_2$,

as shown before. Also we have:

$$\frac{dv^*}{dx} = \frac{-m_1(f - v^*f') - m_2f'}{[(r_2 + m_2x) + v^*\{r_1 + m_1(s - x)\}]f''}$$

from equation (8).

[8] In a diagram, Hoover [2; p. 30] implicity points out this concavity without assuming the substitutability of materials. He also discusses the effect of the substitutability on location [2; pp. 44–46].

R3. If $\phi(s) \geqq 0$, then $M_2(x^* = 0)$ is the optimum location.

R4. If $\phi(0) > 0$, and $\phi(s) < 0$, then calculate the average costs,

$$AC^*(0) = \frac{(r_1 + m_1 s)v^*(0) + r_2}{f(v^*(0))} \text{ at } M_2$$

and

$$AC^*(s) = \frac{r_1 v^*(s) + (r_2 + m_2 s)}{f(v^*(s))} \text{ at } M_1.[9]$$

The one of these two locations which gives the smaller average cost is the optimum location.

The following *propositions* can be deduced by the analysis in this section concerning our *special case* of the optimum location problem.

P1. There is no possibility of an intermediate location.

P2. There is a *unique* optimum location at M_1 or M_2 except for a very rare case where $AC^*(0) = AC^*(s)$.

P3. Since $v^*(0)$ and $v^*(s)$ depend upon r_1 and r_2, as seen by equation (8), the optimum location *does* depend upon the base prices of raw materials.

P4. Since the average cost is independent of the level of output at any location as seen by equations (6) and (7), the optimum location *does not* depend upon the level of output.

P5. In general, the optimum location is *not* the point of minimum transportation cost.[10]

Of course, Proposition 4 does not contradict Moses' finding that the optimum location is dependent upon the level of cutput *if* the production function is not (linear) homogeneous.[11] Proposition 5 will be paraphrased in the next section.

3. DISCUSSION OF THE RESULTS OF SECTION 2

According to Moses, the course of thinking among traditional location theorists has been as follows:

> "[They] assume that there are no geographic variations in the prices or qualities of inputs at alternative sources. [Then] (I) there are no geographic differentials in production costs, and (II) the optimum location is the point of minimum transportation costs."[12]

[9] By dividing equation (6) by equation (7) side by side, we have:

$$AC(x) = \frac{C(x)}{Q} = \frac{\{r_1 + m_1(s - x)\}v + \{r_2 + m_2 x\}}{f(v)}$$

at x.

[10] Tony Smith has correctly pointed out that the *linear homogeneity* assumption may not be essential to the deduction of these propositions, i.e., *P1, P2, P3* and *P5* may be deducible with only the quasi-concavity assumption on the production function, and *P4* may be deducible with the quasi-concavity assumption plus a homogeneity assumption of *some degree* (not necessarily a constant degree). However, note that the quasi-concavity assumption is not exactly equivalent to the assumption shown by expression (5) when the production function is *not* linear homogeneous. Note also that we cannot deduce expression (12) with only a single homogeneity assumption of some degree other than one plus the set of assumptions shown by expressions (3) through (5).

[11] Moses [5; p. 265].

[12] Moses [5; p. 265].

His criticism of this reasoning is that the two conclusions are not generally valid unless an additional assumption about the linear production function (strictly speaking a function with fixed input coefficients) is involved.[13]

Apart from this criticism, the above two conclusions contain a great deal of ambiguity in themselves. First of all, what kind of transportation costs should be minimized in connection with Moses' second conclusion? Naturally, the average transportation cost associated with production and delivery of one unit final product must be the object of minimization. But if there is room for the choice of production technique, we can expect no uniqueness for such an average transportation cost at given location. Even if we reinterpret this statement to mean the ***minimum minimoram*** of the average transportation cost with respect to the location ***and*** the production technique chosen, there is no assurance that the same choice of technique would coincide with a condition of productive efficiency.

By the same token, the first conclusion involves some vagueness concerning the type of production cost to be compared among alternative locations. It must be the "already-minimized" average production cost per unit of final product by the employment of the optimal production technique. This average production cost will be independent of the level of output if we assume a linear homogeneous production function.

Of course, the foregoing ambiguities will completely disappear if we assume fixed input coefficients as Moses says. But there is another way of reinterpreting the two conclusions. First, concerning Moses' first conclusion, we can choose an optimum value of the input ratio, $v = \hat{v}$, without regard to the transportation costs by the usual efficiency condition:

$$\frac{f(\hat{v}) - \hat{v}f'(\hat{v})}{f'(\hat{v})} = \frac{r_2}{r_1} \tag{13}$$

Conclusion (I) implies that $\hat{v}$ is independent of the location of the firm.

Secondly, taking this value of $v = \hat{v}$ as given, we can calculate the transportation cost slope, $\hat{\phi} = - m_1\hat{v} + m_2$, which is constant for $0 \leqq x \leqq s$ in this case. If $\hat{\phi}$ is negative, conclusion (II) leads the firm to locate at M_1, and if $\hat{\phi}$ is positive, the same conclusion leads it to locate at M_2. It is easy to see that the above procedure (and it is the only consistent and unambiguous reinterpretation of the two conclusions without the assumption of fixed input coefficients) lacks general validity as a criterion of optimum location in the sense of overall cost minimization developed in the previous section. For that purpose, it suffices to point out that $\hat{v}$ differs from both of $v^*(0)$ and $v^*(s)$ in *R1*.

However, it is still worthwhile to inquire whether the above rule can be used a proxy procedure for deciding the optimum location, at least as far as the choice between M_1 and M_2 is concerned. By a simple counter-example, we can show that this is not the case. Let us specify the productivity function to be: $f(v) = v^\alpha$ (a Cobb-Douglas function) where α is some constant between 0 and 1. Then we have:

$$\hat{v} = \frac{\alpha}{1-\alpha}\frac{r_2}{r_1}\,; \tag{14}$$

[13] Moses [5; p. 265].

$$v^*(0) = \frac{\alpha}{1-\alpha}\frac{r_2}{r_1 + m_1 s}; \tag{15}$$

$$v^*(s) = \frac{\alpha}{1-\alpha}\frac{r_2 + m_2 s}{r_1}; \tag{16}$$

and

$$\hat{\phi} = -m_1\left(\frac{\alpha}{1-\alpha}\frac{r_2}{r_1}\right) + m_2; \tag{17}$$

$$\phi(0) = -m_1\left(\frac{\alpha}{1-\alpha}\frac{r_2}{r_1 + m_1 s}\right) + m_2; \tag{18}$$

$$\phi(s) = -m_1\left(\frac{\alpha}{1-\alpha}\frac{r_2 + m_2 s}{r_1}\right) + m_2. \tag{19}$$

In addition, we assume that $\hat{\phi} > 0$. Then the "reinterpreted" procedure leads us to a location at M_2.

It is clear that $\phi(0) > 0$ by the above assumption. However, $\phi(s)$ can be negative even under this assumption. If this is the case, we have an indefinite situation, as seen in Table 1, and further information about $AC^*(0)$ and $AC^*(s)$ is needed. See *R4* in Section 2. In fact we have:

$$AC^*(0) = \frac{r}{(1-\alpha)\left(\frac{\alpha}{1-\alpha}\frac{r_2}{r_1 + m_1 s}\right)^{\alpha}}; \tag{20}$$

$$AC^*(s) = \frac{r_2 + \alpha m_2 s}{(1-\alpha)\left(\frac{\alpha}{1-\alpha}\frac{r_2 + m_2 s}{r_1}\right)^{\alpha}}. \tag{21}$$

Let $K(s)$ be the ratio of $AC^*(s)$ to $AC^*(0)$, then,

$$K(s) = \frac{AC^*(s)}{AC^*(0)} = \frac{r_2 + \alpha m_2 s}{r_2}\left[\frac{r_1 r_2}{(r_1 + m_1 s)(r_2 + m_2 s)}\right]^{\alpha}. \tag{22}$$

For very large values of s, $K(s)$ becomes:

$$K(s) \sim C s^{1-2\alpha} \tag{23}$$

where C is some constant.

If $\alpha > \frac{1}{2}$, K may become very small as s increases, in spite of the fact that $K(0) = 1$ and $(dK/ds)_{s=0} > 0$. Therefore, in the case where $\alpha > \frac{1}{2}$ and s is sufficiently large, the optimum location will be M_1 by procedure *R4* in Section 2 and this contradicts the solution obtained by the "reinterpreted" procedure. The latter method does not give us the correct answer, and Proposition *P5* in Section 2 has been further verified. See Figure 2.

Up to this point, there has been very little added to Moses' analysis. He was certainly correct in pointing out that a narrow technological approach to the location problem could be misleading.[14] However, it may be worthwhile to re-emphasize the following findings of Section 2: a) exclusion of intermediate points as the optimum location is due to the concavity of the optimized cost function $C^*(x)$ with respect to the distance variable x, and this concavity is

[14] As an example, we may mention the work of Kuhn and Kuenne [4].

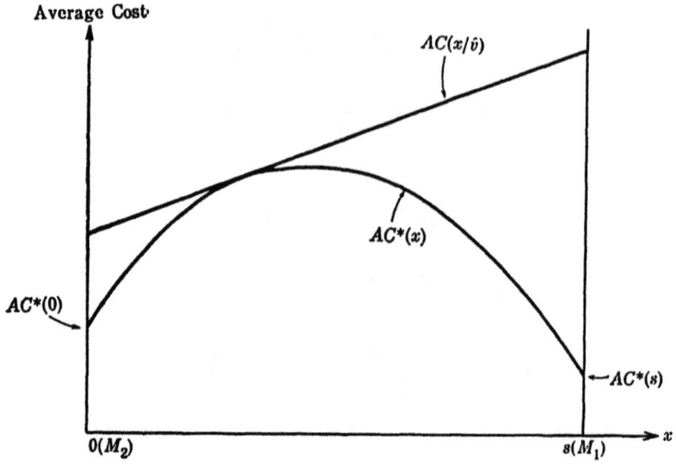

FIGURE 2. Locational Average Cost Curves.

due, in turn, to the concavity of the productivity function $f(v)$, b) in some cases, it is not necessary to compare to average costs at M_1 and M_2 themselves. A shortcut method (*R2* or *R3*) may be available to decide the optimum location of the firm.[15]

4. A CASE OF PROFIT MAXIMIZATION: INTRODUCTION OF THE DEMAND FUNCTION

In this section, we shall consider another case of the firm's locational problem where the following conditions are met:

i) The market for the firm's final product is concentrated at the single point C.

ii) While the first raw material can be produced only at the single site M_1, the second raw material is ubiquitous and can thus be obtained anywhere on the straight line between C and M_1 at a uniform price (see Figure 3).

iii) At the market, C, the firm is facing a demand function for its product which is expressed by a "demand price" function of the following type:

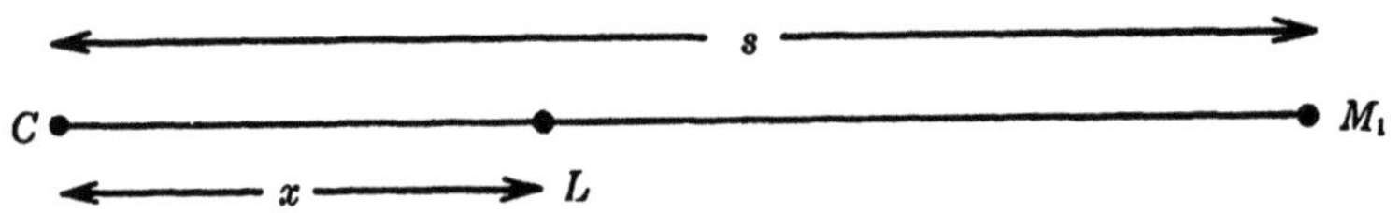

FIGURE 3. Locational Line.

$p(Q)$: the demand price as a function of the quantity demanded, where $p'(Q) < 0$ for all $Q \geqq 0$.

The condition on the second derivative of $p(Q)$ will be specified later. We will use the same notation as that adopted in Section 2 with the following differences:

c: transport rate on the firm's product;

[15] Moses' diagramatical approach does not seem strong enough to clarify these points.

s: distance between C and M_1;
x: distance between C and the firm's location point, $0 \leq x \leq s$.
Under these circumstances, the profit function of this firm will be shown as:

$$\begin{aligned}\pi &= \{p(Q) - cx\}Q - [\{r_1 + m_1(s - x)\}V_1 + r_2V_2] \\ &= \{p(Q) - cx\}Q - [\{r_1 + m_1(s - x)\}v + r_2]\frac{Q}{f(v)} . \qquad (24)\end{aligned}$$

As usual, we consider first the optimum adjustment by the firm at a *given* location. The primary conditions for the maximum of the π-function are:

$$\frac{f(v^*) - v^*f'(v^*)}{f'(v^*)} = \frac{r_2}{r_1 + m_1(s - x)} ; \qquad (25)$$

$$p(Q^*)\left\{1 + \frac{p'(Q^*)}{p(Q^*)}Q^*\right\} = \frac{\{r_1 + m_1(s - x)\}v^* + r_2}{f(v^*)} + cx . \qquad (26)$$

Concerning the secondary condition for the maximum, we may argue as follows: As we see by equation (25), the optimum value of v is determined quite independently of the level of Q. Also, it is easily shown that this value of $v = v^*$, has a profit-maximizing characteristic for any arbitrarily given value of Q. See Footnote 5. Then, in a process of step-wise maximization, v^* can be regarded as a function of Q in the trivial sense that it takes the same value for all possible values of Q, and we have a concentrated objective function as follows:

$$\hat{\pi}(Q; v^*) = \{p(Q) - cx\}Q - [\{r_1 + m_1(s - x)\}v^* + r_2]\frac{Q}{f(v^*)} . \qquad (27)$$

Then we have:

$$\underset{(=0)}{\frac{d\hat{\pi}}{dQ}} = p(Q)\left\{1 + \frac{p'(Q)}{p(Q)}Q\right\} - \left[\frac{\{r_1 + m_1(s - x)\}v^* + r_2}{f(v^*)} + cx\right] \qquad (28)$$

and

$$\frac{d^2\hat{\pi}}{dQ^2} = 2p'(Q) + p''(Q)Q \qquad (29)$$

at $Q = Q^*$.

If $(2p' + p''Q)$ is assumed to be negative for all $Q > 0$, then $\hat{\pi}$ is really a strictly concave function of Q and the secondary condition for the maximum is satisfied. This assumption is not too restrictive with respect to the price elasticity of the inverse function of $p(Q)$, so we shall maintain this assumption henceforth.

iv) $2p'(Q) + p''(Q)Q < 0$ for all $Q > 0$.

In fact, a linear and negatively sloped demand function or a negative exponential demand function certainly satisfies this condition although neither of them is strictly concave.[16]

With Assumption (iv), we can proceed in a fairly straightforward manner. Now equations (25) and (26) give us unique and globally-maximizing values of v

[16] See Stevens and Rydell [8] concerning the classification of demand functions which has a very close relationship to Assumption (iv).

and Q for a given value of x, as well as the optimized profit function $\pi^*(x)$. Again by a theorem of comparative statics we have:

$$\frac{d\pi^*}{dx} = \frac{\partial \pi^*}{\partial x} = \left\{- c + m_1 \frac{v^*}{f(v^*)}\right\} Q^* \tag{30}$$

and

$$\begin{aligned} \frac{d^2\pi^*}{dx^2} &= \frac{m_1\{f(v^*) - v^* f'(v^*)\}}{\{f(v^*)\}^2} \frac{dv^*}{dx} Q^* + \left\{- c + m_1 \frac{v^*}{f(v^*)}\right\} \frac{dQ^*}{dx} \\ &= - \frac{[m_1\{f(v^*) - v^* f'(v^*)\}]^2 Q^*}{[r_2 + v^*\{r_1 + m_1(s - x)\}]\{f(v^*)\}^2 f''(v^*)} \\ &\quad - \frac{1}{\{2p'(Q^*) + p''(Q^*)Q^*\}} \left\{c - m_1 \frac{v^*}{f(v^*)}\right\}^2 . \end{aligned} \tag{31}$$

By expression (5) and Assumption (iv), it is obvious that:

$$\frac{d^2\pi^*}{dx^2} > 0 \qquad \text{for} \quad 0 \leqq x \leqq s , \tag{32}$$

which means that the optimized profit function is strictly convex with respect to x. Therefore any intermediate locations between C and M_1 are again strictly excluded.

Writing $\{- cf(v^*) + m_1 v^*\} = \phi(x)$, we have the following three cases of the optimum location as shown in Table 2. This table is similar to the one presented in Section 2.

TABLE 2. Optimum Location Possibilities.

$\phi(0)$ \ $\phi(s)$	$-$ or 0	+
$-$	$x^* = 0$ (C)	?
0 or +	impossible	$x^* = s$ (M_1)

By this table, we can easily deduce the procedure for determining the optimum location of the firm in this profit maximization problem.

R1. Obtain the values of $v^*(0)$ and $v^*(s)$ by equation (25). Then calculate $\phi(0)$ and $\phi(s)$.

R2. If $\phi(0) \geqq 0$, then $M_1(x^* = s)$ is the optimum location.

R3. If $\phi(s) \leqq 0$, then $C(x^* = 0)$ is the optimum location.

R4. If $\phi(0) < 0$ and $\phi(s) > 0$, then calculate the average cost of production and delivery, i.e.,

$$k(x) = \frac{\{r_1 + m_1(s - x)\}v^* + r_2}{f(v^*)} + cx ,$$

at $x = 0$ and at $x = s$. The one of these two locations which gives the smaller average cost is the optimum location.

The last rule can be verified as follows: At given value of x, the firm first optimizes its input ratio as $v = v^*(x)$ and gets a concentrated objective function in the form:

$$\hat{\pi}(Q;\ x) = \{p(Q) - k(x)\}Q \tag{33}$$

where $k(x)$ is the average cost of production and delivery at x;

$$k(x) = \frac{\{r_1 + m_1(s-x)\}v^* + r_2}{f(v^*)} + cx\,. \tag{34}$$

Then Q is adjusted as $Q = Q^*(x)$ in order to maximize $\hat{\pi}$. Such being the case, Q^* and π^* depend upon x *only through* $k(x)$. In other words, only the value of $k(x)$ is crucial to determine Q^* and π^*. In addition we have:

$$\frac{d\pi^*}{dk} = \frac{\partial\pi^*}{\partial k} = -\,Q^* \qquad \text{for all} \quad k(x); \qquad 0 \leqq x \leqq s \tag{35}$$

for the change of k. Then we can conclude that.

$$\text{if} \quad k(x_1) < k(x_2), \quad \text{then} \quad \pi^*(x_1) > \pi^*(x_2)\,. \tag{36}$$

This result verifies *R4*.

The next five propositions follow those results.

P1. There is no possibility of an intermediate location.

P2. There is a *unique* optimum location at C or M_1 except in the very rare case where $k(0) = k(s)$.

P3. Since $v^*(0)$ and $v^*(s)$ depend upon r_1 and r_2, as seen by equation (25), the optimum location *does* depend upon the base prices of raw materials.

P4. In any case, the optimum location *does not* depend upon the shape and the position of the demand function.

P5. Generally speaking, the optimum location is *not* the point of minimum transportation cost.

It should be noted that we do not need Assumption (iv) as far as the deduction of Proposition 1 is concerned. This is because the selection of the optimum location depends only upon the sign of $d\pi^*/dx$ and the latter is the same as that of $\phi(x) = -\,cf(v^*) + m_1v^*$. It is easy to show the strict convexity of $\phi(x)$ with respect to x. We can then conclude that there is no turning point for $d\pi^*/dx$ from positive to negative between $x = 0$ and $x = s$ so that there is no possibility of an intermediate location. Nevertheless, Assumption (iv) is required as a sufficient condition of profit maximization in our model.

The rest of this section will be devoted to the analysis of a specific case where the demand price function is linear and the production function is of the Cobb-Douglas type, i.e.,

$$p(Q) = a - bQ\,; \tag{37}$$

$$f(v) = v^\alpha\,. \tag{38}$$

In this particular case, we can first determine the values of $v^*(0)$ and $v^*(s)$ by equation (25) as follows:

$$v^*(0) = \frac{\alpha}{1-\alpha}\,\frac{r_2}{r_1 + m_1 s} \tag{39}$$

$$v^*(s) = \frac{\alpha}{1-\alpha}\,\frac{r_2}{r_1}\,. \tag{40}$$

If

$$c \leqq m_1\left(\frac{\alpha}{1-\alpha}\frac{r_2}{r_1+m_1 s}\right)^{1-\alpha} \quad \text{or} \quad c \geqq m_1\left(\frac{\alpha}{1-\alpha}\frac{r_2}{r_1}\right)^{1-\alpha},$$

then there is no further problem about the location of the firm according to *R2* and *R3*. Therefore here we assume that:

$$m_1\left(\frac{\alpha}{1-\alpha}\frac{r_2}{r_1+m_1 s}\right)^{1-\alpha} < c < m_1\left(\frac{\alpha}{1-\alpha}\frac{r_2}{r_1}\right)^{1-\alpha}. \tag{41}$$

By equation (26), we have:

$$Q^*(0) = \frac{1}{2b}\left\{a - \frac{r_2}{(1-\alpha)\left(\frac{\alpha}{1-\alpha}\frac{r_2}{r_1+m_1 s}\right)^{\alpha}}\right\}; \tag{42}$$

$$Q^*(s) = \frac{1}{2b}\left\{a - \frac{r_2}{(1-\alpha)\left(\frac{\alpha}{1-\alpha}\frac{r_2}{r_1}\right)^{\alpha}} - cs\right\}; \tag{43}$$

and then,

$$\pi^*(0) = \frac{1}{4b}\left\{a - \frac{r}{(1-\alpha)\left(\frac{\alpha}{1-\alpha}\frac{r_2}{r_1+m_1 s}\right)^{\alpha}}\right\}^2; \tag{44}$$

$$\pi^*(s) = \frac{1}{4b}\left\{a - \frac{r_2}{(1-\alpha)\left(\frac{\alpha}{1-\alpha}\frac{r_2}{r_1}\right)^{\alpha}} - cs\right\}^2, \tag{45}$$

by equation (24).

The choice between C and M_1 as the optimum location depends upon the relative magnitudes of $\pi^*(0)$ and $\pi^*(s)$. However, as seen by equations (44) and (45), this comparison depends only upon the relative sizes of the terms:

$$\left\{\frac{r_2}{(1-\alpha)\left(\frac{\alpha}{1-\alpha}\frac{r_2}{r_1+m_1 s}\right)^{\alpha}}\right\} \quad \text{and} \quad \left\{\frac{r_2}{(1-\alpha)\left(\frac{\alpha}{1-\alpha}\frac{r_2}{r_1}\right)^{\alpha}} + cs\right\}.$$

This means that the selection of the optimum location is quite independent of the demand condition for the final product of the firm, and we then clearly see the validity of our shortcut rule, *R4*. The demand conditions play no role on the locational decision of the firm *as long as we assume a linear homogeneous production function.*[17]

5. CONCLUSION

The discussions in the preceding sections certainly have not been of a general type. They have been concerned with very specific cases of a firm's locational decision. It may be useful, therefore, to examine briefly some possible courses of generalization of our models.

[17] Since the total delivery cost is a linear function of Q, a homogeneity assumption about the production function other than linear one, will change this result, i.e., the demand conditions are generally relevant to the locational decision unless a *linear* homogeneous production function is assumed by contrast. See footnote 10 for the sake of contrast.

First of all, we have severely limited our scope to the cases of the simple locational straight line. Even the discussion of Weber's "locational triangle" has been avoided. The theoretical reason for this is that in a triangle or a polygon setting, the mathematical expression of distances and the resulting normal equations for optimality become extremely unwieldy and they cannot be readily handled by analytical methods, as has been pointed out by Kuhn and Kuenne.[18] The practical reason, on the other hand, is that as far as we take the existing transportation system for granted, a wide class of locational problems may be translated into the straight line case by an appropriate choice of variables. In that sense, our straight line approach is not so restrictive as might be supposed.

In any event, however, it is unrealistic to adhere to the simple straight line case: we should generalize our models to the triangle or polygon cases: Yet, in those cases, we probably have to be content (for the reasons discussed above) to utilize some algorithm for the numerical solution of the problem, instead of solving it analytically. Even so, it is emphasized that such an algorithm should take factor substitutability into account and not confine itself to the narrow transport cost-minimizing approach. In the terminology used by Kuhn and Kuenne, the potential function Φ and its gradient over the locational triangle must be based on the profit function which is directly related to both demand function and the production function.[19] The advantage of simplification, gained by excluding revenues and costs, other than transport costs, is too small, relative to the subsequent disadvantage of loss of reality. The speed of convergence of the algorithm may actually be increased by the introduction of factor substitutability.

Second, we have ignored the price of land itself in our models. The introduction of the land price into the problem may change some of our propositions such as the extremity of the optimum location. Generalization in this direction is not only interesting but also realistic. However, some words of warning are necessary. First, we must be very cautious when dealing with the land variable as one of the factors of production. A simple addition of this variable to the production function as its third component is sometimes inadequate because of the essential difference between the land and other factors of production, particularly in the case of manufacturing industry. There should therefore be some special treatment of the land variable. Second, and more important, is the relation between rent theory and location theory. If we presume the existence of a land price structure in advance, how can we explain the formation of a rent structure in a particular area? Are we not falling into a pitfall of circular argument?

In order to avoid this dilemma, we require a demand and supply approach to land use, however difficult its construction might be. The work of Alonso is a rare effort in this direction although his discussions are not always rigorous and in some places, they are even misleading.[20] As a further step in this direction, we should examine more rigorously the characteristics of the so-called *bid price curves* in relation to demand and/or production functions. Since real and overwhelming difficulties arise from the infinite heterogeneity of land as an

[18] Kuhn and Kuenne [4; p. 21].

[19] Kuhn and Kuenne [4; p. 25].

[20] Alonso [1].

economic good, some practical method of limiting the number of heterogeneous land groups should be employed with the minimum degree of arbitrariness. It is the author's intention to tackle these problems in the future.

Finally, the locational problem must be re-examined in a dynamic setting. The firm's locational decision is nothing other than an aspect of its investment decision with respect to fixed equipment. Hence, location theory must contain a very long-run perspective and needs to be integrated with the investment theory of the firm. In a recent work, Smith has attempted to integrate investment theory with theory of production.[21] It is now our task to synthesize both these theories with location theory of the firm.

REFERENCES

[1] Alonso, William. *Location and Land Use*. Cambridge, Mass.: Harvard University Press, 1964.

[2] Hoover, Edgar M. *The Location of Economic Activity*. New York: McGraw-Hill, 1948.

[3] Isard, Walter. *Location and Space-Economy*. New York: The Technology Press of M. I. T. and John Wiley and Sons, 1956.

[4] Kuhn, Harold W. and Robert E. Kuenne. "An Efficient Algorithm for the Numerical Solution of the Generalized Weber Problem in Spatial Economics," *Journal of Regional Science*, Vol. 4 (Winter 1962), pp. 21-33.

[5] Moses, Leon N. "Location and the Theory of Production," *Quarterly Journal of Economics*, Vol. 72 (May 1958), pp. 259-272.

[6] Samuelson, Paul A. *Foundations of Economic Analysis*. Cambridge, Mass.: Harvard University Press, 1947.

[7] Smith, Vernon L. *Investment and Production*. Cambridge, Mass.: Harvard University Press, 1961.

[8] Stevens, Benjamin H. and C. Peter Rydell. "Spatial Demand Theory and Monopoly Price Policy," *Papers, Regional Science Association*, Vol. 17 (1966), pp. 195-204.

[21] Smith [7].

Economics, Annals of Economics Department, Tohoku, Vol 31 (1970) 20-42

On a Simple Model of Dynamic Fiscal Policy

by

Noboru Sakashita

In Chapter 5 of his book [5], Hirschman developed a very attractive discussion on the strategy of investment choices in underdeveloped areas. In replacement of the elaborate but hardly applicable "social marginal productivity (SMP)" investment criteria in the past,[1)] he proposed a thory of "efficient sequence" among different investment programs particularly in relation to the selection between investments in Social Overhead Capital and in Directly Productive Activities. For the purpose of practical application, however, we need to make the concept of the efficient sequence itself much more palpable without losing the essence of his unique thinking.

Hirschman's theory does have at least two points of uniqueness. The first one is that it deals with not only the problem of substitution choices among investment programs but also that of postponement choices among them. Then his theory is substantially a dynamic one especially when it is contrasted with the essentially static discussion of investment criteria. Secondly, all types of investments in his model (both the private investment and the public investment) are assumed to be induced investments. Then we have to seek for another exogenous instrument than decision on the public investment itself as an initiating factor of development.

However, it may be unwise to start with a model which contains all components of his freely developed discussion. As an alternative way, we will proceed step by step from a very simple closed model to complicated open ones. In this article, three positive and closed models will be formulated in Section I, and in Section II a normative treatment of the first model in Section I will be studied.

1) See [1], [3] and [4] as examples of the investment criteria discussion. Also see [7]. 37

I. Simple Closed Models

In this section, we treat a simple closed economy of single sector which has two types of capital stock: social overhead capital and private capital for directly productive activities. We call the former "SOC stock" and the latter "DPA (capital) stock". The system of notation is as follows:

K : the amount of DPA stock,

Q : the amount of SOC stock,

Y : the rate of national product,

$\dot{K}=\dfrac{dK}{dt}$: the rate of investment in DPA stock,

$\dot{Q}=\dfrac{dQ}{dt}$: the rate of investment in SOC stock,

$K=\dfrac{K}{Q}$: the DPA-SOC capital ratio,

$F(K, Q)\ (=Y)$: the production function of the economy,

s : the saving ratio of the economy, $0<s<1$,

θ : the rate of tax for public investment.

As common assumptions for all of subsequent models, we assume that

1. All gooods are homogeneous, then a complete price system is not needed in the economy.

2. The production function is continuously twice differentiable with respect to both variables and is subject to constant returns to scale. Then we have a unique productivity function as

$$\text{(1)} \qquad \frac{Y}{Q}=f(k)=F\left(\frac{K}{Q},\ 1\right).$$

Several additional assumptions are made on this productivity function. These are

(i) $\lim_{k\to 0} f(k)=0,\ \lim_{k\to\infty} f(k)=\infty$,

(ii) $0\leqq f'(k)<\infty$ for all k: $0<k<\infty$,

2) As a matter of fact, Assumption (v) is not an independent postulate but is deducible from other assumptions in this set. But we write it here for the sake of referring convenience.

(iii) $f''(k) < 0 \qquad$ for all $k \geqq 0$,

(iv) $\lim_{k \to 0} f'(k) = \infty, \ \lim_{k \to \infty} f'(k) = 0$,

(v) $0 \leqq f(k) - kf'(k) < \infty$ for all k: $0 < k < \infty$ [2])

The second and the fifth assumptions imply that the marginal productivities of DPA stock and of SOC stock are both always nonnegative, and other assumptions are usual regularity conditions on the production function.

In our models, θ is usually restricted to the tax rate only for the purpose of public investment (with an exception of Model I-3). Taxation for current public expendiutre should be included in the consumption of the economy.

I-1. *Model with a Constant Saving Ratio*

Let us first consider a simple situation where both s and θ are fixed constants. In addition we assume that the supply of private (or public) fund is always equal to the demand for private (or public) investment respectively. This assumption does not necessarily imply the presence of an over-all investment plan especially in the DPA subscctor. It means only that the adjustmnt factor of saving and investment is placed in back stage.

Under the circumstances, we have the following process of capital accumulation.

$$\dot{K} = s(1-\theta)Y = s(1-\theta)F(K, Q), \tag{2}$$

$$Q = \theta Y = \theta F(K, Q). \tag{3}$$

By the use of the ratio variable k, these equations are transformed into

$$\dot{k} = \{s(1-\theta) - \theta k\} f(k). \tag{4}$$

If we assume $k(0) > 0$ as the initial condition the process (4) satisfies the Lipschitz conditions, and the existence of the solution is assured. (Recall Assumption (ii).) Letting the right-hand side of (4) be $\phi_1(k)$, we see that

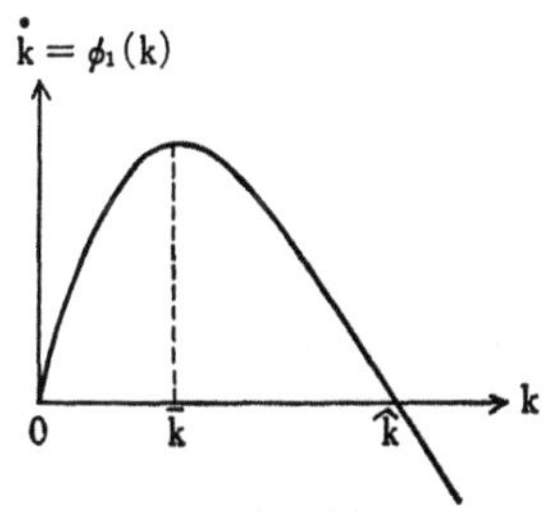

Figure 1

$$\begin{cases} \lim_{k \to 0} \phi_1(k) = 0, \quad \lim_{k \to 0} \phi_1'(k) = \infty, \\ \phi_1(k) < 0 \quad \text{for all } k > \text{some } \bar{k}, \\ \lim_{k \to \infty} \phi_1(k) = -\infty \end{cases} \tag{5}$$

and the stability of this system with regard to the variable k can be visualized as on Figure 1. The long-run equilibrium value of k is

$$\hat{k} = s\,\frac{1-\theta}{\theta} \tag{6}$$

and the balanced growth rate (G) of K and Q is

$$G = \theta f(\hat{k}) \tag{7}$$

in this system.

If we can freely choose the G-maximizing value of θ within the range of [0, 1], it will be given as

$$\theta^* = 1 - \frac{\hat{k}^* f'(\hat{k}^*)}{f(\hat{k}^*)} \tag{8–1}$$

with the unique optimal value of $\hat{k}$ such that[3)]

$$\hat{k}^* = s\,\frac{1-\theta^*}{\theta^*} \tag{8–2}$$

by letting

$$\frac{dG}{d\theta} = f(\hat{k}) - \frac{s f'(\hat{k})}{\theta} = 0$$

and with a condition that

$$\frac{d^2 G}{d\theta^2} = \frac{s^2}{\theta^3} f''(\hat{k}) < 0 \text{ for all } \theta\colon 0<\theta\leqq 1.$$

The elasticity of the productivity function, $\varepsilon = \dfrac{kf'}{f}$, always lies betweeen 0 and 1 by Assumptions (v) and (ii), then we are sure to find the optimal feasible value of θ by Equations (8–1) and (8–2). (See Figure 2.)

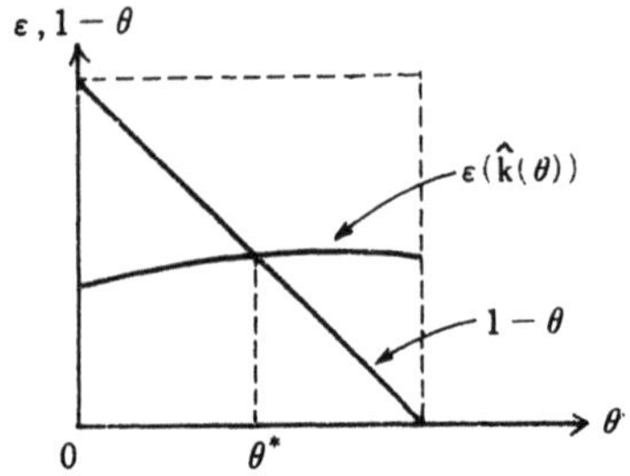

Figure 2

If θ^* is eliminated from (8–1) and (8–2), we have a relation such that

$$s f'(\hat{k}^*) = f(\hat{k}^*) - \hat{k}^* f'(\hat{k}^*) \tag{9}$$

---

3) The same as in Chapter 12 of [2], we can call $\hat{k}^*$ the von Neumann configuration of capital composition, and the corresponding growth rate $G(\hat{k}^*)$ the von Neumann growth rate. (See [2] page 329.) But it must be noticed that our system includes the institutional and behavioral factors (θ and s) of the economy as well as its technological factor, so that the optimal configuration depends not only upon the latter but also upon the former.

at the optimal long-run equilibrium. Equation (9) means that the marginal productivity of DPA stock modified by the saving ratio should be equal to the marginal productivity of SOC stock at the optimal equilibrium.

In the case of the Cobb-Douglas production function, $F(K, Q) = AK^{\alpha}Q^{\beta}$ $(\beta = 1\text{-}\alpha)$, the optimal tax rate is β and the optimal balanced capital ratio is $s\dfrac{\alpha}{\beta}$. This situation implies something like a fair distribution of national product between the private and the public subsectors in the economy.

In reality, however, the feasibe range of θ may be much narrower than between 0 and 1, and sometimes the optimal θ^* may lie outside of the feasible range. In the case of $\theta \in [0, \bar{\theta}]$ where $\bar{\theta} < \theta^*$, we can only choose the maximum $\theta = \bar{\theta}$ within the feasible range as the second best solution.

Although the above model is far from the profound implication of Hirschman's thoery, it could show the existence of the optimal balanced DPA-SOC capital ratio, $\hat{k}^*$, which depends upon the production technology, and the institutional and behavioral factors of the economy by an extremely simple manipulation.

I-2 *Model with a Variable Saving Ratio*

As the first complication, we introducd a kind of changeability in the value of the saving ratio. Let us take s as *an increasing function of the marginal productivity of DPA stock.*[4] Sincc we have already established the properties of the $f'(k)$-function sufficiently, we can treat s as a direct function of k,

(10) $$s = s(k)$$

4) In [6] Inada has shown that if the aggregate utility index is expressed by a function of the Constant Elasticity of Substitution

$$u(y_c, y_I) = A(\delta y_c^{-\gamma} + (1-\delta) y_I^{-\gamma})^{-1/\gamma}$$

where y_c is the amount of consumption goods and y_I is the amount of investment goods, then we obtain a saving ratio such that

$$s = \frac{1}{1 + \left(\frac{\delta}{1-\delta}\right)^{\sigma} p^{\sigma}}$$

where p is the price of investment goods in terms of consumption goods and $\sigma = \frac{1}{1+\gamma}$ $(0 \leqq \sigma \leqq 1)$ is the elasticity of substitution. In our model p is identically unity because of the homogeneity of all goods. In addition if δ which determines the relative evaulation of two kinds of goods is itself a bounded and decreasing function of the marginal productivity of the investment goods, then we have s as an increasing function of the latter. This may be one of the various methods to formulate our saving function. See [6] p. 128.

with the following assumptions:

(vi) s is continuous and differentiable for all $k \geqq 0$,

(vii) $\lim_{k \to 0} s(k) = \bar{\bar{s}}$, $\quad \lim_{k \to \infty} s(k) = \bar{s}$

where $\bar{s}$ and $\bar{\bar{s}}$ are constants such that $0 < \bar{s} < \bar{\bar{s}} < 1$,

(viii) $s' < 0$ and $|s'|$ is bounded for all $k \geqq 0$ [5].

With these additional assumptions, Equation (4) in the preceding section is changed into

$$\dot{k} = \{s(k)(1-\theta) - \theta k\} f(k) \tag{11}$$

which satisfies the Lipschitz conditions for a positive initial condition. The right-hand side of (11), say $\phi_2(k)$, has the following properties just the same as $\phi_1(k)$.

$$\left\{ \begin{array}{l} \lim_{k \to 0} \phi_2(k) = 0, \quad \lim_{k \to 0} \phi_2'(k) = \infty \\ \phi_2'(k) < 0 \text{ for all } k > \text{some } \bar{\bar{k}}, \\ \lim_{k \to \infty} \phi_2(k) = -\infty. \end{array} \right. \tag{12}$$

Then we have a stable equilibrium value of k and the corresponding balanced growth rate such that

$$\frac{\hat{k}}{s(\hat{k})} = \frac{1-\theta}{\theta}. \tag{13}$$

$$G = \theta f(\hat{k}). \tag{14}$$

The derivation of the optimal tax rate is a little more complicated than the previous case. But finally it is shown as the solution of the following equations:

$$\frac{\hat{k}^* f'}{f} \left(\frac{s}{s - s' \hat{k}^*} \right) = 1 - \theta^* \tag{15-1}$$

$$\hat{k}^* = s \frac{1-\theta^*}{\theta^k} \tag{15-2}$$

In this case, however, further assumptions on the shape of the s-function are needed to

5) For instance the following form gives us a saving function of required properties:

$$s = s + (\bar{s} - s)(1 - e^{-f'(k)})$$

provided that $|e^{-f'} \cdot f''|$ *is bounded for all* $k \geqq 0$. Or if the parameter δ in the preceding footnote takes the form that

$$\delta = \bar{\bar{\delta}} + (\bar{\delta} - \bar{\bar{\delta}})(1 - e^{-f(k)})$$

where $0 < \bar{\delta} < \bar{\bar{\delta}} < 1$ and $\bar{\delta}$ and $\bar{\bar{\delta}}$ are constants, then the similar results are obtained under the same presumption. The boundedness of $\{e^{-f} \cdot f''\}$ follows for the Cobb-Douglas production function.

deduce the secondary condition: $\frac{d^2 G}{d\theta^2}<0$. Here we simply assume that $\frac{d^2 G}{d\theta_2}<0$ for all θ: $0\leqq\theta\leqq 1$, then $\mathring{k}^*$ is assumed to be the unique optimal value of $\mathring{k}$.

Let the multiplicand in the left-hand side of (15–1) be $S(\mathring{k})$ in general. It is obvious that

$$0\leqq S(\mathring{k})\leqq 1 \quad \text{for all} \quad \mathring{k}\leqq 0.$$

Then the existence of the optimal tax rate is confirmed again by Equations (15–1) and (15–2).

Similarly to the previous case, we have to be satisfied with the second best solution when the feasible range of θ is narrower than $[0, \theta^*]$.

I–3. *Model with a Variable Proportion of Public Investment*

Now we change the picture to the reverse direction and introduce a changeability of the proportion of public investment. For that purpose θ is redefined as the rate of tax for both of public investment and current public expenditure. The total of the tax receipts will be subdivided into two parts with a ratio of ρ: $1-\rho$. The first part of the government funds is devoted to the public investment and the second part to the current public expenditure.

The crucial assumption which we are going to make is that ρ, the proportion of public investment to the total public expenditure, is *an increasing function of the marginal productivity of SOC stock.* Before introducing this function, let us examine the properties of the related marginal productivity a little further. It was expressed as a function of k such that

(16) $$h(k)=f(k)-kf'(k)$$

By the foregoing assumptions we can show that

(ix) $0\leqq h(k)<\infty$ for all k: $0<k<\infty$

(The same as Assumption (v).),

(x) $h'(k)=-kf''(k)\geqq 0$ for all $k\geqq 0$

(See Assumption (iii).),

(xi) $\lim_{k\to 0} h(k)=0$

(See Assumptions (i) and (ii).).

In addition we can deduce that

(xii) $\lim_{k \to \infty} h(k) = \infty$

as the symmetry of the first part of Assumption (iv).

With these assumptions on $h(k)$, it is easy to take ρ as an increasing function of k directly, i.e.

$$\rho = \rho(k). \tag{17}$$

The assumptions on ρ (k) are

(xiii) ρ is continuous and differentiable for all $k \geqq 0$,

(xiv) $\lim_{k \to 0} \rho(k) = \bar{\rho}, \quad \lim_{k \to \infty} \rho(k) = 1$

where $\bar{\rho}$ is a constant such that $0 < \bar{\rho} < 1$.

(xv) $\rho' > 0$ and $|\rho' k|$ is bounded for all $k \geqq 0$.[6]

Taking s as constant again, we have a new variant of Equation (4) such that

$$\dot{k} = \{s(1-\theta) - \rho(k)\theta(k)\} f(k) \tag{18}$$

which satisfies the Lipschitz conditions for a positive initial condition. The right-hand side of (18), $\phi_3(k)$, has the same properties as $\phi_2(k)$ and $\phi_1(k)$. (Relations (5) or (12).) Again we have a stable equilibrium value of k and the corresponding balanced growth rate.

$$\rho(\hat{k})\hat{k} = s\frac{1-\theta}{\theta} \tag{19}$$

$$G = \rho(\hat{k})\theta f(\hat{k}). \tag{20}$$

The optimum tax rate for this system is derived as the solution of

$$\frac{\hat{k}^* f'}{f}\left(\frac{\rho}{\rho + \rho' \hat{k}^*}\right) + \frac{\rho' \hat{k}^*}{\rho + \rho' \hat{k}^*} = 1 - \theta^* \tag{21-1}$$

and

$$\rho(\hat{k}^*)\hat{k}^* = s\frac{1-\theta^*}{\theta^*}. \tag{21-2}$$

Again we simply assume that $\frac{d^2 G}{d\theta^2} < 0$ for all θ: $0 \leqq \theta \leqq 1$, or assume the uniqueness of the

---

6) An example of the ρ-function which satisfies all of these requirements is

$$\rho = \bar{\rho} + (1-\bar{\rho})(1 - e^{-h(k)})$$

provided that $|e^{-h} \cdot h'k|$ *is bounded for all* $k \geqq 0$.

44 If $f(k) = k^{\alpha}$ and $h(k) = \beta k^{\alpha}$, $(\beta = 1 - \alpha)$, then $|e^{-h} \cdot h'k|$ is bounded for all $k \geqq 0$.

optimal value, $\hat{k}$.* The left-hand side of (21–1) is a weighted average of $\left(\frac{kf'}{f}\right)$ and 1. Letting it be $R(k)$, we have

$$0 \leqq R(\hat{k}) \leqq 1 \quad \text{for all } \hat{k} \geqq 0.$$

Under these conditions the existence of the optimal (total) tax rate is again assured.

In this model we observe a foreshadowing element of the *induced* public investment. The growth rate of SOC stock, $GQ = \rho(k)\theta f(k)$, is an increasing function of k in a duplicated meaning. Because for a fixed value of θ, we have

$$\frac{d\,GQ}{dk} = \rho'\theta f + \rho\,\theta f', \tag{22}$$

and the first term of the right-hand side implies an inducing effect of increased DPA-SOC capital ratio for the investment in SOC stock.

Of course, especially for regional economic problems, the behavior of the induced public investment should be considered not in a closed model of this kind but in an open model of capital flows. Nevertheless, the above model may still be a good example of the fact that we can treat the pressure factor to the public investment even in a simple closed model.

II. The Optimal Path of SOC Accumulation in Closed Model I-1

In Section I we have been concerned with comparative dynamics analyses of closed models. A fatal assumption made there was the constancy of the tax rate (θ) throughout the time. Although this assumption is not unplausible in practical situations, it may be a too rigid one at least in the theoretical framework.

Furthermore though the technique of comparative dynamics is superior to that of comparative statics, still it is not a true substitute for a flexible dynamic theory. For instance, theoretically speaking the system like Equation (4) in the preceding section cannot reach its stable equilibrium within a finite length of time. It can only approach *indefinitely* to the state of $k = \hat{k}$.[7] Of course this is by no means a significant difficulty of the analysis in a practical sense, but in any case we have no particular reason to adhere

7) We can find the same kind of discussion in reference to the comparative statics analysis in Chapter 20 of [10] (pp. 472–473).

45

to the constancy of the tax rate.

In the present section, we wish to formulate a model of a dynamic fiscal policy which leads to the optimal time path of SOC accumulation. For that purpose we adopt the first model of the preceding section with an alternative assumption of the flexible tax rate within certain limits.

In order to avoid the complicated discussions regarding social objectives, we proceed with a target function of the minimum time objective type in which the goal of an economic system is a combination of the optimal DPA-SOC capital ratio and a certain absolute level of SOC stock.[8] In this case the optimal DPA-SOC capital ratio ($\hat{k}^*$ in Section I-1) can be understood as a variant of *the maximum terminal path level* discussed in [13] [8] etc.

Recapitulating the formulation in Section I-1, our economic system is expressed by the following differential equations:

(1) $$\frac{dQ}{dt} = \theta f(k) Q$$

(2) $$\frac{dk}{dt} = \{s(1-\theta) - \theta k\} f(k)$$

with the initial conditions that

(i) $k(0) = k_0 > 0$,

(ii) $Q(0) = Q_0 > 0$,

However, now we can freely choose the value of θ at each time point under a restriction of

(iii) $0 \leqq \theta \leqq \bar{\theta}, \quad \bar{\theta} > \theta^*$,

where θ^* is the optimal tax rate in Section I-1.

Then θ, our control variable, should be considered as a function of time, i.e.

(3) $$\theta = \theta(t).$$

Except at the points of discontinuity of $\theta(t)$, it will be possible to find a set of solutions for the system of (1), (2), and (3).[9] As far as the number of those points of discontinuity is finite, we can construct continuous time paths of k and Q by connecting successive segments

8) I owe the following discussions much to [8].

9) Rigorously speaking, at its points of discontinuity $\theta(t)$ must have its finite limits, i.e.

$$\lim_{\substack{t \to \tau \\ t < \tau}} \theta(t) = \theta(\tau - 0), \qquad \lim_{\substack{t \to \tau \\ t > \tau}} \theta(t) = \theta(\tau + 0)$$

at any point of discontinuity, τ. See [11] p. 10.

of smooth time curves.[10)]

The goal of our system is that

(iv) $k(T)=k^*$,

(v) $Q(T)=Q^*$,

whre T is the terminal time point and k^* is equal to $\hat{k}^*$ in Section I-1. In addition we of course assume that

(vi) $Q_0<Q^*$.

Then our optimizing problem is that

Minimize T with respect to $\theta(t)$ subject to the system of (1) and (2), and a constraint of (iii) with the initial and terminal conditions of (i), (ii), (iv) and (v).

We wish to solve this problem by the use of the Maximum Principle developed in [11]. Theorem 2 in Chapter 1 of the book is especially relevant to our probiem.[11)]

II-1 *Theorems on Optimal Solution*

First of all we formulate a related Hamiltonian Function as

$$H=\psi_1\theta f(k)Q+\psi_2\{s(1-\theta)-\theta k\}f(k)$$

with a ***nonzero time-continuous*** vector of auxiliary variables, $\psi(t)=(\psi_1(t), \psi_2(t))$, time behavior of which is described by

$$\text{(vii)}\quad \begin{aligned} \frac{d\psi_1}{dt}&=-\frac{\partial H}{\partial Q}=-\theta f\psi_1\\ \frac{d\psi_2}{dt}&=-\frac{\partial H}{\partial k}=-\theta f'Q\psi_1-[\{s(1-\theta)-\theta k\}f'-\theta f]\psi_2. \end{aligned}$$

Pontryagin's theorem tells us that for the optimal solution of the above problem the following conditions must be satisfied.

(a) For all t, $0\leqq t\leqq T$, the function $H(\psi(t), x(t), \theta)$

....where $x(t)=(Q(t), k(t))$....attains its maximum at the point $\theta=\theta(t)$:

10) Regarding the method of piecewise solution of a system of differential equations, see [11] pp. 12–13.

11) [11] pp. 20–21.

$$H(\psi(t),\ x(t),\ \theta(t)) = M(\psi(t),\ x(t)).$$

(b) For all t, $0 \leqq t \leqq T$,

$$M(\psi(t),\ x(t)) \geqq 0.$$

The H-function is rewritten as

$$H = [\{\psi_1 Q - \psi_2 (s+k)\}\theta + \psi_2 s] f(k), \tag{4}$$

and we write the first part of the function as

$$\psi_1 Q - \psi_2 (s+k) = \phi(t). \tag{5}$$

by Condition (a) we have

$$\theta(t) = \begin{cases} 0 & \text{if } \phi(t) < 0 \\ \hat{\theta},\ 0 \leqq \hat{\theta} \leqq \bar{\theta}, & \text{if } \phi(t) = 0 \\ \bar{\theta} & \text{if } \phi(t) > 0 \end{cases} \tag{6-1}$$

for all $t \in [0,\ T]$,

or reversely

$$\phi(t) = \begin{cases} \geqq 0 & \text{if } \theta = \bar{\theta} \\ = 0 & \text{if } 0 < \theta < \bar{\theta} \\ \leqq 0 & \text{if } \theta = 0 \end{cases} \tag{6-2}$$

for all $t \in [0, T]$.

Next let us examine the behaviors of our system under particular strategies on θ.

[A]

$\theta = 0$ strategy for some time interval (say, $[0,\ \hat{t}]$) :

$$\frac{d\psi_1}{dt} = 0, \quad \psi_1 \equiv \text{A}, \quad \text{(A is some constant.)}$$

$$\frac{d\psi_2}{dt} = -sf'\psi_2, \quad \psi_2 = \text{B} \exp\left[-\int_0^t sf'\,d\tau\right], \quad \text{(B is some constant.)}$$

$$\frac{dQ}{dt} = 0, \quad Q = Q_0,$$

$$\frac{dk}{dt} = sf(k)$$

$$\phi(t) = AQ_0 - \psi_2 (s+k) = AQ_0 - B \exp\left[-\int_0^t sf'\,d\tau\right](s+k) \leqq 0, \tag{7}$$

48

(8)
$$\frac{d\phi}{dt} = -\frac{d\psi_2}{dt}(s+k) - \psi_2 \frac{dk}{dt}$$
$$= s\left\{sf' - (f - kf')\right\}\psi_2.$$

[B] $\theta = \hat{\theta}$ strategy $(0 < \theta \leqq \bar{\theta})$ for some time interval:

(9)
$$\phi(t) = \psi_1 Q - \psi_2(s+k) \geqq 0 \quad \text{and} \quad \phi(t)\,(\bar{\theta} - \hat{\theta}) = 0$$

(10)
$$\frac{d\phi}{dt} = \frac{d\psi_1}{dt} Q + \psi_1 \frac{dQ}{dt} - \frac{d\psi_2}{dt}(s+k) - \psi_2 \frac{dk}{dt}$$
$$= s\left\{sf' - (f - kf')\right\}\psi_2 + \hat{\theta}(s+k)\phi(t).$$

Definition of the Switching Time of Strategy

If $\theta(t) = \theta_1$ for $t < \hat{t}$, and $\theta(t) = \theta_2$ for $t \geqq \hat{t}$ where θ_1 and θ_2 are two distinct constants, we call the time point $\hat{t}$ a switching time of strategy.

Lemma 1 At any switching time of strategy, ψ_2 must be positive for an optimal solution.

Proof Before and after any switching time $\hat{t}$, $\phi(t)$ changes its sign or remains zero. Then in either case $\phi(\hat{t}) = 0$ by the time-continuity of the $\phi(t)$-function. Then $M(\psi(t), x(\hat{t})) = \psi_2(\hat{t}) sf(k)$ by (4) and it follows that $\psi_2(\hat{t}) \geqq 0$ by Condition (*b*). If $\psi_2(t) = 0$, $\psi_1(\hat{t})$ is also zero because $\phi(\hat{t}) = 0$. It means, however, that $\psi_2(t) = 0$, $\psi_1(t) = 0$ for all $t \geqq \hat{t}$ by (vii). This consequence contradicts the nonzero requirement of vector $\psi(t)$. Then ψ_2 must be positive at any switching time. (q.e.d.)

As the next procedure let us divide the k-Q plane in Figure 1 into two parts by a vertical line upon the point $(k^*, 0)$, and call the set of points (k, Q) where $0 < k < k^*$ and $0 < Q < Q^*$ Region α, the set of them where $k = k^*$ and $0 < Q < Q^*$ Line l, and the set of them where $k > k^*$ and $0 < Q < Q^*$ Region β. By (9) in Section I-1 it is clear that

(11)
$$sf' - (f - kf') \begin{cases} > 0 & \text{if } k \in \text{Region } \alpha \\ = 0 & \text{if } k \in \text{Line } l \\ < 0 & \text{if } k \in \text{Region } \beta. \end{cases}$$

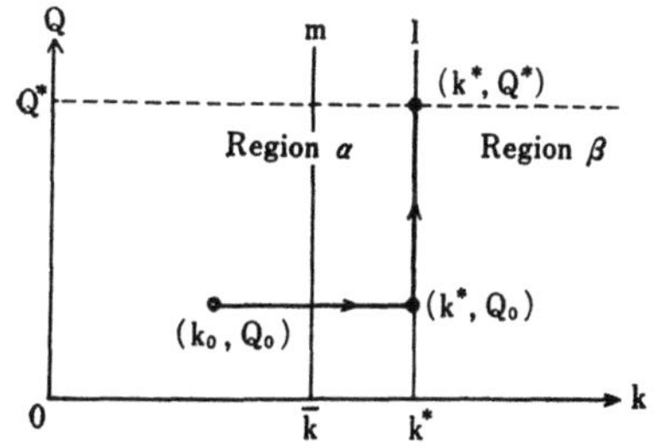

Figure 1

$$k^* = s\frac{1-\theta^*}{\theta^*}$$
$$\bar{k} = s\frac{1-\theta^*}{\bar{\theta}} \qquad (\bar{\theta} > \theta^*)$$

Lemma 2 In Regions α and β we cannot take the $\theta=\hat{\theta}(0<\hat{\theta}<\bar{\theta})$ strategy for nonzero length of time.

Proof During the time interval when this strategy is taken $\phi(t)=0$ by (6–2). By the same reasoning discussed in the proof of Lemma 1, $\psi_2(t)\neq 0$ during this time interval. Then we have $\frac{d\phi}{dt}\neq 0$ by (10) and (11), and $\phi(t)$ must leave zero value immediately. This completes the proof. (q. e. d.)

Let us consider the following three cases separately according to different initial conditions.

Case 1 $(k, Q_0)\in$ Region α.

Lemma 3 In Region α we cannot take the $\theta=\bar{\theta}$ strategy.

Proof If we take the $\theta=\bar{\theta}$ strategy in Region α, we must have at least one switching time inside the same region in the future. Because without such a switching time the system converges to the m-line in Figure 1 as shown in Section I-1, and it cannot reach the terminal point, (k^*, Q^*). Now suppose that $\hat{t}$ is the first switching time. At $\hat{t}$, $\phi(\hat{t})=0$, $\psi_2(\hat{t})>0$, and $\{sf'-(f-kf')\}>0$ by Lemma 1 and (11). Then we have $\left(\frac{d\phi}{dt}\right)_{t=\hat{t}}>0$ and $\phi(t)$ becomes positive immediately, i.e. we are drawn back to the $\theta=\bar{\theta}$ strategy. ((6–1)) This means that we cannot change our strategy from the $\theta=\bar{\theta}$ one to other ones in Region α, so that if we wish to have a feasible solution in that region we cannot take the $\theta=\bar{\theta}$ strategy. (q.e.d.)

By Lemmas 2 and 3 it turns out that the only strategy we can take in Region α for nonzero length of time is the $\theta=0$ policy. Under this strategy $\phi(t)\leqq 0$ and the system proceeds horizontally to the right from the initial point, (k_0, Q_0), as described in Figure 1. Even in this case we must have a switching time in order to get a feasible solution. Therefore the constant B in the solution for $\psi_2(t)$ obtained in [A] must be positive (by Lemma 1), and the constant A which is the solution for $\psi_1(t)$ must be positive too. (Otherwise $\phi(t)$ remains negative forever and we cannot have any switching time.) For those values of A and B, we can solve $\phi(t)$ explicitly as:

$$\phi(t)=AQ_0-B\exp\left[-\int_0^t sf'\,d\tau\right](s+k) \tag{12}$$

$$=AQ_0-B(s+k_0)\exp\left[-\int_0^t \frac{s}{s+k}\{sf'-(f-kf')\}d\tau\right]$$ [12]

Again by Lemmas 2 and 3 we must proceed with the $\theta=0$ strategy until the system reaches Line l.

Lemma 4 On Line l we cannot take the $\theta=\bar{\theta}$ and $\theta=0$ strategies for nonzero length of time.

Proof If we take the $\theta=\bar{\theta}$ strategy on Line l for non-zero length of time, the system is immediately pulled back to Region α with the continuation of the same strategy. Then the system will drop in the same trap as discussed in Lemma 3. On the other hand if the $\theta=0$ strategy is taken for nonzero time duration, the system immediately steps into Region β with the continuation of the same strategy. As will be shown later in Lemma 6 we cannot take the $\theta=0$ policy in Region β. Then both strategies are prohibited on Line l. (q.e.d.)

We give the following lemma without proof.

Lemma 5 The only strategy which we can take on Line l is the $\theta=\theta^*$ strategy.

It may be easily seen that if we take the $\theta=\hat{\theta}$ policy on Line l where $0<\hat{\theta}<\bar{\theta}$ but $\hat{\theta}\neq\theta^*$ for nonzero time duration, we have a situation which contradicts Lemma 2. As shown in Section I-1, θ^* is the tax rate with which the balanced growth on Line l is maintained.

In order that we can take the $\theta=\theta^*$ strategy persistently on Line l, (α) $\phi(t)$ must be zero when the system has reached Line l, and (β) $\phi(t)$ must remains zero on Line l. Let us examine these two requirements.

(α) In the extreme right-hand side of Equation (12), the first term is a positive constant and the absolute value of the second term is decreasing while the system proceeds from (k, Q_0) to (k^*, Q_0). (Remember $\{sf'-(f-kf')\}>0$ in Region α.) Then if we assume appropriate values for A and B, we shall be able to make the value of $\phi(t)$ zero at the time

---

12) $\exp\left[-\int_0^t sf'd\tau\right](s+k)$

$$=(s+k_0)\exp\left[\left\{-\int_0^t sf'd\tau\right\}+\log(s+k)-\log(s+k_0)\right]$$

$$=(s+k_0)\exp\left[\left\{-\int_0^t sf'd\tau\right\}+\left\{\int_0^t \frac{1}{s+k}\frac{dk}{d\tau}\right\}\right]$$

$$=(s+k_0)\exp\left[-\int_0^t s\left(f'-\frac{f}{s+k}\right)d\tau\right]$$

$$=(s+k_0)\exp\left[-\int_0^t \frac{s}{s+k}\left\{sf'-(f-kf')\right\}d\tau\right].$$

point $t=t^*$ when $k(t^*)=k^*$ at the first time. Changing the variable of integration from t to k, we can show the suitable combination of A and B which are unique up to scale as follows:

$$\frac{A}{B}=\frac{(s+k)\exp\{-L(k_0)\}}{Q_0} \tag{13}$$

where

$$L(k_0)=\int_0^{t*}\frac{s}{s+k}\{sf'-(f-kf')\}\,d\tau$$

$$=\int_{k_0}^{k*}\left(\frac{f'}{f}-\frac{1}{s+k}\right)dk.$$

(Remember $\frac{dk}{dt}=sf$ under the $\theta=0$ policy.)

(β) If we maintain the $\theta=\theta^*$ policy on Line l the first term of the extreme right-hand side of (10) remains zero, because $\frac{dk}{dt}=0$ by (2) in this section and (8–2) in Section I-1. Then we have a differential equation such that

$$\frac{d\phi}{dt}=\theta^*(s+k^*)\phi(t)$$

with an initial condition of $\phi(t^*)=0$ given in (α). It is easily seen that

(14) $\phi(t)\equiv 0$ for all $t\geqq t^*$ as far as $\theta(t)\equiv\theta^*$ under these conditions.

At the same time we have

$$\psi_1(t)=A\exp\{-\theta^*f(k^*)(t-t^*)\}>0 \quad \text{for all } t\geqq t^*$$

from (vii) and the condition that $\psi_1(t^*)=A$. Then the nonzero requirement of the vector $\psi(t)$ is satisfied in this phase.

Proceeding with the $\theta=\theta^*$ strategy on Line l, the system can attain the required terminal point (k^*, Q^*) finally. From all of the above discussion, we have the following theorem:

Theorem 1 When the system starts with an initial point in Region α, the optimal strategy for our problem is as follows:

(I) First take the $\theta=0$ strategy untill the DPA-SOC capital ratio, k, attains the value of k.*

(II) At the time point when k attains the value of k,* switch to the $\theta=\theta^*$ strategy and proceed with that strategy until the system reaches the terminal point (k^*, Q^*).

This optimal strategy is a unique one in the sense that there is no other *feasible* strategy which satisfies all of the necessary conditions of the optimality when the initial point lies in Region α. Then as far as there is at least an optimal strategy for our problem, it must be one which we have discovered.[13]

Case 2 $(k_0, Q_0) \in$ Region β.

Lemma 6 In Region β we cannot take the $\theta=0$ strategy.

Proof If we take the $\theta=0$ strategy in Region β, there must be at least one switching time to other strategies by the same reason given in the proof of Lemma 3. Assume the existence of such a switching time as $\hat{t}$. Then we have that

$$\phi(\hat{t})=0,\ \psi_2(\hat{t})>0 \qquad \text{(by Lemma1)},$$

$$sf'-(f-kf')<0 \qquad \text{(by (11))}$$

Then $\frac{d\phi}{dt}<0$ at $\hat{t}$ by (10), and $\phi(t)$ tends to negative so that θ again becomes zero immediately. So we cannot have a switcing time in the real sense if we have once taken the $\theta=0$ strategy. Then the $\theta=0$ strategy cannot be chosen in Region β. (q.e.d.)

By Lemma 2 and Lemma 6, the following lemma is derived immediately.

Lemma 7 The only strategy that is a candidate for the optimal strategy in Region β is the $\theta=\bar{\theta}$ policy.

Now we subdivide Region β into two subregions by a rectangular hyperbola which is derived from the following differential equation:

$$Q=\frac{Q^*\left(k^*-s\frac{1-\bar{\theta}}{\bar{\theta}}\right)}{k-s\frac{1-\bar{\theta}}{\bar{\theta}}} \tag{15}$$

which is derived from the following differential equation:

$$\frac{dQ}{dk}=\frac{\bar{\theta}Q}{s(1-\bar{\theta})-\bar{\theta}k}\,. \tag{15-a}$$

13) It is by no means an easy work to prove the existence of the optimal solution to this kind of problem in general. But for our particular problem it is not so difficult to see the existence. The length of time period is of course bounded from below, and it is a continuous functional with respect to the time function, $\theta(t)$. These two conditions are sufficient to establish the existence of the optimal solution.

with a terminal condition that $Q^*=Q(k^*)$. We can get (15-a) by eliminating dt from two differential equations, (1) and (2).

By this rectangular hyperbola, say n, we have two subregions, Region β-1 (the points on Curve n are included in Region β-1) and Region β-2, and two corresponding subcases. (See Figure 2.)

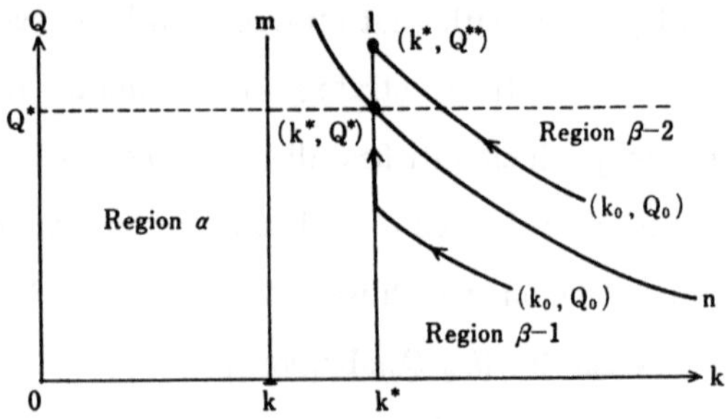

Figure 2

(Case 2-1) $(k_0, Q_0) \in$ Region β-1.

By the foregoing discussion and Lemma 4, the following theorem is established.

Theorem 2 When the system starts with an initial point in Region β-1, the optimal strategy for our problem is as follows:

(I) First take the $\theta=\bar{\theta}$ strategy until the DPA-SOC capital stock ratio, k, attains the value of k.*

(II) At the time point when k attains the value of k,* switch to the $\theta=\theta^*$ strategy and proceed with that strategy until the system reaches the terminal point (k,* Q^*).

If the initial point lies exactly on Curve n, the second strategy becomes unnecessary.

(Case 2-2) $(k_0, Q_0) \in$ Region β-2.

In this case there is no feasible solution to our problem. In other words, the system cannot attain the terminal point by any $\theta=\tilde{\theta}$ strategy where $0\leqq\tilde{\theta}\leqq\bar{\theta}$ or by any combination of these strategies. All avilable paths of capital accumulation lie in the right-hand side of Curve n.

Even in this infeasible case, the $\theta=\hat{\theta}$ policy may be said to possess some kind of optimality. Take the policy and attain some point, say (k^*, Q^{**}), on Line l. Then this strategy would be optimal if the teminal point were given at (k,* Q^{**}). (See Figure 2.)

Lastly we may have a trivial case where the initial point incidentally lies on our "Turnpike", Line l.

Case 3 $(k_0, Q_0) \in$ Line l.

Theorem 3 When the system starts with an initial point on Line l, the optimal strategy for our problem is to take $\theta=\theta^*$ policy until the terminal point is reached.

54 For the optimal solutions in Theorem 2 and 3, we can assert the same kind of

uniqueness property as discussed in the case of Theorem 1.

II-2. *Discussion of the Results*

Although the results obtained in the previous section are those for a very simple normative model with a fixed saving ratio, they still indicate several intresting features of the development strategy through the social overhead investment.

First of all, they have shown the "turnpike" property of the balanced growth path with a tax rate of θ^* and a capital ratio of $k.^*$ It has been already discusssed that k^* may be called the von Neumann configuration for our system.

Secondly, we have seen a drastic change of the optimal strategy in response to the change of the initial point. In Region α we have the shortage of private capital as well as public capital. But as indicated by the value of k, SOC is somewhat abundant in a strictly relative sense. In this case total investment must be devoted to the formation of private capital until the optimal configuration of DPA and SOC is attained. After reaching this optimal capital ratio the system should proceed on the balanced growth path.

On the contrary, we have a relative abundance of private capital in Region β. In this case we must raise the level of SOC investiment as high as possible until the system reaches the same balanced growth path as in the case of Region α.

It seems to me that these conclusions are very plausible from the viewpoint of rational behaviors, but they might be *too* rational from the viewpoint of Hirschman's theory. In chapter 5 of [5], Hirschman has discussed the desirability of a development via shortage of SOC. His argument may be summarized by a slightly modified reproduction of Figure 3 in page 87 of [5]. (See our Figure 3)

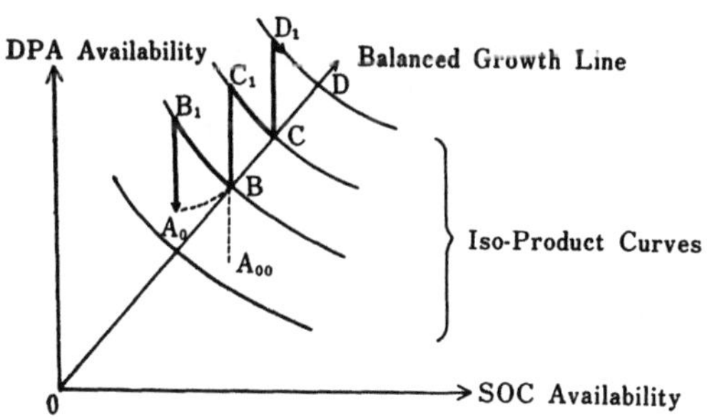

Figure 3

Hirschman more or less favors growth paths like $A_0 B_1 BC_1 CD_1 \ldots$ or weaving "cobweb" paths around the balanced growth line because of a generated public pressure by these strategies to the authorities responsible for SOC formation.[14] On the other hand,

14) [5] p. 88.

the optimal strategies which have been discovered in this paper are ones like $A_0BCD....$or $A_{00}BCD....$depending on the initial condition. (A_0 corresponds to our Region β and A_{00} does to Region α.)

The reason of the difference of our conclusions from his, of course, lies in our treatment of SOC investment as an autonomous factor of economic growth. In his discussion SOC investment is a type of induced investment, but in our model it is an instrument which controls the growth path indicrectly. It is my speculation that this difference will not disappear even if we adopt Model **I-3** in which a bit of induced character is attached to SOC investment.

For the full treatment of Hirschman's implication we may have to formulate an open model of development where SOC investment is capable of being induced as well as DPA investment. At the same time the characterization of the Q-variable as SOC is more or less weak in our single sector model. It will be fairly strengthened in some model of two or more sectors by the adoption of Samuelson-type argument of public goods.[15]

Although we owe further indebtedness to Hirschman for shortcoming in developing a model which corresponds to his thinking exactly, our theory itself has an advantage as a planning theory in a capitalistic economy. Because we have restricted our instrument variable to one which is, in a strict sense, manageable by the government leaving other variables to be determined by th working of the system. In many planning models, on the contrary, an over-all point of view has been adopted by using too many economic variables as instruments.[16] In my opinion such a viewpoint has made these models unrealistic as economic models in a free market system.[17]

II-3. *Derivation of Time-Contours for the Cobb-Douglas Case*[18]

If the production function in our model is specified as Cobb-Douglas type like

$$f(k) = k^{\alpha}, \quad 0<\alpha<1, \tag{16}$$

we shall have a concrete time path of the optimal solution.

(Case 1)

---

15) See [12].

16) As only one example we may mention [9].

17) In this sense a model treated in Chapter 7 of [14] seems to me much more realsitic.

18) For the suggestion of a contour-diagram, I owe to Professor T.A. Reiner of the University of Pennsylvania.

If the initial point of the system happens to be in Region α, we have the following optimal solution.

(17-1)
$$\begin{cases} Q = Q_0 \quad \text{for } t \in [0, \hat{t}] \\ k = (k_0^{\beta} + s\beta t)^{1/\beta} \end{cases}$$

where $\beta = 1 - \alpha$, $\hat{t} = \frac{1}{s\beta}(k^{*\beta} - k^{\beta}_0)$, $k^* = s\frac{\alpha}{\beta}$,

(17-2)
$$\begin{cases} Q = Q_0 \exp\left[k^{*\alpha}\left\{\frac{1}{s}k_0^{\beta} + \beta t\right\} - \frac{\alpha}{\beta}\right] \quad \text{for } t \in [\hat{t}, T]. \\ k = k^* \end{cases}$$

For a given value of the terminal condition on Q, Q,* and a given (minimized) $T(\leqq 0)$, the relationship between k_0 and Q_0 are given that

(18)
$$Q_0 = Q^* \exp\left[\frac{\alpha}{\beta} - k^{*\alpha}\left(\frac{1}{s}k_0^{\beta} + T\right)\right]$$

with the constraints of

(18-a)
$$0 < Q_0 \leqq Q^*, \quad 0 < k_0 \leqq k^{*}$$ [19]

By this equation it is obvious that Q_0 is a decreasing function of k_0 on a time-contour for a given T. Our Case 3 may be also included in Equation (18) without any difficulty.

(Case 2)

If the initial point lies in Region β-1, we can show the optimal solution by an implicit form.

(19-1)
$$\begin{cases} Q = Q_0\left[\frac{k_0 - \bar{k}}{k(t) - \bar{k}}\right] \\ \int_{k_0}^{k(t)} \frac{dx}{\theta(\bar{k} - x)x^{\alpha}} = t \quad \text{for } t \in [0, \hat{t}] \end{cases}$$

where $k^* \leqq k(t) \leqq k_0$, $\bar{k} = s\frac{1-\theta}{\theta}$, $(\bar{k} < k^*)$,

$$\hat{t} = \int_{k_0}^{k^*} \frac{dx}{\theta(\bar{k} - x)x^{\alpha}},$$

---

19) Zero values of k_0 and Q_0 are excluded of coruse for the establishment of the integrability conditions.

$$
(19\text{-}2) \qquad \begin{cases} Q = Q_0\left(\dfrac{k_0 - \bar{k}}{k^* - \bar{k}}\right) \ \exp\left[\beta k^{*\alpha}(t - \hat{t})\right] \quad \text{for } t \in [\hat{t},\ T] \\ k = k^* \end{cases}
$$

The time contour of k_0 and Q_0 for a given T ($\geqq 0$) is as follows:

$$
(20) \qquad Q_0 = Q^*\left(\frac{k^* - \bar{k}}{k_0 - \bar{k}}\right)\exp\left[-\beta k^{*\alpha}(T - \hat{t})\right]
$$

with the constraints of

$$
(20\text{-a}) \qquad \begin{cases} 0 < Q_0 \leqq Q^*, \quad k_0 > k^* \\ Q_0(k_0 - \bar{k}) \leqq Q^*(k^* - \bar{k}).^{20)} \end{cases}
$$

On a particular time-contour we have

$$
(21) \qquad \frac{dQ_0}{dk_0} = -Q^*\frac{k^* - \bar{k}}{(k_0 - \bar{k})^2}\exp\left[-\beta k^{*\alpha}(T - \hat{t})\right]
$$

$$
+ Q^*\frac{k^* - \bar{k}}{k_0 - \bar{k}}\exp\left[-\beta k^{*\alpha}(T - \hat{t})\right]\beta k^{*\alpha}\frac{d\hat{t}}{dk_0}
$$

$$
= Q^*\frac{k^* - \bar{k}}{(k_0 - \bar{k})^2}\exp\left[-\beta k^{*\alpha}(T - \hat{t})\right]\cdot\left\{\frac{\beta}{\theta}\left[\frac{k^*}{k_0}\right]^{\alpha} - 1\right\}.
$$

It is clear that $\dfrac{dQ_0}{dk} < 0$ because $\beta = \theta^* < \theta$ by one of the basic assumptions (Assumption (iii)) and $k^* \leqq k_0$.

By (18) and (20) with their side conditions we can depict the family of time-contours which indicates *an equivalence-relation* among different initial conditions on Figure 2 or Figure 3. Different points on the same time-contour implies that these initial conditions have the same level of accesibility to the final target even though they are quite dissimilar regarding the levels and the proportions of SOC and DPA stocks.

References

[1] Chenery, Hollis, B., "The Application of Investment Criteria", *Quarterly Journal of Economics*, Vol. LXVII, No. 1, February, 1953, pp. 76–96.

[2] Dorfman, Robert, Paul A. Samuelson, and Robert M. Solow, *Linear Programming and Economic Analysis*, New York, McGraw-Hill, 1958.

20) The last constraint corresponds to Equation (14).

[3] Eckstein O., "Investment Criteria for Economic Development and the Theory of Intertemporal Welfare Economics, "*Quarterly Journal of Economics*, Vol. LXXI, No. 1, February, 1957, pp. 56–85.

[4] Galenson, W., and H. Leibenstein, "Investment Criteria, Productivity and Economic Development, "*Quarterly Journal of Economics*, Vol. LXIX, No. 3, August, 1955, pp. 343–370.

[5] Hirschman, Albert O., *The Strategy of Economic Development*, New Haven, Yale University Press, 1958.

[6] Inada, Ken-ichi, "On the Stability of Growth Equilibria in Two-Sector Models, "*Review of Economic Studies*, Vol. XXXI (2), No. 86, April, 1964, pp. 127–142.

[7] King, Timothy, "Development Strategy and Investment Criteria : Complementary or Competitive ?", *Quarterly Journal of Economics*, Vol. LXXX, No. 1, February, 1966, pp.108–120.

[8] Kurz, Mordecai, "Optimal Paths of Captial Accumulation Under the Minimum Time Objective", *Econometrica*, Vol. 33, No. 1, January, 1965, pp. 42–66.

[9] Moses, L.N., "A General Equilbirium Model of Production, Interregional Trade, and Location of Industry" *Review of Economics and Statistics*, Vol. 42, No. 4, November, 1960, pp.373∼397.

[10] Musgrave, Richard A., *The Theory of Public Finance*: *A Study in Public Economy*, New York McGraw-Hill, 1959.

[11] Pontryagin, L.S. and others, *The Mathematical Theory of Optimal Processes*, trans. by K.N. Trirogoff, New York, John Wiley, 1962.

[12] Samuelson, Paul A., "The Pure Theory of Public Expenditures", *Review of Economics and Statistics*, Vol. 36, No. 4, November 1954, pp. 387–389.

[13] Srinivasan, T.N., "On a Two Sector Model of Growth," *Cowles Foundation Discussion Paper*, No. 139, July, 1962.

[14] Tinbergen, J., and H.C. Bos, *Mathematical Models of Economic Growth*, New York, McGraw-Hill, 1962.

International Economic Review, Osaka, Vol. 14 (1973) 372–382

NATIONAL GROWTH AND REGIONAL INCOME INEQUALITY: A CONSISTENT MODEL*

BY NOBORU SAKASHITA AND OSAMU KAMOIKE[1]

IN A RECENT VOLUME of this Review, Fukuchi and Nobukuni have developed an interesting discussion on the trade-off relation between national growth and regional income equality for the Japanese economy [**2**]. Unfortunately, however, their theoretical framework contains some conceptual difficulties which may be itemized as follows:

(I) Question on the admissiblity of the approximation procedure adopted for the deduction of stability condition, which has deprived their stability proof of the global character,

(II) Question on the use of absolute variance of the per capita output as the index of regional income inequality,

(III) Inconsistency between the sum of regional increments of labor or capital and the national increment of them in the model,[2]

(IV) Question on the exogenous treatment of the overall growth rate of capital which should be an endogenous variable of the system.[3]

In this paper we wish to re-examine these crucial points of the Fukuchi-Nobukuni model by its alternative formulation with continuous time variable and regional share variables. The most important conclusion of our analysis is that the model is not unstable in any case if we define the index of income inequality by a relative variance of the per capita output which may be more natural index for the purpose.

1. ALTERNATIVE FORMULATION OF THE MODEL

The original F-N model has been formulated with discrete time variable. This formulation may be convenient for empirical application of the model, but it has produced a somewhat unrealistic effect on the stability condition. The upper part of the stability conditon (28) in [**2**] shows the possibility of an 'overshooting' effect of the interregional factor movement which may be unplausible except for the special case of 'gold rush' in view of the *ceaselessness* in such a movement. The model with continuous time variable is, we think, a

* Manuscript received September 9, 1971; revised August 11, 1972.

[1] The authors are extremely grateful to Professor Kiyoshi Kuga of Osaka University for his valuable comments and suggestions to the earlier version of this paper with which the paper has been fundamentally revised. Also we wish to thank the referees of our paper for their useful comments. Needless to say, however, the authors alone are responsible for any remaining errors.

[2] This inconsistency reveals itself in Equations (2) and (3) in [**2**, (84)], in which

$$\sum_{i=1}^{n} \pi_{i,t-1} E_{i,t-1} \neq 0 \text{ and } \sum_{i=1}^{n} \lambda_{i,t-1} K_{i,t-1} \neq 0 \quad \text{generally.}$$

[3] Besides these conceptual problems their paper contains quite a few misrepresentations or misprints. See [**7**, (2)] for the details.

better description of the reality at least in the theoretical framework.

In addition, the inconsistency and the imposedness of the F-N model discussed before ((III) and (IV)) must be amended by some appropriate device, and these considerations have resulted in the following model using the same system of notation as [**2**].

(i) Production functions:

$$\frac{O_i}{E_i} = q_i^{\gamma}, \quad 0 < \gamma < 1, \qquad i = 1, \ldots, n, \tag{1.1}$$

$q_i \equiv (K_i/E_i)$ the capital-labor ratio in the i-th region, (derived from the Cobb-Douglas production functions (1) in [**2**]).

(ii) Relative shares:

$$x_i \equiv \frac{E_i}{\sum_{j=1}^{n} E_j}, \qquad y_i \equiv \frac{K_i}{\sum_{j=1}^{n} K_j}, \qquad i = 1, \ldots, n. \tag{1.2}$$

Naturally we have

$$\sum_{i=1}^{n} x_i \equiv 1, \qquad \sum_{j=1}^{n} y_i \equiv 1.$$

(iii) Discrepancies in marginal productivities:

$$\pi_i \equiv \frac{\left(\frac{\partial O}{\partial E}\right)_i - \sum_{j=1}^{n} x_j \left(\frac{\partial O}{\partial E}\right)_j}{\sum_{j=1}^{n} x_j \left(\frac{\partial O}{\partial E}\right)_j} \tag{1.3}$$ [4]

$$= \frac{q_i^{\gamma} - \sum_{j=1}^{n} x_j q_j^{\gamma}}{\sum_{j=1}^{n} x_j q_j^{\gamma}} \qquad i = 1, \ldots, n,$$

$$\lambda_i \equiv \frac{\left(\frac{\partial O}{\partial K}\right)_i - \sum_{j=1}^{n} y_j \left(\frac{\partial O}{\partial K}\right)_j}{\sum_{j=1}^{n} y_j \left(\frac{\partial O}{\partial K}\right)_j} \tag{1.4}$$

$$= \frac{q_i^{\gamma-1} - \sum_{j=1}^{n} y_j q_j^{\gamma-1}}{\sum_{j=1}^{n} y_j q_j^{\gamma-1}} \qquad i = 1, \ldots, n.$$

By these formulations we can deduce desirable consistency properties of

$$\sum_{i=1}^{n} \pi_i E_i = 0 \quad \text{and} \quad \sum_{i=1}^{n} \lambda_i K_i = 0.$$

[4] We write $\frac{\partial O_i}{\partial E_i}$ and $\frac{\partial O_i}{\partial K_i}$ as $\left(\frac{\partial O}{\partial E}\right)_i$ and $\left(\frac{\partial O}{\partial K}\right)_i$ for the compactness of notation.

(iv) Growth rates of production factors:

$$(1.5)\qquad \frac{1}{E_i}\frac{dE_i}{dt} = \rho\pi_i + e,\ e = \frac{1}{\sum_{j=1}^{n} E_i}\frac{d\left(\sum_{i=1}^{n} E_i\right)}{dt}, \qquad \rho > 0, i = 1, \ldots, n,$$

in which e is a given constant.

$$(1.6)\qquad \frac{1}{K_i}\frac{dK_i}{dt} = \eta\lambda_i + k, \quad k = \frac{1}{\sum_{i=1}^{n} K_i}\frac{d\left(\sum_{i=1}^{n} K_i\right)}{dt}, \quad \eta > 0, i = 1, \ldots, n,$$

in which k is a variable being endogenously determined later. From (1.5) and (1.6) we have

$$(1.7)\qquad \frac{1}{x_i}\frac{dx_i}{dt} = \frac{1}{E_i}\frac{dE_i}{dt} - e = \rho\left(\frac{q_i^\gamma - \sum_{j=1}^{n} x_j q_j^\gamma}{\sum_{j=1}^{n} x_j q_j^\gamma}\right)$$

$$(1.8)\qquad \frac{1}{y_i}\frac{dy_i}{dt} = \frac{1}{K_i}\frac{dK_i}{dt} - k = \eta\left(\frac{q\, q_i^{\gamma-1} - \sum_{j=1}^{n} x_j q_j^\gamma}{\sum_{j=1}^{n} x_j q_j^\gamma}\right)$$

$q \equiv \dfrac{\sum_{i=1}^{n} K_i}{\sum_{i=1}^{n} E_i}$: the overall capital-labor ratio.

The last relation has been derived using the relation of $q_j = (y_j/x_j)q$.

(v) Saving-investment relation:

$$(1.9)\qquad \frac{d\left(\sum_{i=1}^{n} K_i\right)}{dt} = s\left(\sum_{i=1}^{n} O_i\right) = s\left(\sum_{i=1}^{n} K_i\right)\sum_{i=1}^{n} y_i q_i^{\gamma-1}$$

s: the overall saving ratio.

By (1.9) and the definition of k, we have

$$(1.10)\qquad k = s\sum_{i=1}^{n} y_i q_i^{\gamma-1} = \frac{s}{q}\sum_{i=1}^{n} x_i q_i^\gamma .$$

(vi) Growth rates of capital-labor ratios

For the national economy we have

$$(1.11)\qquad \frac{1}{q}\frac{dq}{dt} = k - e = \frac{s}{q}\sum_{i=1}^{n} x_i q_i^\gamma - e ,$$

by (1.10) and the definition of e.

The relation for the individual regional economy is

$$(1.12)\qquad \frac{1}{q_i}\frac{dq_i}{dt} = \frac{1}{y_i}\frac{dy_i}{dt} - \frac{1}{x_i}\frac{dx_i}{dt} + \frac{1}{q}\frac{dq}{dt}$$

$$= \eta\left(\frac{q\,q_i^{\gamma-1} - \sum_{j=1}^{n} x_j q_j^{\gamma}}{\sum_{j=1}^{n} x_j q_j^{\gamma}}\right) - \rho\left(\frac{q_i^{\gamma} - \sum_{j=1}^{n} x_j q_j^{\gamma}}{\sum_{j=1}^{n} x_j q_j^{\gamma}}\right) + \left(\frac{s}{q}\sum_{j=1}^{n} x_j q_j^{\gamma} - e\right),$$

in view of (1.7), (1.8), (1.11) and $q_j = (y_j/x_j)q$.

(i)—(vi) complete the structure of our model, but one additional assumption will be useful to simplify the analysis: i.e.,

(vii) Assumption on relative shares:

$$(1.13)\qquad \text{Initial } x_i\text{s and } y_i\text{s are all positive.}$$

Under this assumption, we can show that all of x_is and y_is are always positive for any $t > 0$ as will be discussed in Section 3.

Concerning the regional difference of q_i, we shall define the following new variables:

$$(1.14)\qquad \theta_i \equiv \frac{q_i}{q} - 1\,.$$

By (1.13) and (1.14), it is clear that $\theta_i > -1$.

2. BEHAVIOR OF RELATIVE VARIANCE IN PER CAPITA OUTPUT

In the first place we define a weighted absolute variance V of per capita output among regions.[5]

$$(2.1)\qquad V \equiv \mathrm{Var}\left(\frac{O}{E}\right) \equiv \sum_i \left\{x_i\left[\left(\frac{O_i}{E_i}\right) - \sum_j x_j\left(\frac{O_j}{E_j}\right)\right]^2\right\}$$

$$= \sum_i x_i q_i^{2\gamma} - \left(\sum_j x_i q_i^{\gamma}\right)^2$$

As is seen in (2.1), V is the difference of V_a and V_b:

$$(2.2)\qquad V_a = \sum_i x_i q_i^{2\gamma}\,,$$

$$(2.3)\qquad V_b = \left(\sum_i x_i q_i^{\gamma}\right)^2.$$

The time behaviors of V_a and V_b can be derived from (1.7) and (1.12) as:

[5] In the remaining sections, the range of running suffix is always from 1 to n.

$$\left(\sum_i \equiv \sum_{i=1}^{n}\ \ \sum_j \equiv \sum_{j=1}^{n}\ \text{etc.}\right)$$

(2.4)
$$\frac{dV_a}{dt} = \sum_i q_i^{2\gamma}\frac{dx_i}{dt} + 2\gamma\sum_i x_i q_i^{2\gamma-1}\frac{dq_i}{dt}$$
$$= \frac{q^{2\gamma}}{M_\gamma}[(1-2\gamma)\rho\{M_{3\gamma} - M_\gamma\cdot M_{2\gamma}\} + 2\gamma\eta\{M_{3\gamma-1} - M_\gamma\cdot M_{2\gamma}\}]$$
$$+ 2\gamma q^{3\gamma-1}\{sM_{2\gamma}\cdot M_\gamma\} - 2\gamma e q^{2\gamma}M_{2\gamma},$$

(2.5)
$$\frac{dV_b}{dt} = 2(\sum_i x_i q_i^\gamma)\left[\sum_i q_i^\gamma\frac{dx_i}{dt} + \gamma\sum_i x_i q_i^{\gamma-1}\frac{dq_i}{dt}\right]$$
$$= 2q^{2\gamma}[(1-\gamma)\rho\{M_{2\gamma} - M_\gamma^2\} + \gamma\eta\{M_{2\gamma-1} - M_\gamma^2\}]$$
$$+ 2s\gamma q^{3\gamma-1}M_\gamma^3 - 2e\gamma q^{2\gamma}M_\gamma^2,$$

in which M_z is the moment of $(1+\theta_i)$ of z-order, i.e.

(2.6)
$$M_z = \sum_i x_i(1+\theta_i)^z.$$

Using the notation of M_z, V, V_a and V_b themselves are given as

(2.7)
$$V = q^{2\gamma}\{M_{2\gamma} - M_\gamma^2\},\quad V_a = q^{2\gamma}M_{2\gamma},\quad V_b = q^{2\gamma}M_\gamma^2.$$

For the sake of interregional comparison, however, some measure of *relative* variance seems to be more appropriate than absolute one.[6] Because if the per capita income of every region has been doubled then few people would think that regional income disparity has been increased, although an absolute variance index is exactly four times larger than before.

In this context we shall define a relative variance index of per capita output as the square of coefficient of variation, V^*, i.e.

(2.8)
$$V^* \equiv \frac{\operatorname{Var}\left(\frac{O}{E}\right)}{\left\{\sum_i x_i\left(\frac{O_i}{E_i}\right)\right\}^2}$$
$$= \frac{\sum_i x_i\{(1+\theta_i)^\gamma - \sum_j x_j(1+\theta_j)^\gamma\}^2}{\{\sum_i x_i(1+\theta_i)^\gamma\}^2} = \frac{V_a}{V_b} - 1.$$

Combining (2.4), (2.5) and (2.7) the time derivative of V^* will be calculated as:

(2.9)
$$\frac{dV^*}{dt} = \frac{\frac{dV_a}{dt}V_b - \frac{dV_b}{dt}V_a}{V_b^2}$$
$$= \frac{1}{V_b^2}[q^{4\gamma}\{-\rho M_{2\gamma}(M_{2\gamma} - M_\gamma^2) + (1-2\gamma)\rho(M_\gamma M_{3\gamma} - M_{2\gamma}^2)$$
$$+ 2\gamma\eta(M_\gamma M_{3\gamma-1} - M_{2\gamma}M_{2\gamma-1})\}].$$

[6] The behavior of V for very small values of (θ_i) has been examined in [7, (16–18)] and the results similar to those of [2, (88)] have been obtained. This implies the *local* character of the stability proof by Fukuchi and Nobukuni.

We shall examine the signs of three members in the extreme righthand-side of (2.9) in turn.

$$M_{2\gamma} - M_\gamma^2 = \sum_i x_i\{(1+\theta_i)^\gamma - \sum_j x_j(1+\theta_j)^\gamma\}^2 \geqq 0 \tag{2.10}$$

$$\begin{aligned} M_\gamma M_{3\gamma} - M_{2\gamma}^2 &= \sum_i \sum_j x_i x_j (1+\theta_i)^\gamma (1+\theta_j)^{3\gamma} \\ &\quad - \sum_i \sum_j x_i x_j (1+\theta_i)^{2\gamma}(1+\theta_j)^{2\gamma} \\ &= \sum_i \sum_j x_i x_j (1+\theta_i)^\gamma (1+\theta_j)^{2\gamma}\{(1+\theta_j)^\gamma - (1+\theta_i)^\gamma\} \\ &= \sum_{\substack{i \\ (i\neq j \\ i<j)}} \sum_j [x_i x_j (1+\theta_i)^\gamma (1+\theta_j)^{2\gamma}\{(1+\theta_j)^\gamma - (1+\theta_i)^\gamma\} \\ &\quad + x_j x_i (1+\theta_j)^\gamma (1+\theta_i)^{2\gamma}\{(1+\theta_i)^\gamma - (1+\theta_j)^\gamma\}] \\ &= \sum_{\substack{i \\ (i\neq j \\ i<j)}} \sum_j x_i x_j (1+\theta_i)^\gamma (1+\theta_j)^\gamma \\ &\quad \times \{(1+\theta_j)^\gamma - (1+\theta_i)^\gamma\}^2 \geqq 0 \end{aligned} \tag{2.11}$$

$$\begin{aligned} M_\gamma M_{3\gamma-1} - M_{2\gamma} M_{2\gamma-1} &= \sum_i \sum_j x_i x_j (1+\theta_i)^\gamma (1+\theta_j)^{3\gamma-1} \\ &\quad - \sum_i \sum_j x_i x_j (1+\theta_i)^{2\gamma}(1+\theta_j)^{2\gamma-1} \\ &= \sum_i \sum_j x_i x_j (1+\theta_i)^\gamma (1+\theta_j)^{2\gamma-1} \\ &\quad \times \{(1+\theta_j)^\gamma - (1+\theta_i)^\gamma\} \\ &= \sum_{\substack{i \\ (i\neq j \\ i<j)}} \sum_j [x_i x_j (1+\theta_i)^\gamma (1+\theta_j)^{2\gamma-1} \\ &\quad - x_j x_i (1+\theta_j)^\gamma (1+\theta_i)^{2\gamma-1}] \\ &\quad \times \{(1+\theta_j) - (1+\theta_i)\} \\ &= \sum_{\substack{i \\ (i\neq j \\ i<j)}} \sum_j [x_i x_j (1+\theta_i)^\gamma (1+\theta_j)^\gamma \{(1+\theta_j)^{\gamma-1} \\ &\quad - (1+\theta_i)^{\gamma-1}\}\{(1+\theta_j)^\gamma - (1+\theta_i)^\gamma\} \leqq 0\,. \end{aligned} \tag{2.12}$$

Hence, if the elasticity of production γ satisfies the condition of

$$1 - 2\gamma \leqq 0. \quad \text{or} \quad \gamma \geqq \frac{1}{2}. \tag{2.13}$$

(2.10)～(2.12) assure that always $(dV^*/dt) \leqq 0$ and the equality sign holds only if every θ_i is equal to each other, i.e. all θ_is are zero. On the other hand, it can be easily shown by (2.8) that V^* is always positive excepting when all θ_i are zero.

If we regard V^* as a Liapunov function of $\theta(t) = \{\theta_1(t), \ldots, \theta_n(t)\}$, we can conclude by the discussion above that[7]

$$\lim_{t\to\infty} V^*(t) = 0 \tag{2.14}$$

which concomitantly means that

$$\lim_{t\to\infty} \theta_i(t) = 0 \qquad \text{for all } i. \tag{2.15}$$

So we can say that under the assumptions stated the interregional differences of capital-labor ratios will disappear ultimately, and that the coefficient of variation of per capita output as an index of relative income inequality will constantly decrease.

In the case in which (2.13) does not hold or

$$1 - 2\gamma > 0 \quad \text{or} \quad \beta > \frac{1}{2} \tag{2.16}$$

by the notation of [2], we can reformulate the whole process of demonstration in the preceding paragraphs using the average productivity of *capital* and the *labor-capital ratio* ($p_i \equiv E_i/K_i$) in each region as key variables instead of the average productivity of labor and the capital-labor ratio.

Then we may define a relative variance index W^* of the average productivities of capital (O_i/K_i) which corresponds to (2.8) as a function of $p_1, \ldots, p_n$ or their discrepancies from the national labor-capital ratio (p), $\mu_1 = p_1/p - 1, \ldots, \mu_n = p_n/p - 1$. Following the exactly similar process of deductions as adopted above which will not be repeated here, we can reach a conclusion that

$$\lim_{t\to\infty} W^*(t) = 0 \tag{2.17}$$

which indicates that

$$\lim_{t\to\infty} \mu_i(t) = 0 \qquad \text{for all } i, \tag{2.18}$$

under the assumption of (2.16).

By the definition of μ_is, (2.18) implies that interregional differences of labor-capital ratios $p_i (i = 1, \ldots, n)$ will disappear ultimately in this case, and since p_i is the reciprocal of q_i this is equivalent to the convergence of the latter. The convergence of p_is or q_is to a common value shown by (2.15) or (2.18) can be considered as an *indirect* proof of the unconditional convergence of the relative income inequality measure to the value of zero.

3. BEHAVIOR OF RELATIVE SHARES

In the foregoing analysis we have been implicitly assuming that all of the relative shares of labor and capital are positive for any $t > 0$. But this proposi-

[7] See Morishima [5, (30, footnote 1)] which can be immediately applied to our case taking

$$y = \theta, \qquad y_0 = \{0, \ldots, 0\}, \text{ and } V = V^*.$$

tion is deducible from Assumption (1.13) as will be seen in this section.[8]

A slight transformation of (1.7) and (1.8) gives us

$$\frac{dx_i}{dt} = \rho\left(\frac{x_i^{1-\gamma}y_i^\gamma}{\sum_j x_j^{1-\gamma}y_j^\gamma} - x_i\right), \qquad i = 1, \dots, n, \tag{3.1}$$

$$\frac{dy_i}{dt} = \eta\left(\frac{x_i^{1-\gamma}y_i^\gamma}{\sum_j x_j^{1-\gamma}y_j^\gamma} - y_i\right), \qquad i = 1, \dots, n. \tag{3.2}$$

Let us define

$$w = \sum_j x_j^{1-\gamma}y_i^\gamma \tag{3.3}$$

at any time and assume

$$x_i = \text{Min}\,(x_i, y_i) \tag{3.4}$$

for the i-th region without any loss of generality.

Since $w \leqq 1$,[9] we have

$$\frac{dx_i}{dt} \geqq \rho\left(\frac{x_i^{1-\gamma}x_i^\gamma}{w} - x_i\right) = \rho\left(\frac{1-w}{w}\right)x_i \geqq 0\,, \tag{3.5}$$

so it can be said that

$$\frac{dm_i}{dt} \geqq 0 \qquad \text{in which} \qquad m_i = \text{Min}\,(x_i, y_i)\,, \tag{3.6}$$

at any time point and for any region.[10]

Taking $t = 0$ we can say for t^* sufficiently small that

$$\text{Min}\,\{x_i(t^*), y_i(t^*)\} \geqq \text{Min}\,\{x_i(0), y_i(0)\} \tag{3.7}$$

by the proposition (3.6) and the continuity of the solution $x_i(t), y_i(t)$. We may take this t^* as a new starting point to repeat the process again and this succession will lead to the conclusions that

$$\text{Min}\,\{x_i(t), y_i(t)\} \geqq \text{Min}\,\{x_i(0), y_i(0)\} \tag{3.8}$$

for all t and i, and that

$$\begin{cases} \lim\limits_{t\to\infty} x_i(t) \geqq \text{Min}\,\{x_i(0), y_i(0)\} \\ \lim\limits_{t\to\infty} y_i(t) \geqq \text{Min}\,\{x_i(0), y_i(0)\} \end{cases} \qquad \text{for all } i. \tag{3.9}$$

[8] The authors owe to Professor Kuga the detailed suggestions on which the analysis of this section is based.

[9] By the definition of x_i and y_i,

$$w = \sum_i x_i^{1-\gamma}\, y_i^\gamma \leqq \sum_i \{(1-\gamma)x_i + \gamma y_i\} = 1\,.$$

[10] The authors wish to thank one of the referees for his suggestion of the argument that follows.

The former asserts that $x_i(t)$ and $y_i(t)$ are bounded from below for all t and i so that they are always positive under Assumption (1.13). The latter implies that the final states of x_i and y_i are not unique and are dependent on their initial values in this way.[11]

4. CONCLUDING REMARKS

We have obtained some additional results concerning our continuous model of interregional economic growth. This last section will be devoted to outline a couple of them.[12]

(1) For our convergence problem, Kuga has proposed an alternative Liapunov function such that

$$V = \sum_{i=1}^{n} \left[\log\left(\frac{O_i}{E_i}\right) - \log\left(\frac{O_{i+1}}{E_{i+1}}\right)\right]^2$$

in which $O_{n+1}/E_{n+1} \equiv O_1/E_1$. It can be shown that $V \geqq 0$ and $dV/dt \leqq 0$ (both of equalities hold only when all (O_i/E_i)s are equal) which establish the convergence of all (O_i/E_i)s to a common value. Kuga's V function with his relevant proof seems to be much more elegant than our laborious V^* (or W^*) function although its relevance to the inequality measure is more or less roundabout.

Furthermore, by the use of a slightly different type of the Liapunov function, i.e.,

$$V = \sum_{i=1}^{n} [\log q_i - \log q_{i+1}]^2$$

in which $q_{n+1} \equiv q_1$, we can extend the covergence proof to the case of general neoclassical production function $O_i = F(K_i, E_i)$ which satisfies the following conditions:

(i) Continuous twice differentiability,
(ii) Positive marginal productivities of both factors,
(iii) Constant returns to scale, and
(iv) Diminishing rate of substitution.

As for the positivity of

$$x_i(t) \equiv \frac{E_i(t)}{\sum_j E_j(t)}, \qquad y_i(t) \equiv \frac{K_i(t)}{\sum_j K_j(t)}$$

for all t and i, a sufficient condition for it is that the functions $w(q_i) \equiv f(q_i) - q_i f'(q_i)$, and $r^*(p_i) \equiv f'(1/p_i) = f'(q_i)$ in which $f(q_i) \equiv F(q_i, 1)$ and $p_i \equiv E_i/K_i = 1/q_i$ are concave with respect to q_i and p_i respectively. A condition that

[11] In the appendix of [7] we have shown a simulation of the time behavior of x_is and y_is by a discrete time model based on the conditions of the Japanese economy in 1963. The convergence of x_i and y_i to a common value which is definite for each region is relatively quick, and this result also implies a quick disappearance of regional income disparity in theory. Propositions (3.8) and (3.9) are also observable in this simulation. See [7, (22–24)].

[12] The detailed discussions and proofs regarding these remarks are given in [8].

$$f'' > = -qf''' > 2f''$$

is sufficient for the concavity of both of w and r^* functions in turn. The last sufficient condition is satisfied automatically in the case of Cobb-Douglas function.

(2) As for the possible time path of the aggregate capital-labor ratio $q(= \sum_j x_i q_j)$, we can say that

(i) $\lim_{t \to \infty} q(t) = q^*$

in which q^* is capital-labor ratio at the Solow equalibrium as the solution of $sf(q^*) = eq^*$,[13]

(ii) $q(t)$ cannot move from a value smaller than q^* to a value larger than q^*,

(iii) $q(t)$ may show an oscillatory move in the area smaller than q^* for a while.

In the present paper it has been shown that there is no tendency in the regional income disparity to be enlarged over time if we express the latter by the relative measure of per capita output. We can, therefore, say that there is no conflict or trade-off relation between high national economic growth and regional income quality as far as the model of Fukuchi-Nobukuni type is concerned: in other words the free market economy generally does not augment regional disparity.[14]

For explaining the enlarging tendency of the regional income disparity in Japan if such tendency existed at all, we must seek for other types of the model than the F-N's which should emphasize the role of regional allocation of social overhead capital that determines the relative productivity of private capital in each region.[15] Mera identified the cause of regional income inequality with the regional difference of production functions in [4], and we too think that the direction of his analysis might be more promising than that of Fukuchi and Nobukuni.[16]

University of Birmingham, England and Osaka University, Japan
Tohoku University, Japan

[13] R. M. Solow [9].

[14] See [1, (Chapter 2)] for the empirical evidence of this statment for the United States.

[15] As a theoretical example see [6].

[16] In a recent mimeographed paper [3], Fukuchi and Nobukuni themselves have made some theoretical improvements concerning their original model developed in [2]. The new points are:
(i) using continuous time variable instead of the discrete one,
(ii) making over-all saving (or investment) an endogenous variable of the system,
(iii) stating the unconditional convergence of the absolute variance in the long run, and
(iv) introducing the coefficient of variation and stating its unconditional convergence. All of them are quite similar to our treatment in the present paper.

However, this new model by Fukuchi and Nobukuni still contains inconsistency pointed out in the introductory part of our paper ($\sum_i \lambda_i K_i \neq 0$ and $\sum_i \pi_i E_i \neq 0$ in general), and their intensive use of approxmation procedure is again depriving their proof of stability of 'globality' alleged.

REFERENCES

[1] Borts, G. H. and J. L. Stein, *Economic Growth in a Free Market* (New York: Columbia University Press, 1964).
[2] Fukuchi, T. and M. Nobukuni, "An Econometric Analysis of National Growth and Regional Income Inequality," *International Economic Review*, XI (February, 1970), 84–100.
[3] ———, "On the Backwashing Economic Growth," (mimeographed, 1971).
[4] Mera, K., "Trade-off Between Aggregate Efficiency and Interregional Equity: A Static Analysis," *Quarterly Journal of Economics*, LXXXI (Nevember, 1967), 658–674.
[5] Morishima, M., *Equilibrium, Stability, and Growth: A Multisectoral Analysis* (Oxford: The Clarendon Press, 1964).
[6] Sakashita, N., "Regional Allocation of Public Investment," *Papers, Regional Science Association*, XIX (1967), 161–182.
[7] ———, and O. Kamoike, "National Growth and Regional Income Inequality: A Consistent Model," Discussion Paper No. 68, The Institute of Social and Economic Research, Osaka University, July 1971.
[8] ———, "National Growth and Regional Income Inequality: Further Results," Discussion Paper No. 72, The Institute of Social and Economic Research, Osaka University, August 1972.
[9] Solow, R. M. "A Contribution to the Theory of Economic Growth," *Quarterly Journal of Economics*, LXX (February, 1956), 65–94.

[5]

Journal of Regional Science, Arizona, Vol. 14 (1974) 81–87

NATIONAL GROWTH AND REGIONAL INCOME INEQUALITY: FURTHER RESULTS*

Noboru Sakashita and Osamu Kamoike†

An econometric model of interregional growth originated by Fukuchi and Nobukuni [1] has been criticized and revised in a recent paper by the present authors with some interesting conclusions. (See Sakashita and Kamoike [2]). In this note, additional results which have been obtained with regard to our interregional growth model are reported. We use the same notation as Fukuchi-Nobukuni [1] and Sakashita-Kamoike [2].

1. EXTENSION TO THE CASE OF NEOCLASSICAL PRODUCTION FUNCTIONS

It was Kuga's suggestion that a Liapunov function, such that

$$V = \sum_{i=1}^{n} [\log (O_i/E_i) - (O_{i+1}/E_{i+1})]^2$$

in which O_i and E_i are the output and the labor force in the ith region respectively and $(O_{n+1}/E_{n+1}) = (O_1/E_1)$, can be used to deduce the convergence of all (O_i/E_i) to a common value. (See Sakashita and Kamoike [2, pp. 15–16].)

Now we can extend the convergence proof to the case of a general neoclassical production function by the use of almost the same kind of Liapunov function as Kuga's. The production function

$$O_i = F(K_i, E_i) \qquad (i = 1, \cdots, n) \tag{1.1}$$

where K_i is the capital stock in the ith region should satisfy the conditions of: (i) continuous twice differentiability, (ii) positive marginal productivities of both factors, (iii) constant returns to scale, and (iv) diminishing rate of substitution.

By (iii) we can write

$$O_i/E_i = f(q_i), \qquad q_i = K_i/E_i, \qquad f(q_i) = F(q_i, 1) \tag{1.2}$$

and (ii) implies

$$r(q_i) \equiv \partial O_i/\partial K_i = f'(q_i) > 0 \tag{1.3}$$

---

* The authors wish to thank Professors Kiyoshi Kuga, Mitsugu Nakamura, and Mikiro Otsuki for their valuable comments on earlier versions of this paper.

† Professor, Institute of Social and Economic Research, Osaka University and visiting lecturer at the University of Birmingham; and Assistant Professor of Economics, Tohoku University, respectively.

Date received: November, 1972; revised, June, 1973.

(1.4) $$w(q_i) \equiv \partial O_i/\partial E_i = f(q_i) - q_i f'(q_i) > 0$$

and we have

(1.5) $$f''(q_i) < 0$$

by (iv).

The system of differential equations which corresponds to that of (1.8), (1.9), and (1.13) in Sakashita and Kamoike [2] will be

(1.6) $$\dot{x}_i/x_i = \rho\{[w(q_i)/\textstyle\sum_j x_j w(q_j)] - 1\} \equiv \rho\pi_i, \qquad x_i = E_i/\textstyle\sum_j E_j$$

(1.7) $$\dot{y}_i/y_i = \eta\{[qr(q_i)/\textstyle\sum_j x_j q_j r(q_j)] - 1\} \equiv \eta\lambda_i, \qquad y_i = K_i/\textstyle\sum_j K_j$$

(1.8) $$\dot{q}_i/q_i = \eta\lambda_i - \rho\pi_i + s[\textstyle\sum_j x_j f(q_j)/\textstyle\sum_j x_j q_j] - e$$

where s is the saving ratio, and e is the constant growth rate of the total labor force, and in which $q = \sum_j K_j/\sum_j E_j = \sum_j x_j q_j$ and $\dot{X} = dX/dt$ in general.

We define a V function of Kuga's type as

(1.9) $$V = \textstyle\sum_{i=1}^{n} (\log q_i - \log q_{i+1})^2$$

in which $q_{n+1} = q_1$, then we have

(1.10) $$\dot{V} = 2\textstyle\sum_{i=1}^{n} (\log q_i - \log q_{i+1})[(\dot{q}_i/q_i) - (\dot{q}_{i+1}/q_{i+1})]$$

Since

(1.11) $$\begin{aligned} \text{sign}(\lambda_i - \lambda_j) &= \text{sign}\{r(q_i) - r(q_j)\} = -\text{sign}(q_i - q_j) \\ \text{sign}(\pi_i - \pi_j) &= \text{sign}\{w(q_i) - w(q_j)\} = \text{sign}(q_i - q_j) \end{aligned}$$

and

(1.12) $$(\dot{q}_i/q_i) - (\dot{q}_j/q_j) = \eta(\lambda_i - \lambda_j) - \rho(\pi_i - \pi_j) \qquad \text{for all } i \text{ and } j$$

we can say that

(1.13) $$\text{sign}[(\dot{q}_i/q_i) - (\dot{q}_j/q_j)] = -\text{sign}(q_i - q_j) = -\text{sign}(\log q_i - \log q_j)$$

Therefore we have the conditions

(1.14) $$\dot{V}\begin{cases} = 0 & \text{if } q_i = q_{i+1} \quad \text{for all } i \\ < 0 & \text{otherwise} \end{cases}$$

and

(1.15) $$V\begin{cases} = 0 & \text{if } q_i = q_{i+1} \quad \text{for all } i \\ > 0 & \text{otherwise} \end{cases}$$

These lead to the conclusion

(1.16) $$\lim_{t\to\infty} q_i = q^* \qquad \text{for all } i$$

in which q^* is a common value for all i.

As for the positivity of $x_i(t)$ and $y_i(t)$ for all t and i, the concavity of $w(q_i)$ and $r^*(p_i)$ is a sufficient condition, where $r^*(p_i) = r(1/p_i)$ and $p_i = E_i/K_i = 1/q_i$. Under this condition we can show that

$$(1.17)\qquad \begin{cases} \text{If } x_i \leqslant y_i \qquad (q_i \gtrless q = \sum_j x_j q_j) \\ w(q_i) \gtrless w(\sum_j x_j q_j) \gtrless \sum_j x_j w(q_j), \quad \text{then } \dot{x}_i/x_i \gtrless 0 \end{cases}$$

$$(1.18)\qquad \begin{cases} \text{If } x_i \gtrless y_i \qquad (p_i \gtrless p = \sum_j y_j p_j) \\ r^*(p_i) \gtrless r^*(\sum_j y_j p_j) \gtrless \sum_j y_j r^*(p_j), \quad \text{then } \dot{y}_i/y_i \gtrless 0 \end{cases}$$

by (1.6) and an equivalent of (1.7), i.e.

$$(1.19)\qquad \dot{y}_i/y_i = \eta\{[r^*(p_i)/\textstyle\sum_j y_j r^*(p_j)] - 1\}$$

Propositions (1.17) and (1.18) assure the same conclusion as (5.5) in Sakashita and Kamoike [2],[1] if we assume the positivity of the initial x_i and y_i.

Since

$$(1.20)\qquad w''(q_i) = -[f''(q_i) + q_i f'''(q_i)]$$

$$(1.21)\qquad r^{*\prime\prime}(p_i) = q_i^3[q_i f'''(q_i) + 2f''(q_i)]$$

if f is thrice differentiable, a condition that

$$(1.22)\qquad f'' > -qf''' > 2f''$$

is sufficient for the concavity of both w and r^*. The last sufficient condition is satisfied automatically in the case of the Cobb-Douglas function $O_i = K_i^{\gamma} E_i^{1-\gamma}$ since

$$(1.23)\qquad \gamma(\gamma - 1) > (2 - \gamma)\gamma(\gamma - 1) > 2\gamma(\gamma - 1)$$

2. TIME PATH OF THE AGGREGATE CAPITAL-LABOR RATIO

In this section we analyze the possible time paths of the aggregate capital-labor ratio q. The differential equation for q is expressed as

$$(2.1)\qquad \dot{q} = s\textstyle\sum_j x_j f(q_j) - eq$$

It is assumed that a Solow equilibrium, defined by the value of $q^* > 0$ which satisfies

$$(2.2)\qquad sf(q^*) - eq^* = 0,$$

exists uniquely. (Solow [3].)

Since f is strictly concave and $x_j > 0$ for all j, if some q_j's are not equal to each other,[2] the following relation holds

$$\textstyle\sum_j x_j f(q_j) < f(\sum_j x_j q_j) = f(q)$$

[1] The conclusion is that $dm_i/dt \geqslant 0$ for all t and i in which $m_i = \min(x_i, y_i)$.

[2] If the initial values of q_j are all equal, (2.1) becomes $\dot{q} = sf(q) - eq$, which is the same equation as that of Solow's model and q^* is stable. If the $q_i(0)$'s are not all equal, since the system of differential equations of q_j and x_j ($j = 1, \cdots, n$) satisfies the Lipschiz conditions, the solution is unique and $q_j(t)$ cannot be equalized in a finite time interval. So we can assume $\forall t, \exists i, j, q_i(t) \neq q_j(t)$ hereafter.

Therefore

$$\dot{q} = s\textstyle\sum_j x_j f(q_j) - eq \leqslant sf(q) - eq$$

(Equality in the last relation holds only when all q_j are equal to q.) We examine the various possibilities.

(a) When $q = q^*$.

$$\dot{q}_{(q=q^*)} \leqslant sf(q^*) - eq^* = 0$$

(Equality in the first relation holds only when all q_j are equal to q^*.) Thus we can see that $q(t)$ cannot move from a value smaller than q^* to a value larger than q^*, i.e., once $q(t) < q^*$ then $\forall\ \tau \geqslant t$, $q(\tau) < q^*$.

(b) When $q > q^*$.

Since

$$\dot{q} \leqslant sf(q) - eq < (q - q^*)[sf'(q^*) - e] = -(q - q^*)(sw^*/q^*) < 0$$

where $w^* = f(q^*) - q^*f'(q^*) > 0$, $q(t)$ approaches q^* from above as $t \to \infty$.[3]

(a) and (b) imply that a common value to which all $q_j(t)$ converge is q^* or a value smaller than q^*.

(c) When $q(t) < q^*$.

(c-1) When $\exists T$, $\forall t \geqslant T$, $q_j(t) \leqslant q^*$ for all j, i.e., after a sufficiently long time passes, all q_j become smaller than q^*. In this case, for $t \geqslant T$ $sf(q_j) - eq_j > 0$ for all j which implies $\dot{q} = \sum_j x_j[sf(q_j) - eq_j] > 0$ for $t \geqslant T$. Hence in this case $\lim_{t\to\infty} q(t) = q^*$ from below.[4]

---

[3] If we assume $\lim_{t\to\infty} q(t) = q^* + \epsilon$, in which ϵ is a positive constant, then $\dot{q} < -\epsilon sw^*/q^*$. Integrating from 0 to T, we get $q(T) < q(0) - (\epsilon sw^*/q^*)T$. When T is taken sufficiently large, $q(T)$ becomes negative which contradicts the fact $q \geqslant 0$. Hence $\lim_{t\to\infty} q(t) \to q^*$ if $q(t) > q^*$.

[4] Let us assume $\lim_{t\to\infty} q(t) = q^* - \epsilon$ in which ϵ is a small positive constant in this case (ϵ cannot be "large" because of the converging properties of all q_j to a common value). If we express (2.1) as

$$\dot{q} = s\textstyle\sum_j x_j f[q + \delta_j(t)] - eq \tag{2.1'}$$

we have $\lim_{t\to\infty} \delta_j(t) = 0$ for all j by the discussion in Section 1. (2.1′) is further transformed as

$$\begin{aligned}
\dot{q} &= s\textstyle\sum_j x_j\{f(q) + f'[q + \theta_j(\delta_j)\delta_j]\delta_j\} - eq & [0 < \theta_j(\delta_j) < 1]\\
&= sf[q^* - \xi(t)] - e[q^* - \xi(t)] + s\textstyle\sum_j x_j f'(q + \theta_j\delta_j)\delta_j & \\
& & [\xi(t) = q^* - q(t) > \epsilon > 0] \quad (2.1'')\\
&= -\{sf'[q^* - \rho(\xi)\xi(t)] - e\}\xi(t) + s\textstyle\sum_j x_j f'(q + \theta_j\delta_j)\delta_j & \\
& & [0 < \rho(\xi) < 1]
\end{aligned}$$

Since $\lim_{t\to\infty} \xi(t) = \epsilon > 0$ and $\lim_{t\to\infty} \delta_j(t) = 0$, the first term in the extreme right-hand side of (2.1″) will dominate the second term in the same side after some large $t = T$. Therefore

$$\dot{q} \geqq -\{sf'[q^* - \rho(\xi)\xi(t)] - e\}\xi(t) > -\{sf'[q^* - \rho(\epsilon)\epsilon] - e\}\epsilon \tag{2.1'''}$$

for all $t > T$. (The second relation comes from the "smallness" of ϵ.) But (2.1‴) contradicts the premise that $\lim_{t\to\infty} q(t) = q^* - \epsilon$ because its extreme right-hand side is a positive constant. Hence $\lim_{t\to\infty} q(t) = q^*$ in this case also.

(c-2) When $\forall t, \exists \tau \geqslant t, \exists i, q_i(\tau) > q^*$, i.e. we cannot find such a T as is defined in (c-1). Since $\forall j, q_j(t) \to$ a common value as $t \to \infty$; that common value must be q^*.

Summing up (a)–(c):

(i) $\lim_{t\to\infty} q(t) = q^*$

(ii) $q(t)$ cannot move from a value smaller than q^* to a value larger than q^*,

(iii) $q(t)$ may show an oscillatory move in the area smaller than q^* for a while.

3. THE COBB-DOUGLAS, TWO-REGION CASE WITH PUBLIC CAPITAL

This section will be devoted to a non-rigorous discussion of the Cobb-Douglas, two-region case in which room for public policy is introduced by the inclusion of public capital and public investment.

The new production function is

$$(3.1)\qquad O_i = K_i^{\gamma} S_i^{\delta} E_i^{1-\gamma-\delta}, \qquad \gamma > 0, \delta > 0, 1-\gamma-\delta > 0, i = 1, 2$$

where K_i is the private capital stock in the ith region, and S_i is the public (social) capital stock in the ith region. The average productivity of labor is

$$(3.2)\qquad O_i/E_i = q_i^{\gamma} r_i^{\delta}$$

where $q_i = K_i/E_i$ and $r_i = S_i/E_i$.

For interregional movements of "private" factors of production, the same mechanism will be used as in Section 1 of Sakashita and Kamoike [2].

$$(3.3)\qquad dE_1/dt = \{\rho[(1-x)(q_1^{\gamma} r_1^{\delta} - q_2^{\gamma} r_2^{\delta})/\hat{\theta}] + e\} E_1$$

$$(3.4)\qquad dE_2/dt = \{\rho[x(q_2^{\gamma} r_2^{\delta} - q_1^{\gamma} r_1^{\delta})/\hat{\theta}] + e\} E_2$$

where $x = E_1/(E_1 + E_2)$ and $\hat{\theta} = xq_1^{\gamma} r_1^{\delta} + (1-x) q_2^{\gamma} r_2^{\delta}$. Also

$$(3.5)\qquad dK_1/dt = \{\eta[(1-y)(q_1^{\gamma-1} r_1^{\delta} - q_2^{\gamma-1} r_2^{\delta})/\hat{w}] + k\} K_1$$

$$(3.6)\qquad dK_2/dt = \{\eta[y(q_2^{\gamma-1} r_2^{\delta} - q_1^{\gamma-1} r_1^{\delta})/\hat{w}] + k\} K_2$$

where $y = K_1/(K_1 + K_2)$, $\hat{w} = yq_1^{\gamma-1} r_1^{\delta} + (1-y) q_2^{\gamma-1} r_2^{\delta}$,[5] and

$$(3.7)\qquad k = (1/K)(dK/dt) = s(1-\tau)[q_1^{\gamma-1} r_1^{\delta} y + q_2^{\gamma-1} r_2^{\delta}(1-y)]$$

(τ will be defined immediately.)

The total amount of public investment is determined by a constant "tax" rate τ

$$(3.8)\qquad dS/dt = \tau(O_1 + O_2)$$

[5] Professor M. Otsuki pointed out that the factor which determines the interregional private capital movement is not $\partial O_i/\partial K_i$ as we suppose but it should be $[O_i - (\partial O_i/\partial E_i)E_i]/K_i$ in each region. Even if this is correct, (3.5) and (3.6) may not change because $\partial O_i/\partial K_i$ and $[O_i - (\partial O_i/\partial E_i)E_i]/K_i$ are proportional to each other in our model.

It is our thinking that the exact definition of the rate of return to private capital depends on the charge and redistribution policy adopted by the public sector and there should be no unique specification. Our definition may be all right if the public sector charges a price which is equal to $\partial O_i/\partial S_i$ to the users of S_i and redistributes the revenue immediately among the nation-wide consumers.

and the growth rate of public capital in each region will be

$$(3.9)\qquad (1/S_1)(dS_1/dt) = (\lambda\tau/z)[q_1^{\gamma}r_1^{\delta-1}z + q_2^{\gamma}r_2^{\delta-1}(1-z)]$$

$$(3.10)\qquad (1/S_2)(dS_2/dt) = [(1-\lambda)\tau/(1-z)][q_1^{\gamma}r_1^{\delta-1}z + q_2^{\gamma}r_2^{\delta-1}(1-z)]$$

in which $z = S_1/(S_1 + S_2)$ and $\lambda = (dS_1/dt)[(dS_1/dt) + (dS_2/dt)]$. In (3.9) and (3.10), λ is a crucial policy variable which affects the path of interregional growth and inequality.

Henceforth we shall confine ourselves to a case in which the central government insists on a fixed and "status quo" allocation of public investment, i.e. $\lambda \equiv z$ for all t.

In this status quo case, we have the following growth equations for the "relative" variables

$$(3.11)\qquad R \equiv r_2/r_1, \qquad Q \equiv q_2/q_1, \qquad \theta \equiv R/Q \equiv (S_2/K_2)/(S_1/K_1)$$

Denoting $G(X)$ for $\dot{X}/X$, in general,

$$(3.12)\qquad G(R) = G(r_2) - G(r_1) = [G(S_2) - G(E_2)] - [G(S_1) - G(E_1)]$$
$$= (\rho/\vartheta)(q_1^{\gamma}r_1^{\delta} - q_2^{\gamma}r_2^{\delta})$$

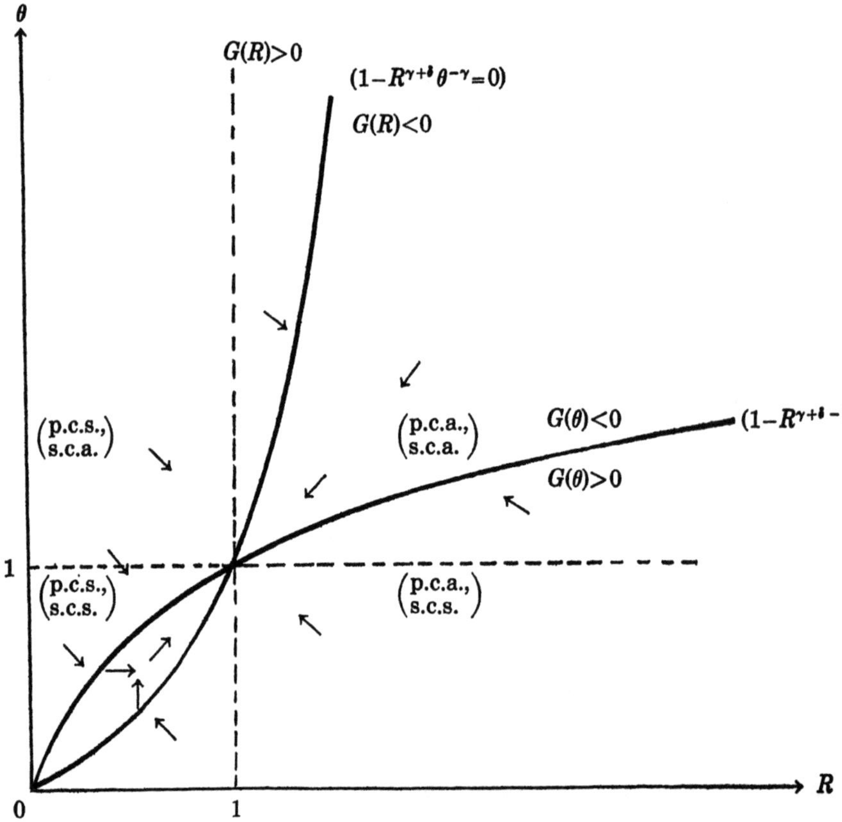

FIGURE 1: Phase Diagram of R and θ.

(3.13) $$G(Q) = G(q_2) - G(q_1) = [G(K_2) - G(E_2)] - [G(K_1) - G(E_1)] = (\eta/\hat{w})(q_2^{\gamma-1}r_2^{\delta} - q_1^{\gamma-1}r_1^{\delta}) + (\rho/\hat{v})(q_1^{\gamma}r_1^{\delta} - q_2^{\gamma}r_2^{\delta})$$

(3.14) $$G(\theta) = G(R) - G(Q) = (\eta/\hat{w})(q_1^{\gamma-1}r_1^{\delta} - q_2^{\gamma-1}r_2^{\delta}).$$

From (3.12) and (3.14), we have

(3.15) $$G(R) = \phi(t)(1 - R^{\gamma+\delta}\theta^{-\gamma})$$

(3.16) $$G(\theta) = \psi(t)(1 - R^{\gamma+\delta-1}\theta^{1-\gamma})$$

in which $\phi(t)$ and $\psi(t)$ are functions always positive. Using (3.15) and (3.16), a phase diagram of R and θ can be depicted as in Figure 1.

In this diagram, abbreviations like "p.c.s." or "s.c.a." mean that "private capital is (relatively) scarce *for Region 2*" or "social capital is (relatively) abundant *for Region 2*" and so on. The diagram shows that the system will again approach complete equality of r_i and q_i in the long run under our assumption of status quo public investment allocation. (The point where $R = \theta = 1$.)

In this case, however, the final values of x_i and y_i are independent of their initial values and are equalized to the values of policy variables $z_i (\equiv \lambda_i)$. This character may be easily reproduced in the generalized multi-region case. The regional inequality of per capita output will of course disappear at the converging point.

REFERENCES

[1] Fukuchi, T. and M. Nobukuni. "An Econometric Analysis of National Growth and Regional Income Inequality," *International Economic Review*, 11 (1970), 84–100.

[2] Sakashita, N. and O. Kamoike. "National Growth and Regional Income Inequality: A Consistent Model," *Discussion Paper No. 68*, The Institute of Social and Economic Research, Osaka University, July, 1971. See also *International Economic Review*, 14 (1973), 372–382.

[3] Solow, R. M. "A Contribution to the Theory of Economic Growth," *Quarterly Journal of Economics*, 70 (1956), 65–94.

London Papers in Regional Science, London, Vol. 5 (1975) 31–51

Distributional Bias in the Welfare Pricing of Public Transport Service

N.SAKASHITA
Osaka University

1 Introduction

Recently the problem of transit pricing has taken the form of an operational programming model. One can see this tendency by comparing the clear-cut discussions by Marchand (1968) or Sherman (1971) with the rather clumsy treatment of a similar subject by Rees (1968). In particular Sherman analyzed the pricing problem between two urban transit modes private automobiles and public buses—which were mutually substitutable in consumption and also mutually interdependent in production through congestion effect. His model is fairly general and can deal equally well with the situations of peak traffic or off-peak traffic. As a programming model, it includes the aspect of income redistribution by one set of instrumental variables, so that it can be considered as an attempt at synthesizing the problems of welfare pricing and compensatory income redistribution.

Generality, however, must pay its own price. First, his formulation of the individual utility functions implies a situation where people are using two transit modes *simultaneously*, which is quite unlikely, particularly in the case of peak-time commuter traffic. Second, and more important, his use of consumer income as an instrumental variable is seemingly unrealistic because it is very unlikely that an income redistribution policy would be performed specifically in connection with the pricing policy of commuter trips. This method was succeeded in a follow-up paper by Abe (1973) which dealt with the problem of pricing mutually substitutable peak and off-peak traffic.

In another series of papers Feldstein (1972a; 1972b) analyzed the problem of distributional equity in public prices and reached a very interesting conclusion which indicated an optimal departure from the well-known marginal-cost pricing approach and which was *derived independently from* the budget constraint—contrary to the case by Rees (1968) or by Baumol and Bradford (1970). Feldstein's method of analysis is, however, that of a partial equilibrium analysis; it therefore should be extended by the general equilibrium method in order to be contrasted with Sherman's theory for example.

The most rigorous treatment of the optimal pricing policy in the public sector was given by Diamond and Mirrlees (1971a; 1971b) using the concept of an indirect social-welfare function. Their analysis can be regarded as a basic theory of public-pricing practice, so applied versions of their analysis will be worthwhile investigating. The distributional aspect of the optimal pricing policy was made somewhat obscure in their model because of the assumption of zero initial incomes for the household sector. This aspect must be clarified as the generalization of Feldstein's theory.

In the present paper, a model which is simple and specific, but which still has the characteristics of a general equilibrium model, will be formulated and analyzed with regard to the public-transport pricing practice for a medium-sized city in order to derive some policy conclusions. This model can be considered as a modification of Sherman's model *with fixed income distribution*, or an extension of Feldstein's model to a general equilibrium setting, or a practical application of the theory by Diamond and Mirrlees with special emphasis on the distributional aspect. Anyhow, this analysis is supposed to be a first step towards the integration of welfare pricing theory and public-investment decision theory.

2 The setting

2.1 Consumption

All consumers are divided into two groups: private-car users and public-bus users. Furthermore, each consumer in the same group is assumed to have the same utility function and the same income level. Needless to say, these extraordinary assumptions are made merely for the sake of analytical simplicity, and there will be no serious loss of generality and also no serious difficulty in generalizing the model to more realistic cases. We denote the number of consumers in the ith group by n^i $(i = 1, 2)$.

The utility function of a consumer in each group is expressed as:

$$u^1 = u^1(t_a/n^1, x^1/n^1) , \tag{1}$$

$$u^2 = u^2(t_b/n^2, x^2/n^2) , \tag{2}$$

where

t_a is the total mileage consumed by private-car users,

t_b is the total mileage consumed by public-bus users,

x^i is the total amount of the composite commodity (excluding travel) consumed by the ith group as a whole [(1)].

u^1 and u^2 are assumed to be strictly concave, continuous, and twice differentiable with respect to both arguments.

Income distribution to the first and second groups is predetermined by a *fixed* set of income variables, y^1 and y^2. These income variables are also regarded as numeraire. An explanation of this treatment is to assume a Robertsonian time-lag structure between income and consumption.

(1) The consumers in each group are supposed to adjust their travel miles, t_a/n^1, or t_b/n^2, by the location of their residence and the frequency of their commuting, business, and shopping trips as a whole household; and by doing so they derive different levels of satisfaction. Since group 1 consumes only t_a and x^1, and group 2 only t_b and x^2, there is no need to attach superscripts 1 and 2 to the variables t_a and t_b.

The price system of the economy in the period next to the income-generation period is determined subject to this given income distribution.

It is natural to assume that the consumers in group 1 are richer than those in group 2, so that the ratio y^2/y^1 should be less than the ratio n^2/n^1. If we denote the prices of x, t_a, and t_b by P_x, P_a, and P_b, the budget constraints for the consumers are:

$$P_x \frac{x^1}{n^1} + P_a \frac{t_a}{n^1} = \frac{y^1}{n^1} , \tag{3}$$

$$P_x \frac{x^2}{n^2} + P_b \frac{t_b}{n^2} = \frac{y^2}{n^2} . \tag{4}$$

The subjective equilibrium of consumers are expressed by

$$\frac{\partial u^i}{\partial (x^i/n^i)} = \lambda^i_* P_x , \qquad i = 1, 2 \tag{5}$$

$$\frac{\partial u^1}{\partial (t_a/n^1)} = \lambda^1_* P_a , \tag{6}$$

$$\frac{\partial u^2}{\partial (t_b/n^2)} = \lambda^2_* P_b , \tag{7}$$

in which λ^i_* is the marginal utility of income for a consumer in the ith group. The conditions in equations (3)–(7) are used to derive *aggregate* demand functions:

$$x^1 = x^1(P_x, P_a | y^1) , \tag{8}$$

$$x^2 = x^2(P_x, P_b | y^2) , \tag{9}$$

$$t_a = t_a(P_x, P_a | y^1) , \tag{10}$$

$$t_b = t_b(P_x, P_b | y^2) . \tag{11}$$

We can express the utility functions of equations (1) and (2) as $U^1(t_a, x^1)$, $U^2(t_b, x^2)$ since n^1 and n^2 are given constants. Then the maximization of U^1 and U^2 under the constraints,

$$P_x x^1 + P_a t_a = y^1 \tag{12}$$

and

$$P_x x^2 + P_b t_b = y^2 , \tag{13}$$

gives the *same* demand functions as equations (8)–(11) and the maximum conditions corresponding to equations (5)–(7), that is

$$\frac{\partial U^i}{\partial x^i} = \lambda^i P_x , \qquad i = 1, 2 \tag{14}$$

$$\frac{\partial U^1}{\partial t_a} = \lambda^1 P_a , \tag{15}$$

and

$$\frac{\partial U^2}{\partial t_b} = \lambda^2 P_b \ , \tag{16}$$

where $\lambda^i = \lambda^i_* / n^i$.

Therefore we use the simpler relations of equations (12)–(16) instead of equations (3)–(7) in the analysis of indirect social-welfare functions which follows.

2.2 Production

Average input requirements to produce t_a and t_b are expressed by g_a and g_b, both of which are dependent upon $(t_a + wt_b)$ by convex, continuous, and twice-differentiable functions in which w is a constant weight factor:

$$g_a = g_a(t_a + wt_b) \ , \tag{17}$$

$$g_b = g_b(t_a + wt_b) \ , \tag{18}$$

and the total intermediate input, g, is represented as

$$g = g_a t_a + g_b t_b \ . \tag{19}$$

In addition, we assume a convex, continuous, and twice-differentiable transformation function between x and g,

$$F(x, g) = 0 \ , \qquad x = x^1 + x^2 \ . \tag{20}$$

A more explicit and convenient form of equation (20) may be, with appropriate functional forms of f and g,

$$K - f(x) - h(g) = 0 \ , \tag{21}$$

where K is a constant. We shall use equation (21) in the following analysis.

2.3 Market

In principle we assume competitive free markets and profit-maximization behaviour of the firms producing the composite commodity (x) and intermediate and primary inputs (g and K). For the private-car service we assume that the average cost is borne by the users themselves.

As a price of public services, P_b can be determined as $\hat{P}_b$ by the government, regardless of the related cost of production. On the other hand, P_a and P_x are able to deviate from their costs of production by a system of commodity taxes. Then we have

$$P_a = \pi_g g_a + \hat{s}_a \ , \tag{22}$$

$$P_x = \pi_k f'(x) + \hat{s}_x \ , \tag{23}$$

where π_g and π_k are the market prices of the intermediate input, g, and the primary input, K, and $\hat{s}_a$ and $\hat{s}_x$ are the aforementioned commodity taxes.

The relation between π_g and π_k may be given as

$$\pi_g = \pi_k h'(g) \tag{24}$$

with the use of equations (17)–(19). Combination of equations (8)–(11), (21), and (22)–(24) brings forth the following single equilibrium condition for K and three price equations concerning π_g, π_k, P_x, and P_a:

from equations (8)–(11) and (21):

$$K = f[x(P_x, P_a, \hat{P}_b)] + h\{g[t_a(P_x, P_a), t_b(P_x, \hat{P}_b)]\} ; \tag{25}$$

from equations (10), (11), and (24):

$$\pi_g = \pi_k h'\{g[t_a(P_x, P_a), t_b(P_x, \hat{P}_b)]\} ; \tag{26}$$

from equations (8), (9), and (23):

$$P_x = \pi_k f'[x(P_x, P_a, \hat{P}_b)] + \hat{s}_x ; \tag{27}$$

from equations (10), (11), (17), and (22):

$$P_a = \pi_g g_a[t_a(P_x, P_a), t_b(P_x, \hat{P}_b)] + \hat{s}_a . \tag{28}$$

Therefore we have four equations for four unknown price variables, P_x, P_a, π_g, and π_k, so that specification of $\hat{P}_b$, $\hat{s}_x$, and $\hat{s}_a$ completely defines a consistent system of absolute prices taking income variables as the numeraire. Alternatively we can take P_x and P_a with $\hat{P}_b$ as the controlled policy variables instead of $\hat{s}_x$ and $\hat{s}_a$, but then there will be one degree of freedom among π_k, π_g, $\hat{s}_x$, and $\hat{s}_a$ in this approach, which will be adopted in the following discussion. [In other words, there are infinite number of combinations of π_k, π_g, $\hat{s}_x$, and $\hat{s}_b$ brought in by this degree of freedom which will produce a given set of P_x, P_a, and P_b which satisfies equation (25).]

3 Basic welfare maximization problem

Under the conditions given by equations (8)–(11), (14)–(16), (17)–(19), and (21) we can formulate a first-best welfare maximization problem without institutional and administrative constraints, that is all price variables are able to be freely adjusted.

First we postulate a simple social-welfare function,

$$W = \beta^1 U^1 + \beta^2 U^2 , \tag{29}$$

with unspecified β^1 and β^2. Then our problem is given as:

Problem 1

Maximize

$$W(t_a, x^1, t_b, x^2) = W(P_x, P_a, P_b) , \quad \text{with respect to } P_x, P_a, P_b, \text{ subject to}$$

$$f(x^1 + x^2) + h[g_a(t_a + wt_b)t_a + g_b(t_a + wt_b)t_b] - K = 0 \quad : \quad \mu_k \tag{30}$$

in which μ_k is a Lagrangian multiplier. Apparently $W(P_x, P_a, P_b)$ is an indirect social-welfare function defined by Diamond and Mirrlees (1971b) so we can use the results of their theorem to derive optimality conditions (see Diamond and Mirrlees, 1971b, p.274, theorem 5).

The first-order conditions for the above problem are [2]:

$$\beta^1\left(\frac{\partial U^1}{\partial t_a}\frac{\partial t_a}{\partial P_x}+\frac{\partial U^1}{\partial x^1}\frac{\partial x^1}{\partial P_x}\right)+\beta^2\left(\frac{\partial U^2}{\partial t_b}\frac{\partial t_b}{\partial P_x}+\frac{\partial U^2}{\partial x^2}\frac{\partial x^2}{\partial P_x}\right)$$
$$-\mu_k h'\left[g'_a\left(\frac{\partial t_a}{\partial P_x}+w\frac{\partial t_b}{\partial P_x}\right)t_a+g_a\frac{\partial t_a}{\partial P_x}+g'_b\left(\frac{\partial t_a}{\partial P_x}+w\frac{\partial t_b}{\partial P_x}\right)t_b+g_b\frac{\partial t_b}{\partial P_x}\right]$$
$$-\mu_k f'\left(\frac{\partial x^1}{\partial P_x}+\frac{\partial x^2}{\partial P_x}\right)=0 \quad : \quad \frac{\partial \Phi}{\partial P_x} \tag{31}$$

$$\beta^1\left(\frac{\partial U^1}{\partial t_a}\frac{\partial t_a}{\partial P_a}+\frac{\partial U^1}{\partial x^1}\frac{\partial x^1}{\partial P_a}\right)-\mu_k h'\left(g'_a\frac{\partial t_a}{\partial P_a}t_a+g_a\frac{\partial t_a}{\partial P_a}+g'_b\frac{\partial t_a}{\partial P_a}t_b\right)$$
$$-\mu_k f'\frac{\partial x^1}{\partial P_a}=0 \quad : \quad \frac{\partial \Phi}{\partial P_a} \tag{32}$$

$$\beta^2\left(\frac{\partial U^2}{\partial t_b}\frac{\partial t_b}{\partial P_b}+\frac{\partial U^2}{\partial x^2}\frac{\partial x^2}{\partial P_b}\right)-\mu_k h'\left(g'_a w\frac{\partial t_b}{\partial P_b}t_a+g_b w\frac{\partial t_b}{\partial P_a}t_b+g_b\frac{\partial t_b}{\partial P_b}\right)$$
$$-\mu_k f'\frac{\partial x^2}{\partial P_b}=0 \quad : \quad \frac{\partial \Phi}{\partial P_b}. \tag{33}$$

For equations (31)-(33) to be true necessary conditions for optimality, a certain 'constraint qualification' is required—the validity of which depends on the form of the utility functions as well as on the characteristics of the production possibility. We assume the fulfilment of this qualification. (See appendix 1 for details on this point.)

Partial differentiation of equations (12) and (13) with respect to P_x, P_a, and P_b generates a set of relations such as

$$x^1+P_x\frac{\partial x^1}{\partial P_x}+P_a\frac{\partial t_a}{\partial P_x}=0\,,\quad \dots,\quad \dots. \tag{34}$$

By equations (34) and (14)-(16), equations (31)-(33) are simplified as

$$\beta^1\lambda^1x^1+\beta^2\lambda^2x^2=-\mu_k\left[h'\left(\frac{\partial t_a}{\partial P_x}\frac{\partial g}{\partial t_a}+\frac{\partial t_b}{\partial P_x}\frac{\partial g}{\partial t_b}\right)+f'\left(\frac{\partial x^1}{\partial P_x}+\frac{\partial x^2}{\partial P_x}\right)\right], \tag{35}$$

$$\beta^1\lambda^1t_a=-\mu_k\left[h'\left(\frac{\partial t_a}{\partial P_a}\frac{\partial g}{\partial t_a}\right)+f'\frac{\partial x^1}{\partial P_a}\right], \tag{36}$$

$$\beta^2\lambda^2t_b=-\mu_k\left[h'\left(\frac{\partial t_b}{\partial P_b}\frac{\partial g}{\partial t_b}\right)+f'\frac{\partial x^2}{\partial P_b}\right], \tag{37}$$

(2) Φ is the Lagrangian form associated with Problem 1:

$$\Phi=W-\mu_k(f+h-K)\,,$$

in which W, f, and h are (indirect) functions of P_x, P_a, and P_b.

where

$$\frac{\partial g}{\partial t_a} = g'_a t_a + g_a + g'_b t_b \ , \tag{38}$$

$$\frac{\partial g}{\partial t_b} = g'_b w t_a + g_b + g'_b w t_b \ ; \tag{39}$$

that is the marginal social costs of producing t_a and t_b in terms of the intermediate input.

If we define direct and cross partial elasticities of the demand functions in equations (8)-(11) by

$$e^1_{xx} = -\frac{\partial x^1}{\partial P_x}\frac{P_x}{x^1} \ , \qquad e_{xa} = \frac{\partial x^1}{\partial P_a}\frac{P_a}{x^1} \ ,$$

and so on (negative sign for direct elasticities and positive sign for cross elasticities), the following relations are derived [(3)],

$$P_x = \frac{\mu_k}{\beta^1\lambda^1 x^1 + \beta^2\lambda^2 x^2}\left[f'\left(e^1_{xx}x^1 + e^2_{xx}x^2\right) - h'\left(e_{ax}t_a\frac{\partial g}{\partial t_a} + e_{bx}t_b\frac{\partial g}{\partial t_b}\right)\right] , \tag{40}$$

$$P_a = \frac{\mu_k}{\beta^1\lambda^1}\left[h'\left(e_{aa}\frac{\partial g}{\partial t_a}\right) - f' e_{xa}\frac{x^1}{t_a}\right] , \tag{41}$$

$$P_b = \frac{\mu_k}{\beta^2\lambda^2}\left[h'\left(e_{bb}\frac{\partial g}{\partial t_b}\right) - f' e_{xb}\frac{x^2}{t_b}\right] . \tag{42}$$

Due to the effect of distributional bias embodied in the price variables, we do not see straightforward equalization of prices and marginal costs. The terms $\mu_k h' \partial g/\partial t_a$ and $\mu_k h' \partial g/\partial t_b$ are proportional to the social opportunity cost of producing t_a or t_b. However, the presence of $\beta^i\lambda^i$ and the fact that $e_{aa} \neq 1$, $e_{bb} \neq 1$, and $e_{xa} \neq 0$, $e_{xb} \neq 0$ in general make P_a and P_b not proportional to the corresponding marginal social costs [(4)].

(3) In our model, we cannot use such relations as $P_a K_{aa} + P_x K^1_{xa} = 0$, in which K_{aa} and K^1_{xa} are the Slutsky terms of the first utility function, in order to simplify maximizing conditions, because the income variables y^1 and y^2 are fixed. See Sherman (1971, p.570) and the next section of this paper.

(4) If we neglect the cross-elasticity terms of equations (41) and (42), we derive a simple relation,

$$\frac{(P_a - m_a)/P_a}{(P_b - m_b)/P_b} = \frac{e_{bb}(\beta^1\lambda^1 - e_{aa})}{e_{aa}(\beta^2\lambda^2 - e_{bb})} ,$$

where

$$m_a = \mu_k h' \frac{\partial g}{\partial t_a} ,$$

$$m_b = \mu_k h' \frac{\partial g}{\partial t_b} .$$

This relation is very close to equation (7) in Feldstein (1972a, p.34).

The net revenue for the government under the optimal pricing is calculated as

$$R = P_b t_b + \hat{s}_a t_a + \hat{s}_x (x^1 + x^2) - \pi_g g_b t_b$$
$$= (P_b - \pi_k h' g_b) t_b + (P_a - \pi_k h' g_a) t_a + (P_x - \pi_k f')(x^1 + x^2) . \qquad (43)$$

R can be evaluated using equations (40)-(42) together with the explicit value of μ_k in the optimizing problem and the explicit value of π_k in the market solution [equations (25)-(28)]. However, the government has flexibility in determining the value of π_k indirectly as mentioned before (see section 2) so the budget constraint is not a real problem to it (see appendix 3).

Now let us consider a particular case in which U^1 and U^2 are represented by log-linear functions:

$$U^1 = \text{constant} + \alpha^1 \log t_a + (1 - \alpha^1) \log x^1 , \qquad (44)$$

$$U^2 = \text{constant} + \alpha^2 \log t_b + (1 - \alpha^2) \log x^2 . \qquad (45)$$

Then apparently

$$\lambda^i = \frac{1}{y^i} , \qquad i = 1,2$$

$$e_{xx} = e_{aa} = e_{bb} = 1 ,$$

and all cross elasticities of the demand functions vanish. Equations (40)-(42) in this case are

$$P_x = \frac{\mu_k f' [(1 - \alpha^1) y^1 + (1 - \alpha^2) y^2]}{(1 - \alpha^1) \beta^1 + (1 - \alpha^2) \beta^2} , \qquad (46)$$

$$P_a = \mu_k \frac{y^1}{\beta^1} \left(h' \frac{\partial g}{\partial t_a} \right) , \qquad (47)$$

$$P_b = \mu_k \frac{y^2}{\beta^2} \left(h' \frac{\partial g}{\partial t_b} \right) . \qquad (48)$$

The marginal (social) cost pricing is justified only when $(y^2/y^1) = (\beta^2/\beta^1)$, but this case is most unlikely because it was suggested before that $(y^2/y^1) < (n^2/n^1)$, and we should postulate that $(\beta^2/\beta^1) \approx (n^2/n^1)$ from the viewpoint of social equity. The condition $(y^2/y^1) < (\beta^2/\beta^1)$ implies greater than marginal (social) cost pricing for private cars and less than marginal (social) cost pricing for public buses. Such pricing policy seems to be very natural from the distributional viewpoint. Finally μ_k is determined so as to make the quantities demanded, $x^1(\mu_k)$, $x^2(\mu_k)$, $t_a(\mu_k)$, and $t_b(\mu_k)$, equal to their feasible maximums as defined by equations (17)-(21).

Equations (40)-(42) or (46)-(48) strongly suggest a distortion of efficient pricing introduced by a distributional consideration. Sufficiency of the above conditions will be discussed in appendix 2, and the fulfilment of the budget condition for the government will be examined in appendix 3 with regard to a special case.

4 Welfare maximization with adjustable income and gain of welfare

If we can adjust y^1 and y^2 as well as price variables in problem 1, a zeroth-best solution with marginal cost pricing will be established. The new problem is:

4.1 *Problem 0*

Maximize

$W(P_x, P_a, P_b, y^1, y^2)$, with respect to P_x, P_a, P_b, y^1, y^2, subject to

equation (30). This is a constraint-free maximization problem which was dealt with in Marchand (1968) and Abe (1973).

Now we have the following first-order condition in addition to equations (31)-(33):

$$\beta^1\left(\frac{\partial U^1}{\partial t_a}\frac{\partial t_a}{\partial y^1}+\frac{\partial U^1}{\partial x^1}\frac{\partial x^1}{\partial y^1}\right)-\mu_k h'\left(\frac{\partial g}{\partial t_a}\frac{\partial t_a}{\partial y^1}\right)-\mu_k f'\frac{\partial x^1}{\partial y^1}=0\ , \tag{49}$$

$$\beta^2\left(\frac{\partial U^2}{\partial t_b}\frac{\partial t_b}{\partial y^2}+\frac{\partial U^2}{\partial x^2}\frac{\partial x^2}{\partial y^2}\right)-\mu_k h'\left(\frac{\partial g}{\partial t_a}\frac{\partial t_b}{\partial y^2}\right)-\mu_k f'\frac{\partial x^2}{\partial y^2}=0\ . \tag{50}$$

Partial differentiation of equations (12) and (13) with respect to y^1 and y^2, combined with equations (14)-(16), changes equations (49) and (50) into

$$\beta^1\lambda^1=\mu_k\left[h'\left(\frac{\partial g}{\partial t_a}\frac{\partial t_a}{\partial y^1}\right)+f'\frac{\partial x^1}{\partial y^1}\right]\ , \tag{51}$$

$$\beta^2\lambda^2=\mu_k\left[h'\left(\frac{\partial g}{\partial t_b}\frac{\partial t_b}{\partial y^2}\right)+f'\frac{\partial x^2}{\partial y^2}\right]\ . \tag{52}$$

Comparison of equation (36) with equation (51), or equation (37) with equation (52), leads us to deduce such relations as

$$h'\frac{\partial g}{\partial t_a}\underbrace{\left(\frac{\partial t_a}{\partial y^1}t_a+\frac{\partial t_a}{\partial P_a}\right)}_{K_{aa}}=-f'\underbrace{\left(\frac{\partial x^1}{\partial P_a}+\frac{\partial x^1}{\partial y^1}t_a\right)}_{K_{xa}}\ , \tag{53}$$

in which K_{aa} and K_{xa} are Slutsky terms in the theory of consumer behaviour. By a well-known theorem, we have [5]

$$P_a K_{aa}+P_x K_{xa}\equiv 0\ , \tag{54}$$

[5] See Samuelson (1953, p.105, footnote 11); in Samuelson's case, $P_a K_{aa}+P_x K_{ax}\equiv 0$ is proved by an expansion, by columns, of a determinant, but of course an expansion by rows in the present case yields the same result.

which leads to

$$\frac{P_a}{P_x} = \frac{h'}{f'}\frac{\partial g}{\partial t_a}\,, \tag{55}$$

and similarly we also have

$$\frac{P_b}{P_x} = \frac{h'}{f'}\frac{\partial g}{\partial t_b}\,. \tag{56}$$

Equations (55) and (56) show that the principle of marginal cost pricing is (finally!) established in this zeroth-best problem. Furthermore, rewriting the right-hand sides of equations (51) and (52) and using equations (55) and (56) we have

$$\beta^1\lambda^1 = \frac{\mu_k}{P_x}f'\left(P_a\frac{\partial t_a}{\partial y^1}+P_x\frac{\partial x^1}{\partial y^1}\right) = \frac{\mu_k f'}{P_x}\,, \tag{57}$$

$$\beta^2\lambda^2 = \frac{\mu_k}{P_x}f'\left(P_b\frac{\partial t_b}{\partial y^1}+P_x\frac{\partial x^1}{\partial y^1}\right) = \frac{\mu_k f'}{P_x}\,. \tag{58}$$

Again partial differentiation of equations (12) and (13) is used. Then we have the supreme-best situation that (see Marchand, 1968, pp.260–273; Abe, 1973, p.58)

$$\beta^1\lambda^1 = \beta^2\lambda^2\,. \tag{59}$$

We note that this optimum with marginal cost pricing is attainable *only when* the government can manage income redistribution *and* can produce exact equalization between the consumer price and the corresponding marginal costs. Any violation of these conditions leads to a suboptimum compared to this supreme optimum. (For instance, average cost pricing of private-car service, that is $P_a = \pi_g g_a$.)

Now let us evaluate, using the results of appendix 3, the gain in welfare brought about by the shift from problem 1 to problem 0 in a special case where we have log-linear utility functions and a linear structure of technology.

The optimized social welfare in the case of appendix 3 is expressed as

$$\begin{aligned}\hat{W} = \beta^1U^1+\beta^2U^2 &= \text{constant}+\beta^1(1-\alpha^1)\log y^1+\beta^2(1-\alpha^2)\log y^2\\ &\quad -[\beta^1(1-\alpha^1)+\beta^2(1-\alpha^2)]\log[(1-\alpha^1)y^1+(1-\alpha^2)y^2]\end{aligned} \tag{60}$$

in the light of equations (44), (45), (A10)–(A14). We can assume $y^1+y^2 \equiv \beta^1+\beta^2 \equiv 1$ without loss of generality, and equation (60) is then transformed into

$$\begin{aligned}\hat{W} &= \text{constant}+\beta^1(1-\alpha^1)\log y^1+(1-\beta^1)(1-\alpha^2)\log(1-y^1)\\ &\quad -[\beta^1(1-\alpha^1)+(1-\beta^1)(1-\alpha^2)]\log[(1-\alpha^1)y^1+(1-\alpha^2)(1-y^1)]\,. \end{aligned}\tag{61}$$

90 It is easily seen that $\hat{W}$ attains its maximum $\hat{W}^*$ (the optimum optimorum)

at $y^{1*} = \beta^1$ (and $y^{2*} = \beta^2$). This optimum optimorum corresponds to the supreme best, derived in the present section, in which $\beta^1\lambda^1 = \beta^2\lambda^2$, because $\lambda^{i*} = 1/y^{i*}$ here so we have $\beta^1\lambda^{1*} = \beta^2\lambda^{2*} = 1$. The gain of welfare brought by a shift from fixed values of y^1 and y^2 to the adjusted values of y^{1*} and y^{2*} (that is the shift from problem 1 to problem 0) is given as

$$\begin{aligned} G(y^1) = \hat{W}^* - \hat{W} = {} & \beta^1(1-\alpha^1)(\log\beta^1 - \log y^1) + (1-\beta^1)(1-\alpha^2) \\ & \times [\log(1-\beta^1) - \log(1-y^1)] - [\beta^1(1-\alpha^1) + (1-\beta^1)(1-\alpha^2)] \\ & \times \{\log[(1-\alpha^1)\beta^1 + (1-\alpha^2)(1-\beta^1)] - \log[(1-\alpha^1)y^1 \\ & + (1-\alpha^2)(1-y^1)]\}\,. \end{aligned} \tag{62}$$

It is obvious that $G = 0$ and $(\mathrm{d}G/\mathrm{d}y^1) = 0$ at $y^1 = \beta^1$, and

$$\frac{\mathrm{d}}{\mathrm{d}y^1}\left(\frac{\mathrm{d}G}{\mathrm{d}y^1}\right) > 0$$

everywhere within $0 < y^1 < 1$. This result implies that there is a potential loss of welfare in problem 1 compared to problem 0, due to the constraint of unadjustable nominal incomes except for a very special case, where $y^1 = \beta^1$ by accident.

5 Public transport as a necessary good

There may be several ways to introduce the concept of necessary goods to the theory of consumer behaviour. A familiar way is to define a necessary good according to the values of income and of the price elasticities of demand for it. However, here we adopt a different approach.

5.1 *Case* A

For the second group, the bus transport is a necessary good up to a fixed amount of t_b^0, probably as commuting trips. Then the consumers in the second group maximize $U^2(t_b, x^2)$ subject to the budget constraint of

$$P_x x^2 + P_b t_b = y^2 - P_b t_b^0\,. \tag{63}$$

The same maximum conditions as equations (14) and (16) follow, but differentiation of equation (63) with respect to P_b gives

$$P_x \frac{\partial x^2}{\partial P_b} + t_b + P_b \frac{\partial t_b}{\partial P_b} = -t_b^0\,. \tag{64}$$

For the corresponding welfare maximization problem (problem 1a) the conditions given in equations (40) and (41) are unchanged, but equation (42) is replaced by

$$P_b = \frac{\mu_k}{\beta^2\lambda^2}\left[h'\left(e_{bb}\frac{t_b}{t_b + t_b^0}\right)\frac{\partial g}{\partial t_b} - f' e_{xb}\frac{x^2}{t_b + t_b^0}\right]. \tag{65}$$

It is a good conjecture from equation (65) to consider that P_b will be lowered in problem 1a compared to its counterpart in problem 1.

We will prove this fact only for the special case of linear and log-linear assumptions adopted in appendix 3. In this case we have

$$P_b = \mu_k \frac{y^2 - P_b t_b^0}{\beta^2}\left[h\frac{\alpha^2(y^2-P_b t_b^0)}{\alpha^2(y^2-P_b t_b^0)+P_b t_b^0}\right]g_b \tag{66}$$

$$\mu_k = \frac{1}{K}\left\{\beta^1+\beta^2(1-\alpha^2)+hg_b\left[\frac{\alpha^2(y^2-P_b t_b^0)}{P_b}+t_b^0\right]\right\}, \tag{67}$$

then an implicit form for P_b is

$$P_b = \frac{\alpha^2 g_b h}{K\beta^2}\left\{[\beta^1+\beta^2(1-\alpha^2)]\frac{(y^2-P_b t_b^0)^2}{\alpha^2(y^2-P_b t_b^0)+P_b t_b^0}+hg_b\frac{\alpha^2(y^2-P_b t_b^0)^2}{P_b}\right\}$$

$$= H(P_b, t_b^0)\,. \tag{68}$$

It is easy to show that

$$\frac{\partial H}{\partial P_b} < 0\,, \qquad \text{and } \frac{\partial H}{\partial t_b^0} < 0\,,$$

provided that

$$y^2 - P_b t_b^0 > 0$$

so that

$$\frac{dP_b}{dt_b^0} < 0\,. \tag{69}$$

Therefore, if the public transport is taken as a necessary good up to a certain amount for the low income group, it will have the effect of lowering its optimal price. This is a very plausible conclusion.

5.2 *Case* B

Usually the captive part of public transport, t_b^0 is charged a price differing from P_b, as in the case of commuters' passes. Such price discrimination generates a totally different solution to our welfare maximization problem (problem 1b).

Now the budget constraint for the second group becomes

$$P_x x^2 + P_b t_b = y^2 - r t_b^0\,, \tag{70}$$

for a given set of P_x, P_b, and r. Partial differentiation of equation (70) by r gives

$$P_x\frac{\partial x^2}{\partial r}+P_b\frac{\partial t_b}{\partial r} = -t_b^0\,. \tag{71}$$

r must obey a natural constraint of $r \geqslant 0$, but we shall neglect this constraint for the moment. Partial differentiation of the Lagrangian form of problem 1 with respect to r gives us

$$\beta^2\lambda^2 t_b^0 = -\mu_k\left[h'\left(\frac{\partial t_b}{\partial r}\frac{\partial g}{\partial t_b}\right)+f'\frac{\partial x^2}{\partial r}\right]. \tag{72}$$

Denoting $y^2 - rt_b^0 = \tilde{y}^2$ as an exogenous variable to the consumer, equation (72) can be expressed as

$$\beta^2\lambda^2 = \mu_k\left[h'\left(\frac{\partial g}{\partial t_b}\right)\frac{\partial t_b}{\partial \tilde{y}^2} + f'\frac{\partial x^2}{\partial \tilde{y}^2}\right], \tag{73}$$

because

$$\frac{\partial \tilde{y}^2}{\partial r} = -t_b^0 .$$

Comparison of equation (73) with equation (37) results in

$$\frac{P_b}{P_x} = \frac{h'}{f'}\frac{\partial g}{\partial t_b} \tag{74}$$

by the same procedure as equations (53)–(56), and again, by equations (73) and (74), we have

$$\beta^2\lambda^2 = \frac{\mu_k}{P_x}f' . \tag{75}$$

On the other hand, the condition in equation (35) is transformed into

$$\begin{aligned}\beta^1\lambda^1x^1 + \beta^2\lambda^2x^2 &= -\mu_k\left[h'\left(\frac{\partial t_a}{\partial P_x}\frac{\partial g}{\partial t_a} + \frac{\partial t_b}{\partial P_x}\frac{P_b f'}{P_x h'}\right) + f'\left(\frac{\partial x^1}{\partial P_x} + \frac{\partial x^2}{\partial P_x}\right)\right] \\ &= -\mu_k\left[h'\left(\frac{\partial t_a}{\partial P_x}\frac{\partial g}{\partial t_a}\right) + f'\frac{\partial x^1}{\partial P_x} + f'\left(\frac{P_b}{P_x}\frac{\partial t_b}{\partial P_x} + \frac{\partial x^2}{\partial P_x}\right)\right] \\ &= -\mu_k\left[h'\left(\frac{\partial t_a}{\partial P_x}\frac{\partial g}{\partial t_a}\right) + f'\frac{\partial x^1}{\partial P_x}\right] + \frac{\mu_k}{P_x}f'x^2 \end{aligned} \tag{76}$$

by using equation (74) and the partial differentiation of equation (13). By using equation (75), equation (76) becomes

$$\beta^1\lambda^1x^1 = -\mu_k\left[h'\left(\frac{\partial t_a}{\partial P_x}\frac{\partial g}{\partial t_a}\right) + f'\frac{\partial x^1}{\partial P_x}\right], \tag{77}$$

and comparison of equation (77) with equation (36) accordingly gives us

$$h'\frac{\partial g}{\partial t_a}\left(\frac{\partial t_a}{\partial P_x}t_a - \frac{\partial t_a}{\partial P_a}x^1\right) = f'\left(\frac{\partial x^1}{\partial P_a}x^1 - \frac{\partial x^1}{\partial P_x}t_a\right), \tag{78}$$

$$h'\frac{\partial g}{\partial t_a}(K_{ax}t_a - K_{aa}x^1) = f'(K_{xa}x^1 - K_{xx}t_a) . \tag{79}$$

Recalling such relations as equation (54) with equation (79), we can conclude that

$$\frac{P_a}{P_x} = \frac{h'}{f'}\frac{\partial g}{\partial t_a} . \tag{80}$$

Here we see the revival of marginal cost pricing in equations (74) and (80), and it is just one more step to reach the conclusion[6]:

$$\beta^1\lambda^1 = \beta^2\lambda^2 \, . \tag{81}$$

The above process of solving problem 1 for the free range of r (positive or negative) convinces us that this is nothing less than an alternative method of redistributing nominal incomes, that is, a variant of problem 0. Since t_b^0 might be relatively small, the condition in equation (81) apparently implies a negative (optimal) r. If we reintroduce a nonnegativity constraint for r, the (sub)optimal r should be zero since $\partial W/\partial r$ may be negative at $r = 0$.

We have almost established a theoretical basis, by solving problem 1b, for the assertion that the price of a public service which is a necessary good in a strong sense should be null.

6 Second-best maximization under the absence of commodity taxes in the private sector

If it is impossible for the government to impose $\hat{s}_a$ and $\hat{s}_x$, it must solve problem 1 with an additional constraint of

$$P_x h'(g) g_a = P_a f'(x) \quad : \quad \mu \text{ (Lagrangian multiplier)} \, , \tag{82}$$

which is derived from equations (26)-(28) when $\hat{s}_a = \hat{s}_x = 0$.

Exactly speaking, equation (82) corresponds to the following case with an arbitrary, single, proportional tax $\hat{\theta}$,

$$P_a = (1+\hat{\theta})\pi_g g_a \, , \tag{i}$$

$$P_x = (1+\hat{\theta})\pi_k f' \, . \tag{ii}$$

These equations, however, define a unique value of $(1+\hat{\theta})\pi_k$ with equations (25) and (26) for a given *consistent* set of P_x, P_a, and $\hat{P}_b$ as discussed below. For a given $\hat{P}_b$, equation (25) defines a functional relationship between P_x and P_a, that is

$$P_x = \phi(P_a | \hat{P}_b) \, . \tag{iii}$$

On the other hand, equations (26), (i), and (ii) define another relationship between the same variables by eliminating $(1+\hat{\theta})\pi_k$ and π_g, that is

$$P_x = \psi(P_a | \hat{P}_b) \, , \tag{iv}$$

and we generally get a unique solution of (P_a, P_x), by equations (iii) and (iv), which defines a unique $(1+\hat{\theta})\pi_k$ in turn. The only possible adjustments between $\hat{\theta}$ and π_k are those that do not change this given value of $(1+\hat{\theta})\pi_k$. (This adjustment may be useful to meet the budget constraint for the government, but it has no effect on P_x

(6) The condition in equation (36) is transformed into

$$\beta^1\lambda^1 t_a = -\mu_k \left[h' \frac{\partial t_a}{\partial P_a} \frac{\partial g}{\partial t_a} + \frac{f'}{P_x}\left(-t_a - P_a \frac{\partial t_a}{\partial P_a} \right) \right]$$

$$= \frac{\mu_k}{P_x} f' t_a + \mu_k \left(\frac{P_a}{P_x} f' - h' \frac{\partial g}{\partial t_a} \right) \frac{\partial t_a}{\partial P_a} = \beta^2\lambda^2 t_a$$

by equations (75) and (80), to give equation (81).

and P_a.) By the above discussion, we see that $\hat{P}_b$ is the single effective policy variable in problem 2 and that other price variables (P_x and P_a) are derived from the constraints in equations (30) and (82) for a given $\hat{P}_b$.

6.1 *Problem 2*

Maximize equation (29) = $W(P_x, P_a, P_b)$ with respect to P_x, P_a, P_b, subject to equations (30) and (82). The conditions in equations (31)–(33) are now modified as follows:

$$\text{equation (31):} \quad \ldots + \mu\left[-h'(g)g_a - P_x h'(g)g_a'\left(\frac{\partial t_a}{\partial P_x} + w\frac{\partial t_b}{\partial P_x}\right)\right] = 0\,, \tag{83}$$

$$\text{equation (32):} \quad \ldots + \mu\left[f'(x) - P_x h'(g)g_a'\left(\frac{\partial t_a}{\partial P_a}\right)\right] = 0\,, \tag{84}$$

$$\text{equation (33):} \quad \ldots + \mu\left[-P_x h'(g)g_a' w\left(\frac{\partial t_b}{\partial P_b}\right)\right] = 0\,. \tag{85}$$

We also have

$$\mu_k h' \to \mu_k h' + \mu P_x h''(g)g_a\,, \qquad \mu_k f' \to \mu_k f' - \mu P_a f''(x)\,.$$

An implicit formulation for P_x, P_a, and P_b is given by:

$$\begin{aligned} P_x = \frac{1}{\beta^1\lambda^1x^1+\beta^2\lambda^2x^2}\Bigg\{&\mu_k\left[f'(e_{xx}^1x^1+e_{xx}^2x^2) - h'\left(e_{ax}t_a\frac{\partial g}{\partial t_a} + e_{bx}t_b\frac{\partial g}{\partial t_b}\right)\right] \\ &- \mu\Bigg[P_x h''g_a\left(e_{ax}t_a\frac{\partial g}{\partial t_a} + e_{bx}t_b\frac{\partial g}{\partial t_b}\right) + P_a f''(e_{xx}^1x^1+e_{xx}^2x^2) \\ &+ P_x h'g_a + P_x h'g_a'(e_{ax}t_a + we_{bx}t_b)\Bigg]\Bigg\} \end{aligned} \tag{86}$$

$$\begin{aligned} P_a = \frac{1}{\beta^1\lambda^1}\Bigg[&\mu_k\left(h'e_{aa}\frac{\partial g}{\partial t_a} - f'e_{xa}\frac{x^1}{t_a}\right) \\ &+ \mu\left(P_x h''g_a e_{aa}\frac{\partial g}{\partial t_a} + P_a f''e_{xa}\frac{x^1}{t_a} + f'\frac{P_a}{t_a} + P_x h'g_a'e_{aa}\right)\Bigg] \end{aligned} \tag{87}$$

$$\begin{aligned} P_b = \frac{1}{\beta^2\lambda^2}\Bigg[&\mu_k\left(h'e_{bb}\frac{\partial g}{\partial t_b} - f'e_{xb}\frac{x^2}{t_b}\right) \\ &+ \mu\left(P_x h''g_a e_{bb}\frac{\partial g}{\partial t_b} + P_a f''e_{xb}\frac{x^2}{t_b} + P_x h'g_a'we_{bb}\right)\Bigg]\,. \end{aligned} \tag{88}$$

Ignoring the terms h'' and f'' with an assumption of a linear technology, we obtain expressions for three price variables that are a little more explicit:

$$\begin{aligned} &P_x\left\{1 + \frac{\mu}{\beta^1\lambda^1x^1+\beta^2\lambda^2x^2}[h'g_a + h'g_a'(e_{ax}t_a + we_{bx}t_b)]\right\} \\ &\quad = \frac{\mu_k}{\beta^1\lambda^1x^1+\beta^2\lambda^2x^2}\left[f'(e_{xx}^1x^1+e_{xx}^2x^2) - h'\left(e_{ax}f_a\frac{\partial g}{\partial t_a} + e_{bx}t_b\frac{\partial g}{\partial t_b}\right)\right] \end{aligned} \tag{89}$$

$$P_a\left(1 - \frac{\mu f'}{\beta^1\lambda^1 t_a}\right) = \frac{1}{\beta^1\lambda^1}\left[\mu_k\left(h'e_{aa}\frac{\partial g}{\partial t_a} - f'e_{xa}\frac{x^1}{t_a}\right) + \mu P_x h'g_a'e_{aa}\right] \tag{90}$$

and

$$P_b = \frac{1}{\beta^2\lambda^2}\left[\mu_k\left(h'e_{bb}\frac{\partial g}{\partial t_a} - f'e_{xb}\frac{x^2}{t_b}\right) + \mu P_x h' g_a' w e_{bb}\right]. \tag{91}$$

Since group 1, as the higher-income class, should be charged more for private-car mileage (P_a) than the average private cost in the first-best optimum; a gap d, such as $P_a f' - P_x h' g_a - d \doteq 0$, will increase the social welfare W. Therefore we can conjecture that μ is negative. (This conjecture is affirmed in a special case discussed below.)
Then equations (89)-(91) suggest higher P_x, and lower P_a and P_b, compared to the case of the first best, that is equations (40)-(42).

Finally let us consider again the simplest case, in which we have (1) linear technology, (2) log-linear utility functions, and (3) constant input requirements for t_a and t_b. This might be a case of no interest if we can adjust income distribution, y^1 and y^2, freely because the average cost (= marginal cost) pricing for P_a will result in a first-best optimum in that case, that is with no difference between the first-best and the second-best solutions.

In our model, however, the second best with the average-cost pricing constraint for P_a is still inferior to the first best, where such a constraint does not exist because of indirect income redistribution through pricing policies.

Now we have:

$$P_x\left[1 + \frac{\mu h' g_a P_x}{(1-\alpha^1)\beta^1 + (1-\alpha^2)\beta^2}\right] = \frac{\mu_k f'[(1-\alpha^1)y^1 + (1-\alpha^2)y^2]}{(1-\alpha^1)\beta^1 + (1-\alpha^2)\beta^2}, \tag{92}$$

$$P_a\left(1 - \frac{\mu f' P_a}{\alpha^1\beta^1}\right) = \frac{\mu_k y^1}{\beta^1} h' g_a \tag{93}$$

$$P_b = \frac{\mu_k y^2}{\beta^2} h' g_b. \tag{94}$$

By dividing equation (93) by equation (92), it is shown that

$$P_a\left[1 - \frac{\mu P_a f'}{\alpha^1\beta^1}\right] \Big/ P_x\left[1 + \frac{\mu h' g_a P_x}{\beta^1(1-\alpha^1) + \beta^2(1-\alpha^2)}\right] = \frac{y^1(1-\alpha^1)\beta^1 + (1-\alpha^2)\beta^2}{\beta^1(1-\alpha^1)y^1 + (1-\alpha^2)y^2}\frac{h' g_a}{f'}. \tag{95}$$

With the use of the constraint of $P_x h' g_a = P_a f' = \rho$, equation (95) is transformed into

$$\left(1 - \frac{\mu\rho}{\alpha^1\beta^1}\right) \Big/ \left(1 + \frac{\mu\rho}{\bar\beta}\right) = \frac{y^1}{\beta^1}\frac{\bar\beta}{\bar y} \tag{96}$$

where

$$\bar\beta = (1-\alpha^1)\beta^1 + (1-\alpha^2)\beta^2,$$

and

$$\bar{y} = (1-\alpha^1)y^1 + (1-\alpha^2)y^2 .$$

Then μ is solved as:

$$\mu = \left(1 - \frac{y^1}{\beta^1}\frac{\bar{\beta}}{\bar{y}}\right) \Big/ \rho\left(\frac{1}{\alpha^1\beta^1} + \frac{y^1}{\beta^1\bar{y}}\right) . \qquad (97)$$

It is easily shown that

$$\frac{y^1}{\beta^1}\frac{\bar{\beta}}{\bar{y}} > 1 ,$$

so we can confirm that μ is negative [7]. Only in the case of $(y^1/\beta^1) = (y^2/\beta^2)$ do we have $\mu = 0$, and this is the sole case in which the average-cost pricing for P_a is justified as the first-best solution [compare equations (92)-(94), with $\mu = 0$, to equations (46)-(48)].

References

Abe, M. A., 1973, "The peak load pricing problem in urban transportation", *Kikan Riron Keizaigaku (The Economic Studies Quarterly)*, 24 (2), December, 54-62.

Baumol, W. J., Bradford, D. F., 1970, "Optimal departures from marginal cost pricing", *American Economic Review*, 60 (3), June, 265-283.

Diamond, P. A., Mirrlees, J. A., 1971a, "Optimal taxation and public production 1: production efficiency", *American Economic Review*, 61 (1), March, 8-27.

Diamond, P. A., Mirrlees, J. A., 1971b, "Optimal taxation and public production 2: tax rules", *American Economic Review*, 61 (3), June, 261-278.

Feldstein, M. S., 1972a, "Distributional equity and the optimal structure of public prices", *American Economic Review*, 62 (1), March, 32-36.

Feldstein, M. S., 1972b, "Equity and efficiency in public sector pricing: the optimal two-part tariff", *Quarterly Journal of Economics*, 86 (2), May, 175-187.

Marchand, M., 1968, "A note on optimal tolls in an imperfect environment", *Econometrica*, 36 (3-4), July-October, 575-581.

Rees, R., 1968, "Second-best rules for public enterprise pricing", *Economica*, 35, August, 260-273.

Samuelson, P. A., 1953, *Foundations of Economic Analysis* (Harvard University Press, Cambridge, Mass.).

Sherman, R., 1971, "Congestion, interdependence and urban transit fares", *Econometrica*, 39 (3), May, 565-576.

[7] Let $(y^1/\beta^1) = s_1$, $(y^2/\beta^2) = s^2$. Then

$$\frac{y^1}{\beta^1}\frac{\bar{\beta}}{\bar{y}} = s_1 \frac{(1-\alpha^1)\beta^1 + (1-\alpha^2)\beta^2}{(1-\alpha^1)\beta^1 s^1 + (1-\alpha^2)\beta^2 s^2} = s_1 \Big/ \frac{s^1 w^1 + s^2 w^2}{w^1 + w^2}$$

where

$$w^i = (1-\alpha^i)\beta^i , \qquad i = 1,2 .$$

We assume $s^1 > s^2$, so we can say

$$\frac{y^1}{\beta^1}\frac{\bar{\beta}}{\bar{y}} = s^1 \Big/ \left(\frac{s^1 w^1 + s^2 w^2}{w^1 + w^2}\right) > 1 .$$

APPENDIX 1

Constraint qualification for problem 1

In Diamond and Mirrlees (1971b) a general maximization problem for an indirect social welfare function was given as:

$$\begin{aligned} &\text{Maximize } V[X(q)] \, , \qquad \text{subject to} \\ &G \; : \; g[X(q)] \leqslant 0 \, , \qquad \text{and } q \geqslant 0 \, . \end{aligned} \tag{A1}$$

Then the relevant constraint qualification is as follows: There is *no* pair of price vectors (r, q) for which

$$\left.\begin{aligned} &X(q) \text{ maximizes } rx \text{ for } x \text{ in } G \, , \\ &r \neq 0 \, , \quad \text{and} \\ &rX'(q) \geqslant 0 \, . \end{aligned}\right\} \tag{A2}$$

[See Diamond and Mirrlees (1971b, p.274)—r is denoted by p there, however.] In our problem, the vector X is (x, t_a, t_b), the vector q is (P_x, P_a, P_b), and the constraint set G is defined by equation (30).

The fulfilment of equation (A2) is, however, dependent upon the form of U^1 and U^2, and is not easily verified. On the other hand, it is easy to find r in our case:

$$r = \left[\lambda f'(x), \lambda h' \frac{\partial g}{\partial t_a}, \lambda h' \frac{\partial g}{\partial t_b} \right] , \tag{A3}$$

where λ is a positive multiplier.

In the special case of log-linear utility functions analyzed in the present paper, the matrix $X'(q)$ is expressed by

$$\begin{bmatrix} \dfrac{\partial X}{\partial P_x} & \dfrac{\partial X}{\partial P_a} & \dfrac{\partial X}{\partial P_b} \\[2ex] \dfrac{\partial t_a}{\partial P_x} & \dfrac{\partial t_a}{\partial P_a} & \dfrac{\partial t_a}{\partial P_b} \\[2ex] \dfrac{\partial t_b}{\partial P_x} & \dfrac{\partial t_b}{\partial P_a} & \dfrac{\partial t_b}{\partial P_b} \end{bmatrix} = \begin{bmatrix} - & 0 & 0 \\[2ex] 0 & - & 0 \\[2ex] 0 & 0 & - \end{bmatrix} \tag{A4}$$

as a special case of gross substitutes market. It is obvious that $rX'(q)$ is always a strictly negative vector, that is, the constraint qualification is unquestionably satisfied in this special case.

APPENDIX 2

Functional form of the indirect social welfare function

The existence of an optimum solution to problem 1 can be established (see Diamond and Mirrlees, 1971a, p.21, theorem 1). The uniqueness of the solution, however, is not easily seen without further specification of the related functions. As a matter of fact, such proof of uniqueness is not necessary for the analysis of the properties of optimal prices because the conditions in equations (40)–(42) are proved to be the true necessary conditions for the optimum.

In general, $U^1[t_a(P_x,P_a), x^1(P_x,P_a)]$ and $U^2[t_b(P_x,P_b), x^2(P_x,P_b)]$ are not concave functions of P_x, P_a, and P_b. However, these price variables are subject to a particular relation derived from

$$K-f[x^1(P_x,P_a)+x^2(P_x,P_b)]-h\{g[t_a(P_x,P_a)+t_b(P_x,P_b)]\} = 0\,, \qquad \text{(A5)}$$

so that W finally becomes a function of any two of P_x, P_a, and P_b.

In order to see this point more closely, let us formulate a simpler problem in which

$$U^i = \alpha^i \log t^i + (1-\alpha^i)\log x^i\,, \qquad i = 1,\ldots,n \qquad \text{(A6)}$$

$$P_t t^i + P_x x^i = y^i\,, \qquad i = 1,\ldots,n \qquad \text{(A7)}$$

$$K-fx-ht = 0\,, \qquad x = \sum_{i=1}^{n} x^i\,, \quad t = \sum_{i=1}^{n} t^i\,. \qquad \text{(A8)}$$

Then we have

$$\frac{1}{P_x} = \frac{1}{f\sum_i(1-\alpha^i)y^i}\left(K-\frac{h}{P_t}\sum_i\alpha^i y^i\right) \qquad \text{(A9)}$$

and

$$U^i = \text{constant}+\alpha^i\log q_t+(1-\alpha^i)\log\left(K-h\sum_i\alpha^i y^i q_t\right) \qquad \text{(A10)}$$

where

$$q_t = \frac{1}{P_t}\,.$$

Maximization of $W = \sum_i \beta^i U^i q_t$ is conditioned by

$$\frac{\mathrm{d}W}{\mathrm{d}q_t} = \sum_i \beta^i\frac{\mathrm{d}U^i}{\mathrm{d}q_t} = \frac{\sum_i\beta^i\alpha^i}{q_t} - \frac{h\sum_i\alpha^i y^i}{K-h\left(\sum_i\alpha^i y^i\right)q_t}\sum_i\beta^i(1-\alpha^i) = 0 \qquad \text{(A11)}$$

which gives the optimal prices of

$$P_t = \frac{1}{q_t} = h\frac{\sum_i\alpha^i y^i}{\sum_i\alpha^i\beta^i}\frac{\sum_i\beta^i}{K} \qquad \text{(A12)}$$

$$P_x = f\frac{\sum_i(1-\alpha^i)y^i}{\sum_i(1-\alpha^i)\beta^i}\frac{\sum_i\beta^i}{K}\,. \qquad \text{(A13)}$$

The secondary condition is shown as

$$\frac{d^2W}{dq_t^2} = -\frac{\sum_i \beta^i\alpha^i}{q_t^2} - \frac{h^2\left(\sum_i \alpha^i y^i\right)^2 \sum_i \beta^i(1-\alpha^i)}{\left[K-h\left(\sum_i \alpha^i y^i\right)q_t\right]^2} < 0\,, \tag{A14}$$

so W is a strictly concave function of q_t. Therefore equation (A11) gives the global maximum of the problem, and $(dW/dP_t) = 0$ gives the same maximum in this case.

Equations (A12) and (A13) show closer similarity to Feldstein's formula [see footnote (4)].

APPENDIX 3

Explicit solution of μ_k and budget constraint for the government: a special case

Let us assume for problem 1: log-linear utility functions, as in equations (44) and (45); $h^i = h$ = constant; $\partial g/\partial t_a = g_a$ = constant; $\partial g/\partial t_b = g_b$ = constant; $f^i = f$ = constant. Then we get

$$x^i = \frac{[(1-\alpha^1)\beta^1 + (1-\alpha^2)\beta^2]}{\mu_k f[(1-\alpha^1)y^1 + (1-\alpha^2)y^2]}(1-\alpha^i)y^i\,, \qquad i = 1,2 \tag{A15}$$

$$t_a = \frac{1}{\mu_k}\frac{\alpha^1\beta^1}{hg_a}\,, \tag{A16}$$

$$t_b = \frac{1}{\mu_k}\frac{\alpha^2\beta^2}{hg_b}\,. \tag{A17}$$

Replacing x^i, t_a and t_b in equation (30) with the above equations, we obtain an explicit solution of μ_k:

$$\mu_k = \frac{\beta^1+\beta^2}{K}\,, \tag{A18}$$

and the optimal system of prices is expressed, by equations (46)–(48), as

$$P_x = \frac{(1-\alpha^1)y^1 + (1-\alpha^2)y^2}{(1-\alpha^1)\beta^1 + (1-\alpha^2)\beta^2} f\left(\frac{\beta^1+\beta^2}{K}\right)\,, \tag{A19}$$

$$P_a = \frac{y^1}{\beta^1} hg_a\left(\frac{\beta^1+\beta^2}{K}\right)\,, \tag{A20}$$

$$P_b = \frac{y^2}{\beta^2} hg_b\left(\frac{\beta^1+\beta^2}{K}\right)\,. \tag{A21}$$

Using equations (26)–(28) we can calculate the values of taxes conditioned by π_k, that is

$$\hat{s}_x = f\left[\frac{(1-\alpha^1)y^1 + (1-\alpha^2)y^2}{(1-\alpha^1)\beta^1 + (1-\alpha^2)\beta^2}\left(\frac{\beta^1+\beta^2}{K}\right) - \pi_k\right]\,, \tag{A22}$$

and

$$\hat{s}_a = hg_a\left[\frac{y^1}{\beta^1}\left(\frac{\beta^1+\beta^2}{K}\right)-\pi_k\right] . \tag{A23}$$

Therefore, the final task of the government is to define the value of π_k which, for instance, makes its net revenue just zero.

The net revenue for this particular case is given by equation (43):

$$R = (y^1+y^2)-\pi_k K , \tag{A24}$$

so a desirable level of π_k is

$$\pi_k = \frac{y^1+y^2}{K} , \tag{A25}$$

which obviously implies a positive $\hat{s}_a$ under the conditions of problem 1.

In other words $\hat{P}_b$, $\hat{s}_x$, and $\hat{s}_a$, calculated by equations (A21)–(A23) and (A25), will bring forth an optimal price system of P_a, P_x, π_k, and π_g with zero net revenue for the government by the market mechanism defined by equations (25)–(28).

Environment and Planning A, London, Vol. 11 (1979) 1105–1114

Urban growth analysis in postwar Japan: fact findings on the distribution of urban population †

N Sakashita¶
Institute of Social and Economic Research, Ōsaka University, Suita, Ōsaka 565, Japan
Received 12 December 1978, in revised form 23 May 1979

Abstract. This paper is an excerpt from a book written by three authors, Sakashita, Asano, and Irie (1979), in which a multidimensional analysis of the urban growth in postwar Japan has been made. After a brief introduction, an analysis that involves the use of several kinds of Hoover indices for the set of all Japanese cities over the period 1955–1975 is made, with a view to demonstrating the strong tendency of the population to concentrate in the metropolitan area. Application of the theoretical lognormal and Pareto distributions is then discussed. The paper closes with a theoretical consideration that coordinates the observations presented.

1 Introduction

The present paper is an excerpt from Sakashita et al (1979), in which many aspects of the urban growth in postwar Japan are comprehensively analyzed. Here attention is concentrated on the problem of the distribution of urban population, which in turn leads to the problem of urban size distribution.

In the next section an analysis that uses Hoover indices for the set of all cities in Japan over the period 1955–1975 is performed in order to show the strong tendency of the population to concentrate in big cities in that period.

In the third section an attempt to apply the theoretical lognormal and Pareto distributions is discussed, with some success for the Pareto distribution. A theoretical foundation which coordinates the results of the two preceding sections is demonstrated in the final section.

2 Hoover indices analysis of population concentration

The Hoover index is defined as follows for the set of regions in a nation:

$$H = \tfrac{1}{2}\sum_{i=1}^{n} |x_i - s_i| , \tag{1}$$

where

x_i is the ratio of the population in the ith region to the national population,
s_i is the ratio of the area in the ith region to the national area, and
n is the number of regions that form the nation.

In the present study, the set of all cities in Japan is taken as a 'nation', thus excluding rural areas. Let x_{ij} be the ratio of the population of the jth city in the ith prefecture (the state-level administrative unit of Japan) to the 'national' population, and s_{ij} be the ratio of the area of the same city to the 'national' area. Then we will have the following three categories of Hoover indices.

Intraprefecture Hoover index of the ith prefecture

$$H_i^{A} = \tfrac{1}{2}\sum_{j} \left| \frac{x_{ij}}{x_{i\cdot}} - \frac{s_{ij}}{s_{i\cdot}} \right| , \tag{2}$$

† This paper was originally prepared for and read at the World Regional Development and Planning Conference held at the University of Tsukuba, 21–23 August 1978.

¶Present address: Institute of Socio-Economic Planning, University of Tsukuba, Sakura, Ibaraki 300-31, Japan

Table 1. Hoover indices for urban population.

	Prefectures	Number of cities	H_i^A 1955	1960	1965	1970	1975
1	Hokkaidō	32	0·38482587	0·39268615	0·41397742	0·43588565	0·46204758
2	Aomori	8	0·21690809	0·21932130	0·22449669	0·23136027	0·22709716
3	Iwate	13	0·18641011	0·20283941	0·22068452	0·24195009	0·26276676
4	Miyagi	11	0·36681640	0·41364166	0·43338442	0·43857715	0·42743919
5	Akita	9	0·21940312	0·22654955	0·23905450	0·25888279	0·28005576
6	Yamagata	13	0·25994993	0·23280678	0·24422212	0·25653341	0·27121005
7	Fukushima	10	0·03701725	0·03876407	0·04920625	0·06743969	0·08191577
8	Ibaraki	18	0·23341028	0·23067587	0·25824219	0·28746745	0·30198470
9	Tochigi	12	0·36885936	0·38477689	0·34127881	0·35766660	0·36456189
10	Gumma	11	0·21927051	0·22557112	0·23292965	0·24227588	0·24572859
11	Saitama	38	0·20363916	0·23526503	0·27596778	0·29545317	0·30298017
12	Chiba	26	0·28106718	0·31561393	0·39350541	0·42222346	0·45439036
13	Tōkyō	27	0·43193967	0·41974824	0·38919473	0·34538124	0·31248094
14	Kanagawa	18	0·27304485	0·29693160	0·28532149	0·26088579	0·24788566
15	Niigata	20	0·30349909	0·32038449	0·33824039	0·35529870	0·37033360
16	Toyama	9	0·30123207	0·30981589	0·32509252	0·33495117	0·34452272
17	Ishikawa	8	0·23477686	0·24557595	0·26603486	0·28377804	0·29853142
18	Fukui	7	0·30370725	0·31655896	0·33011096	0·34387203	0·35665069
19	Yamanashi	7	0·32169677	0·33633706	0·35577670	0·37284752	0·38185361
20	Nagano	17	0·26092073	0·25932815	0·27254611	0·28340319	0·28487029
21	Gifu	13	0·34224507	0·37476741	0·37750546	0·37929974	0·38323168
22	Shizuoka	21	0·27770377	0·28317697	0·28966591	0·29124188	0·28994164
23	Aichi	30	0·36080998	0·37880481	0·36876774	0·34396247	0·32049633
24	Mie	13	0·25329623	0·26603366	0·28084688	0·29333570	0·30163111
25	Shiga	7	0·11670805	0·10349055	0·10265659	0·10608827	0·11601101
26	Kyōto	10	0·47638188	0·48309228	0·49363683	0·50250673	0·50554065
27	Ōsaka	31	0·47054148	0·46597263	0·42349048	0·37361935	0·32751768
28	Hyōgo	21	0·36631067	0·38558425	0·39534072	0·39034739	0·37909972
29	Nara	9	0·15555287	0·15088456	0·16192865	0·20179503	0·22383926
30	Wakayama	7	0·24045135	0·24836898	0·26657138	0·28595350	0·29418127
31	Tottori	4	0·22862180	0·23303417	0·24017839	0·24172094	0·24465735
32	Shimane	8	0·20364374	0·20790284	0·22529554	0·24644432	0·25875888
33	Okayama	10	0·28180880	0·29599552	0·31078139	0·33414051	0·34464077
34	Hiroshima	12	0·26911902	0·29772116	0·31610440	0·33157384	0·31653669
35	Yamaguchi	14	0·24930688	0·24217774	0·24383310	0·24729416	0·25173406
36	Tokushima	4	0·27003554	0·28963572	0·30326014	0·31467616	0·32222212
37	Kagawa	5	0·06907220	0·09570967	0·11803594	0·13432417	0·14271252
38	Ehime	12	0·26079853	0·27610350	0·29292620	0·30292841	0·32098106
39	Kōchi	9	0·39345505	0·41087446	0·44553970	0·47852265	0·50033760
40	Fukuoka	20	0·22852102	0·24822606	0·26697557	0·27320452	0·25314493
41	Saga	7	0·20961008	0·21412077	0·24861585	0·28546126	0·30279843
42	Nagasaki	8	0·33743506	0·29701116	0·33093369	0·34506709	0·33077342
43	Kumamoto	11	0·34951199	0·36902869	0·39291709	0·41875935	0·43667860
44	Ōita	11	0·22894012	0·23324507	0·26469770	0·29335339	0·33322995
45	Miyazaki	9	0·25467126	0·26526840	0·29661706	0·32785379	0·35230270
46	Kagoshima	14	0·26039959	0·28111743	0·31461346	0·34837954	0·37665171
47	Okinawa	10	0·50371761	0·52303421	0·53740167	0·54332213	0·55181076
48	within prefecture (H^A)	644	0·31924793	0·33197674	0·33742336	0·33318781	0·32703526
49	between prefectures (H^B)		0·32383332	0·34440217	0·38525962	0·38525962	0·39127330
50	Hoover index (H)		0·42604214	0·44739090	0·47091735	0·48735709	0·49360782

where

$$x_{i.} = \sum_j x_{ij} , \qquad s_{i.} = \sum_j x_{ij} ;$$

interprefecture Hoover index

$$H^{\mathrm{B}} = \tfrac{1}{2}\sum_i |x_{i.} - s_{i.}| ; \tag{3}$$

national Hoover index

$$H = \tfrac{1}{2}\sum_i \sum_j |x_{ij} - s_{ij}| . \tag{4}$$

For the period of 1955–1975, three categories of Hoover indices are calculated at intervals of five years, as shown in table 1, for 644 cities distributed among forty-seven prefectures of Japan. [These 644 cities conform to the set of all cities of Japan in 1975, and include the Special Municipal District (twenty-three Kus, or subdistricts) of the Tōkyō prefecture. There are now 646 cities in Japan.] In addition, in the bottom three rows of table 1 some aggregated indices are presented. In row 48 a weighted average of the forty-seven values of H_i^{A}, defined by equation (2), is calculated with the use of the city population of each prefecture as a weight, that is, weighted average of H_i^{A}

$$H^{\mathrm{A}} = \sum_i x_{i.} H_i^{\mathrm{A}} \Big/ \sum_i x_{i.} . \tag{5}$$

In row 49 the time series of H^{B} is given, and that of H is shown in row 50.

From this table we observe that the national Hoover index (H) has steadily increased from 0·43 in 1955 to 0·49 in 1975, which implies a strict tendency of population concentration in big cities. From 1970 to 1975, however, the *speed* of increase of H has dropped sharply, which may imply the halt of this concentration tendency in recent years. The interprefecture Hoover index (H^{B}) shows almost the same time pattern as the national index, by starting from 0·32 in 1955 and ending at 0·39 in 1975.

On the other hand, the weighted average of intraprefecture Hoover indices H^{A} shows quite a different time pattern from H or H^{B}. The value of H^{A} is almost constant at 0·33. However, further analysis of H^{A} for individual prefectures is needed. The forty-seven prefectures can be clearly divided into three groups according to the time pattern of H_i^{A}. The first group, with H_i^{A} showing a tendency to rise, consists of twenty-nine prefectures which are usually categorized as relatively backward areas. The second group, which show a tendency for H_i^{A} to decrease, contains four large metropolitan areas only: Tōkyō, Kanagawa, Aichi, and Ōsaka. The third group consists of fourteen prefectures with almost constant values of H_i^{A} which can be classified as 'intermediate' areas. (See table 2 for the complete list of these three groups.)

In table 3 the weighted averages of H_i^{A} in each group are shown. It is impressive to see that the metropolitan areas of group 2 now have the smallest value of the weighted average of intraprefecture Hoover indices. It can be said that these areas are now the most uniformly inhabited prefectures in the nation.

If H is regressed on H^{A} and H^{B} by the time series of table 1, the following single and multiple estimates are obtained:

$$H = 0{\cdot}10337 + \underset{(82\cdot3)}{0{\cdot}99794 H^{\mathrm{B}}} , \qquad \widetilde{R}^2 = 0{\cdot}9994 , \tag{6}$$

$$H = 0{\cdot}0801344 + \underset{(100\cdot49)}{0{\cdot}987590 H^{\mathrm{B}}} + \underset{(2\cdot049)}{0{\cdot}0818371 H^{\mathrm{A}}} , \qquad \widetilde{R}^2 = 0{\cdot}9997 . \tag{7}$$

The figures in parentheses are t values of the estimated coefficients and $\tilde{R}^2$ is the coefficient of determination adjusted for degree of freedom.

It is clear from equations (6) and (7) that the change in the value of H is almost completely explained by the change in the value of H^{B} without considering the value of H^{A}. The fixity of H^{A} can be explained by the offset between the values of H_i^{A} for group 1 and group 2. The latter group has only four prefectures but their weights in terms of urban population are quite large.

Finally a variational analysis of the national Hoover index was attempted. We can call a city in which $x_{ij} > s_{ij}$ a (relatively) densely populated city, and a city in which $x_{ij} < s_{ij}$ a (relatively) sparsely populated city. The difference between the values of H for year t and year $t+5$ can be divided into four components:

(1) the difference for the group of cities (M) that are densely populated both in year t and in year $t+5$ (variation for group M),

(2) the difference for the group of cities (N) that are sparsely populated both in year t and in year $t+5$ (variation for group N),

(3) the difference for the group of cities (V) that are densely populated in year t but are sparsely populated in year $t+5$ (variation for group V),

(4) the difference for the group of cities (W) that are sparsely populated in year t but are densely populated in year $t+5$ (variation for group W).

The mathematical expression for the above division is as follows:

$$\begin{aligned}\Delta H(t, t+5) &= \tfrac{1}{2}\sum_i [|x_i(t+5)-s_i(t+5)| - |x_i(t)-s_i(t)|] \\ &= \tfrac{1}{2}\Big\langle \sum_{i\in M} \{[x_i(t+5)-s_i(t+5)] - [x_i(t)-s_i(t)]\} \\ &\quad + \sum_{i\in N} \{[s_i(t+5)-x_i(t+5)] - [s_i(t)-x_i(t)]\} \\ &\quad + \sum_{i\in V} \{[s_i(t+5)-x_i(t+5)] - [x_i(t)-s_i(t)]\} \\ &\quad + \sum_{i\in W} \{[x_i(t+5)-s_i(t+5)] - [s_i(t)-x_i(t)]\}\Big\rangle . \end{aligned} \tag{8}$$

The results of this variational analysis are given in table 4. In the third column of each subtable, the percentage contribution of each respective group is calculated. The main conclusions derived from this table are as follows. For each five-year variation, major contributions are made by the variation for groups M and N, and we can conjecture that there has been a constant flow of people from sparsely populated

Table 2. Allocation of prefectures to groups.

Group	Prefectures					
1	Hokkaidō	Ibaraki	Ishikawa	Wakayama	Ehime	Oita
	Iwate	Saitama	Fukui	Shimane	Kōchi	Miyazaki
	Akita	Chiba	Yamanashi	Okayama	Fukuoka	Kagoshima
	Yamagata	Niigata	Mie	Tokushima	Saga	Okinawa
	Fukushima	Toyama	Nara	Kagawa	Kumamoto	
2	Tōkyō					
	Kanagawa					
	Aichi					
	Ōsaka					
3	Aomori	Gumma	Shizuoka	Hyōgo	Yamaguchi	
	Miyagi	Nagano	Shiga	Tottori	Nagasaki	
	Tochigi	Gifu	Kyōto	Hiroshima		

to densely populated cities for these periods. In addition, the numbers of cities in group V and group W decrease from one period to the next, and this may mean a polarization phenomenon in the urban size distribution that will finally result in a two-peak distribution of urban size. At the same time, recent variation for group M is loosing its weight rapidly and, in contrast, variation for group W is becoming more prominent, which means a revival of medium-sized cities.

In Japan many people talk about the U-turn and J-turn phenomena of population in the first half of the 1970s [see Kuroda (1977) for example]. However, as a global phenomenon which can be reflected in the Hoover indices, there has been a strong tendency of concentration of urban population *until* 1975. If there was a global dispersion phenomenon of urban population, it should have started *after* 1975, that is, it should be a very recent reversal of the tendency.

Table 3. H^A for different groups.

Group	1955	1960	1965	1970	1975
1	0·26009264	0·27513578	0·30210897	0·32384859	0·33982480
2	0·40557617	0·40615676	0·37762687	0·33712606	0·30496361
3	0·31520516	0·32630140	0·33602341	0·34252708	0·33890549

Table 4. Variational analysis of Hoover indices.

Period	Group	Number of cities	ΔH	Percentage contribution to total ΔH
1955-1960	M	263	0·011645	54·5440
	N	356	0·009801	45·9122
	V	18	−0·000084	−0·3902
	W	7	−0·000014	−0·0659
Total		644	0·021349	100·0000
1960-1965	M	265	0·011576	49·2013
	N	362	0·012331	52·4114
	V	5	−0·000221	−0·9369
	W	12	−0·000159	−0·6757
Total		644	0·023527	100·0000
1965-1970	M	268	0·008034	48·8652
	N	362	0·008150	49·5734
	V	9	−0·000065	−0·3957
	W	5	0·000322	1·9571
Total		644	0·016440	100·0000
1970-1975	M	270	0·002879	46·0511
	N	366	0·003295	52·7164
	V	3	0·000021	0·3375
	W	5	0·000056	0·8950
Total		644	0·006251	100·0000

3 Urban size distribution and its change

In order to derive an urban size distribution of the Japanese cities in a *smoothed form* for each year, histograms were first constructed by the following steps:

Step 1 Transform the population size of each city i into a common logarithm z_i.

Step 2 Set intervals like (3·85, 3·95], (3·95, 4·05] ... for the values of z_i, with interval size 0·1, such that the central values of the intervals are 3·90, 4·00, ... Call these intervals I_k, $k = 1, ..., L$.

Step 3 Let the frequency of cities which belong to the kth interval be f_k, and construct a histogram for each year with the combination of (I_k, f_k), $k = 1, ..., L$.

Five histograms are constructed by this procedure (but are not shown here)—one diagram for each year of 1955, 1960, 1965, 1970, and 1975. The skewness of the logarithmic urban size distribution is rather obvious from these diagrams; nevertheless I shall proceed to the application of a lognormal distribution to each of these histograms [see Simon (1955) for the justification of the lognormal distribution].

First the mean $\bar{z}$ and the variance σ_z^2 are calculated from the histogram (not from the original data of cities). Then the probability density function $\phi(u)$ of a normal distribution $N(\bar{z}, \sigma_z^2)$ is specified and the theoretical value of relative frequency p_k is computed for the interval I_k by the following formula:

$$p_k = \int_{u \in I_k} \phi(u)\, du \,. \tag{9}$$

However, the following treatment is given to the extreme parts of the size distribution. (1) On the side of minimum size, if np_h (n is the total number of cities) is more than 0·5 for some h and if $p_i \leqslant p_h$ and $p_i < 0{\cdot}5$ for $i < h$, a new minimum interval size 1 is defined and its probability is given by

$$p_1^* = \sum_{i \leqslant h} p_i \,. \tag{10}$$

(2) On the side of maximum size, if np_g is more than 0·5 for some g and if $p_i \leqslant p_g$ and $p_i < 0{\cdot}5$ for $i > g$, a new maximum interval size L and its probability are defined by

$$p_L^* = \sum_{i \geqslant g} p_g \,. \tag{11}$$

(3) After the above procedures, the intermediate intervals are renumbered and the whole intervals are redefined as $I_1, I_2, ..., I_L$, in which I_1 is the interval of minimum size and I_L is the interval of maximum size. The actual frequency f_k^* and corresponding theoretical probability p_k^* of interval I_k are calculated for $k = 1, 2, ..., L$.

Now the following χ^2 test can be performed under a null hypothesis that z_i obeys a normal distribution. If the hypothesis is valid, the following statistic S must obey a χ^2 distribution with $(L-3)$ degrees of freedom:

$$S = \sum_{k=1}^{L} \frac{(f_k^* - np_k^*)^2}{np_k^*} \,. \tag{12}$$

The results of the χ^2 test are summarized in table 5. It is clear from these results that it is out of the question to apply lognormal distributions to the urban size distribution of postwar Japan.

The next task is to try Pareto distributions on the truncated urban size distribution that starts from the mode (the maximum frequency) interval. Let $F(P)$ be the relative frequency of cities with population size more than P for this truncated range.

Table 5. χ^2 test for the application of a lognormal distribution to the actual urban size distribution.

	1955	1960	1965	1970	1975
Degrees of freedom $(L-3)$	17	16	15	15	17
S	267·78	290·14	293·01	325·46	257·66
5% critical value	27·60	26·30	25·00	25·00	27·60
1% critical value	33·40	32·00	30·60	30·60	33·40
χ^2 distribution with $(L-3)$ degrees of freedom:					
accept or reject	reject	reject	reject	reject	reject

Then we have the following formula of the Pareto distribution [see Beckmann (1958) for the derivation of the Pareto distribution]:

$$F(P) = AP^{-a} , \tag{13}$$

and its log transformation

$$\lg F(P) = b - a \lg P , \qquad b = \lg A . \tag{14}$$

Table 6 shows the actual frequency table of urban distribution for 1965 with its theoretical counterpart calculated from the least-squares regression of equation (14) with use of the actual frequency table as data. However, the least-squares regression used here is a constrained one to make $\hat{F}(P) = 0$ when $\lg P = 4 \cdot 6$ [the mode interval; see Johnston (1972, pages 157–159)].

The results of the constrained least-squares regressions are shown in table 7, and the results of the related χ^2 tests are summarized in table 8. In this χ^2 test, the same adjustment of the extreme intervals is carried out as in the case of the lognormal application. Judging from these tables, we can conclude that the application of the Pareto distribution to the truncated urban size distributions shows a relatively good performance. We can accept the null hypothesis for 1960 and 1965.

Table 6. Application of Pareto distribution to urban size distribution, 1965.

Result of ordinary least squares

$$\lg F(P) = \underset{\hat{b}}{5 \cdot 829614} - \underset{\hat{a}}{1 \cdot 266721} \lg P \Rightarrow F(P) = 671295 \cdot 9 P^{-1 \cdot 266721}$$

lg *P*	*P*	Range	Absolute frequency	F(*P*) cumulative percentage	$\hat{F}(P)$ estimated cumulative percentage	Estimated absolute frequency
4·6	39811	less than 44668	128	100·000	99·999	120·927
4·7	50119	44669- 56234	86	73·222	74·701	90·334
4·8	63096	56235- 70794	70	55·230	55·802	67·481
4·9	79433	70795- 89125	42	40·586	41·685	50·409
5·0	100000	89126- 112201	31	31·799	31·139	37·656
5·1	125893	112202- 141253	26	25·314	23·261	28·130
5·2	158489	141254- 177827	23	19·874	17·377	21·013
5·3	199526	177828- 223872	24	15·063	12·981	15·697
5·4	251189	223873- 281838	15	10·042	9·697	11·726
5·5	316228	281839- 354813	9	6·904	7·244	8·759
5·6	398107	354814- 446683	10	5·021	5·411	6·543
5·7	501187	446684- 562341	3	2·929	4·042	4·888
5·8	630957	562342- 707945	1	2·301	3·019	3·651
5·9	794328	707946- 891250	3	2·092	2·256	2·728
6·0	1000000	891251-1122018	1	1·464	1·685	2·038
6·1	1258925	1122019-1412537	2	1·255	1·259	1·522
6·2	1584893	1412538-1778279	0	0·837	0·940	1·137
6·3	1995262	1778280-2238721	2	0·837	0·702	0·849
6·4	2511886	2238722-2818382	0	0·418	0·525	0·634
6·5	3162278	2818383-3548133	1	0·418	0·392	0·474
6·6	3981072	3546134-4466835	0	0·209	0·293	0·354
6·7	5011872	4466836-5623413	0	0·209	0·219	0·264
6·8	6309573	5623414-7079457	0	0·209	0·163	0·198
6·9	7943282	7079458 and over	1	0·209	0·122	0·583

χ test

Sample: 478; degrees of freedom: 17; $\chi = 17 \cdot 48$; 5% level: 27·60; 1% level: 33·40.

From table 7 we can observe that the fitted Pareto distribution is making counter-clockwise movements over time except for 1970 when the mode urban size is different. In other words, A and a of equation (13) are decreasing over time. This point will be further discussed in the next section.

Table 7. Results of the constrained least-squares regression $\lg F(P) = b - a \lg P$, $b = \lg A$.

	Estimates		Mode urban size
	$\hat{b}$	$-\hat{a}$	
1955	6·190515	−1·345764	$10^{4 \cdot 6}$
1960	5·982411	−1·300524	$10^{4 \cdot 6}$
1965	5·826914	−1·266721	$10^{4 \cdot 6}$
1970	5·557865	−1·235081	$10^{4 \cdot 5}$
1975	5·783712	−1·257329	$10^{4 \cdot 6}$

Table 8. χ^2 test for the application of a Pareto distribution to the actual urban size distribution.

	S[a]	Sample size	Degrees of freedom[b]
1955	27·30**	466	16
1960	22·68***	471	17
1965	17·48***	478	17
1970	39·50*	614	19
1975	41·11*	524	18

[a] See equation (12) for the expression of S. [b] (Number of intervals) − 3.
* Rejected at 1% level. ** Rejected at 5% level; accepted at 1% level.
*** Accepted at 1% and 5% levels.

4 A theoretical consideration

Let us assume that the urban size distribution of postwar Japan can be approximated by a Pareto distribution with the following formula, which is identical to equation (13) except for the use of the absolute number of cities G(P) instead of the relative frequency F(P):

$$G(P) = AP^{-a}, \qquad a > 1. \tag{15}$$

If P_0 denotes the population size of the city of minimum size, the total number of cities, n, is approximated by

$$n = AP_0^{-a}, \tag{16}$$

and the value of parameter A is calculated as

$$A = nP_0^a. \tag{17}$$

Therefore the number of cities with population size *less* than P, H(P), is expressed by

$$H(P) = n\left[1 - \left(\frac{P}{P_0}\right)^{-a}\right], \tag{18}$$

and the relative frequency (probability) function of the urban size distribution takes the form of

$$h(P) = \frac{1}{n}\frac{dH(P)}{dP} = aP_0^a P^{-a-1}. \tag{19}$$

Now let us assume for the sake of simplicity that all of the n cities have the same area size. Then $h(P)\,dP$ corresponds to s_i defined in section 2 for the interval

$[P, P+dP]$ since all cities have the same area size. On the other hand, the counterpart of x_i in the same section is $q(P)\,dP$, in which $q(P)$ is the relative frequency function of population. The total (urban) population Q is calculated from equation (19) as

$$Q = n\int_{P_0}^{\infty} aP_0^a P^{-a}\,dP = \frac{a}{a-1}nP_0\,, \tag{20}$$

and the corresponding $q(P)$ is

$$q(P) = anP_0^a P^{-a}\Big/\frac{a}{a-1}nP_0 = (a-1)P_0^{a-1}P^{-a}\,, \tag{21}$$

by equation (19).

The sparsely populated city defined in section 2 is a city with P for which $h(P) > q(P)$, and the densely populated city is a city with P for which $h(P) < q(P)$. Obviously $h(P_0) > q(P_0)$ by equations (19) and (21), so that there will be a breaking-point population $P^\dagger$ at which

$$\left.\begin{array}{ll} h(P^\dagger) = q(P^\dagger) & \\ h(P) > q(P)\,, & \text{for } P < P^\dagger\,, \\ h(P) < q(P)\,, & \text{for } P > P^\dagger\,. \end{array}\right\} \tag{22}$$

The actual value of $P^\dagger$ is derived from equations (19) and (21) as

$$P^\dagger = \frac{a}{a-1}P_0\,. \tag{23}$$

Under these circumstances, a theoretical Hoover index can be calculated for the intercity population distribution which is characterized by a Pareto distribution. The formula for this Hoover index is

$$\hat{H} = \tfrac{1}{2}\left\{\int_{P_0}^{P^\dagger} [h(P)-q(P)]\,dP + \int_{P^\dagger}^{\infty} [q(P)-h(P)]\,dP\right\}. \tag{24}$$

In order to evaluate the actual value of $\hat{H}$ by using equations (19) and (21), we first obtain the indefinite integral of

$$K(P) = \int [h(P)-q(P)]\,dP\,, \tag{25}$$

which results in

$$\begin{aligned} K(P) &= \int [ap_0^a P^{-a-1} - (a-1)P_0^{a-1}P^{-a}]\,dP \\ &= aP_0^a\left(\frac{P^{-a}}{-a}\right) - (a-1)P_0^{a-1}\left(\frac{P^{1-a}}{1-a}\right) \\ &= -P_0^a(P^{-a}) + P_0^{a-1}P^{1-a}\,. \end{aligned} \tag{26}$$

By using the result of equation (26), $\hat{H}$ of equation (24) is given as

$$\begin{aligned} \hat{H} &= \tfrac{1}{2}\{[K(P)]_{P_0}^{[a/(a-1)]P_0} + [-K(P)]_{[a/(a-1)]P_0}^{\infty} \\ &= \frac{(a-1)^{a-1}}{a^a}\,. \end{aligned} \tag{27}$$

Two important propositions can be deduced from the above results.

(1) The Hoover index which is derived from the Pareto distribution of urban size is independent of the population of the city of minimum size, P_0, as well as of the total number of cities, n. It is a function of (the absolute value of) *slope a* only.

(2) When the absolute value of slope, a, decreases, the value of the Hoover index increases.

The second proposition can be proved as follows. Let the natural logarithm of $\hat{H}$ be λ, then λ is expressed by

$$\lambda = (a-1)\ln(a-1) - a\ln a\,. \tag{28}$$

Therefore we have

$$\begin{aligned}\frac{d\lambda}{da} &= \ln(a-1) + \frac{a-1}{a-1} - \ln a - \frac{a}{a} \\ &= \ln(a-1) - \ln a < 0\,,\end{aligned} \tag{29}$$

so that a decrease in a raises the value of $\hat{H}$.

In section 2 we observed a continuous increase of the Hoover index for the distribution of urban population in postwar Japan. This phenomenon corresponds to a counterclockwise movement of the fitted Pareto distribution over time, as observed in section 3. These two observations are theoretically coordinated in the discussion of this section.

In table 9 the values of $\hat{H}$ are presented, particularly for 1960 and 1965, when the fit of the Pareto distribution was better than for other years, and are compared with the actual H calculated in section 2. Because of the existence of the truncated part in the Pareto distribution, we can by no means observe strict coincidence of $\hat{H}$ and H. Nevertheless, their proportionality is clearly shown in the fourth column of table 9, and this result is very interesting from the viewpoint of applicability of this theoretical framework.

Table 9. Calculation of theoretical Hoover index.

	a	$\hat{H} = \dfrac{(a-1)^{a-1}}{a^a}$	H in table 1	Ratio of $\hat{H}$ to H
1955	1·345764	0·46448	0·42604	1·090
1960	1·300524	0·49508	0·44739	1·107
1965	1·266721	0·52101	0·47092	1·106
1970[a]	1·235081	0·54819	0·48736	1·125
1975	1·257329	0·52876	0·49361	1·071

[a] In 1970 the city size of the peak frequency is different from the other years.

Acknowledgements. The author wishes to thank Mr Norio Asano of the Japan IBM Company for the computer work and helpful comments on the original version of the paper.

References

Beckmann M J, 1958 "City hierarchies and the distribution of city size" *Economic Development and Cultural Change* **6** 243–248

Johnston J, 1972 *Econometric Method* second edition (McGraw-Hill, New York)

Kuroda T, 1977 "Migration, distribution of population and development in Japan" paper presented at the Shinkansen Conference of IIASA, Laxenburg, Austria; available as an unpublished discussion paper, Department of Economics, Nihon University, Tōkyō, Japan

Sakashita N, Asano N, Irie S, 1979 *Urban Growth Analysis in Postwar Japan* Research Series 32, Economic Research Institute, Economic Planning Agency, Tōkyō (in Japanese)

Simon H, 1955 "On a class of skew distribution functions" *Biometrica* **42** 425–440

International and Interregional Conflict: Analytic Approaches, ed. by W. Isard
and Y. Nagao, Cambridge (1983) 139–146

Resolution of Mutual Loss Conflict Induced by the Embargo Threat

Noboru Sakashita

The response by resource-importing countries to the embargo threat of resource-exporting countries, which takes the form of a precautionary cutback of the quantity imported or of additional storage of imported resources, was, for example, analyzed by Nordhaus (1974), and Tolley and Wilman (1977). But neither article considered the impact of reduced imports on the world market, which might suppress the international equilibrium price of the resource in question. This impact will hurt the trading position of exporting countries, who as a group are forced to adopt monopolistic behavior in order to maintain the level of international price. This behavior will induce further contraction of that resource on the world trade market.

This chapter attempts to analyze these secondary and tertiary effects of an embargo threat and also to search for some instruments to solve this mutual loss conflict in the world (north-south) trade market. The first section analyzes the behavior of a resource-importing country under the embargo threat. The change of international trade equilibrium when exporting countries show passive response is discussed in the second section. Further shrinkage of the world trade market when exporting countries assume a monopolistic behavior is examined in the third section. Finally, in the fourth section, possible resolution of resultant mutual loss conflict is discussed, which then leads to the chapter's conclusion.

ANALYSIS OF AN IMPORTING COUNTRY

Imagine a resource-importing country which has a long-run demand function of the following linear form:

$$q_0 = a - bp_0, \qquad p_0 = \bar{p} + t, \tag{8-1}$$

where

q_0: quantity imported during non-embargo period,
p_0: domestic price of the resource during non-embargo period,
$\bar{p}$: international price of the resource,
t: rate of import tariff.

The short-run demand function starting from an initial combination of (p_0, q_0) can be expressed as:

$$q_1 - q_0 = -b\lambda(p_1 - p_0), \tag{8-2}$$

where

q_1: quantity imported during embargo period,
p_2: domestic price during embargo period,
λ: ratio of the short-run price coefficient to the long-run price coefficient, $0 < \lambda < 1$.[1]

Apparently, the loss in the economy as a whole induced by an import tariff, L_T, is expressed as:

$$L_T = \tfrac{1}{2}t\,[(a - b\bar{p}) + \{a - b(\bar{p} + t)\}] - t\{a - b(\bar{p} + t)\}$$
$$= \tfrac{1}{2}bt^2 \tag{8-3}$$

The first term in the middle line of equation (8–3) shows the decrease in demander's surplus, and the second term expresses the revenue from the import tariff which offsets the surplus loss. On the other hand, the loss evoked by the realization of the embargo, L_E, is given by the following formula:

$$L_E = \tfrac{1}{2}(p_1 - p_0)(q_1 + q_0)$$
$$= \frac{1}{2}\,\frac{(1-\mu)}{b\lambda}\,q_0(\mu + 1)q_0 = \frac{(1-\mu^2)}{2b\lambda}\{a - b(\bar{p} + t)\}^2, \tag{8-4}$$

1. The difference between long-run and short-run demand functions is, of course, the fixedness of certain factors of production in the latter case which are employed by the resource demander as a producer of some final commodity. Even if the demander is supposed to be a consumer, we can assume the presence of similar "factors" in the consumption activities.

where

μ: given contraction rate of import during embargo period,

$$q_1 = \mu q_0, \qquad 0 < \mu < 1.$$

The content of L_E is, needless to say, the decrease in demander's surplus when the quantity of the resource supplied is suddenly cut to q_1 from q_0. Here we are assuming that the gain from the short-run increase of resource price is entirely taken by foreign traders and not by domestic traders.

The total loss evoked by the possibility (not by the realization) of an embargo and corresponding import-cutback policy of the importing country, is the sum of (8–3) and (8–4), that is,

$$L(t) = L_T + \pi L_E = \tfrac{1}{2} bt^2 + \theta\{a - b(\bar{p} + t)\}^2, \tag{8–5}$$

where

π: given realization probability of embargo

$$\theta = \frac{\pi(1-\mu^2)}{2b\lambda}$$

The optimal rate of import tariff which minimizes $L(t)$ is given by:

$$t^* = \frac{2\theta(a - b\bar{p})}{1 + 2\theta b}$$

after letting

$$\frac{dL(t)}{dt} = 0.$$

Now we assume the following values for the parameters:

$$\pi = 0.2, \quad \lambda = 0.2, \quad a = 10, \quad b = 0.8, \quad \mu = 0.75 \quad (\theta \cong 0.27). \tag{8–7}$$

Then the optimal rates of import tariff under the different values of international price of the resource are shown in Table (8–1).

Table 8–1. Optimal Rates of Import Tariff and Related Quantities

	$\bar{p}$	t^*	$\bar{p} + t^*$	q_0	$q(\bar{p})$ [a)]	$q(\bar{p}) - q_0$ [b)]
Case 1	\$1.50	\$3.32	\$4.82	6.14	8.8	2.66
Case 2	\$7.00	\$1.66	\$8.66	3.07	4.4	1.33

Table 8–2. Calculation of Losses under Alternative Trade Policies for Case 1

	t	q_0	L_T	πL_E	L
1. Laissez-faire	0	8.80	0	20.91	20.91
2. Optimal tariff	3.32	6.14	4.41	10.19	14.60
3. Autarky (no import)	11	0	48.40	0	48.40

Table 8–1 implies that the sensitivity of import-cutback policy is a decreasing function of the initial international price of the resource, $\bar{p}$.

Calculation of the losses under alternative trade policies are shown in Table 8–2 for Case 1. Of course, the loss is minimized under the optimal rate of import tariff.

We should notice with Table 8–2 that the cost of an autarchy policy is much bigger than that of a laissez-faire policy in this case, which can be a warning to the extremist on the side of a "foreign independence" policy.

ANALYSIS OF EXPORTING COUNTRIES AND CONTRACTED EQUILIBRIUM

Here we introduce a long-run supply function LRS:

$$q^S = -0.2 + 6p \qquad (8\text{–}8)$$

which produces the long-run international equilibrium price $\bar{p} = 1.5$ assumed earlier combined with the long-run demand function LRD given in the previous section:

$$q^D = 10 - 0.8p. \qquad (8\text{–}9)$$

Under the import-cutback policy employed by the importing country, however, the assumed equilibrium price, $\bar{p} = 1.5$, never realizes. Therefore, in the presence of an embargo threat, actual equilibrium of the world resource market is given as a solution of the following three equations:

$$\tilde{q} = 10 - 0.8(\tilde{\tilde{p}} + t^*) \qquad \text{LDR} \qquad (8\text{–}10)$$

$$\tilde{q} = -0.2 + 6\tilde{\tilde{p}} \qquad \text{LSR} \qquad (8\text{–}11)$$

$$t^* = 3.804 - 0.304\tilde{\tilde{p}} \qquad \text{optimal tariff policy.} \qquad (8\text{–}12)$$

We can contrast the international equilibrium with an embargo threat–(8–10), (8–11), (8–12)–with the same without that threat– (8–8) and (8–9)–as follows:

$$\tilde{\bar{p}} = 1.09, \quad t^* = 3.47, \quad \tilde{q} = 6.35 \qquad \text{with embargo threat} \tag{8–13}$$

$$\bar{p} = 1.5, \quad t = 0, \quad \bar{q} = 8.8 \qquad \text{without embargo threat} \tag{8–14}$$

The losses borne by both parties caused by the transition from a state without an embargo threat to one with an embargo threat *which is not realized* will be calculated as follows:

$$L_D = \tfrac{1}{2}\{(\tilde{\bar{p}} + t^*) - \bar{p}\}\{q^D(\bar{p} + t^*) + q^D(\bar{p})\} - t^* \cdot q^D(\tilde{\bar{p}} + t^*) = 1.1632 \tag{8–15}$$

The loss for the exporting countries are:

$$L_S = \tfrac{1}{2}(\bar{p} - \tilde{\bar{p}})\{q^s(\bar{p}) + q^s(\tilde{\bar{p}})\} = 3.0942 \tag{8–16}$$

Obviously the cost of an embargo threat hurts exporting countries themselves more severely if they do not take further retaliatory action after the threat in this case.

MONOPOLISTIC BEHAVIOR BY EXPORTING COUNTRIES

Under the circumstance just described, the exporting countries will realize that the *effective* demand function which they face is the following one deduced by the substitution of (8–12) into (8–10):

$$q = 6.957 - 0.557p \tag{8–17}$$

The marginal revenue associated with this effective demand function is:

$$MR = p + \frac{dp}{dq}q = 12.500 - 3.594q \tag{8–18}$$

and the corresponding marginal cost as derived from equation (8–11) is:

$$MC = 0.033 + 0.167q \tag{8–19}$$

The exporting countries will adopt monopolistic behavior in which they equate *MR* and *MC* given in equations (8–18) and (8–19), with the resultant equilibrium quantity and price:

$$\hat{p} = 6.543, \quad \hat{t}^* = 1.813, \quad \hat{q} = 3.315 \tag{8–20}$$

The *absolute* gain for the exporting countries in this situation is calculated as follows:

$$\hat{G}_S = \hat{p}\hat{q} - \int_0^{\hat{q}} (MC)\, dq = 20.665 \tag{8–21}$$

The *absolute* gain for the importing country is also calculated as follows:

$$\hat{G}_D = \int_0^{\hat{q}} (12.5 - 1.25q)\, dq - (\hat{p} + \hat{t}^*)\hat{q} + \hat{t}^*\hat{q} = 12.880 \tag{8–22}$$

Corresponding absolute gains for both parties in the case of no-threat and no-tariff are given as follows:

$$\bar{G}_S = \bar{p}\bar{q} - \int_0^{\bar{q}} (MC)\, dq = 6.453 \tag{8–23}$$

$$\bar{G}_D = \int_0^{\bar{q}} (12.5 - 1.25) q\, dq - \bar{p}\bar{q} = 48.4. \tag{8–24}$$

The world gain, which is the sum of G_S and G_D, naturally decreases from 54.853 to 33.545 when both parties move from the laissez-faire situation to the tariff and monopoly situation. We should notice, however, that the distribution of the world gain is more drastically changed from one situation to the other.

COMPARISON OF POLICIES AND RESOLUTION OF THE CONFLICT

Comparison of equations (8–14), (8–13), and (8–20) shows us the course of retaliatory actions initiated by the embargo threat of exporting countries, which reduces sequentially the quantity imported. We can construct the pay-off matrix shown in Table 8–3 associated with alternative policies adopted by the importing country and the exporting countries.

The pay-off matrix as shown in Table 8–3 is clearly that of a non-zero-sum game, and from this matrix a possible resolution of the mutual loss conflict can be derived. An incentive for exporting

Table 8–3. Pay-off Matrix

Exporting Countries \ *Importing Country* (G_D / G_s)	*No Tariff*	*Tariff*	*No Tariff and Transfer*
No threat	48.4 / 6.453 (A)		34.188 / 20.665 (D)
Threat		47.237 / 3.359 (B)	
Threat and monopolistic behavior		12.880 / 20.665 (C)	

Note. In this pay-off matrix, the values of pay-off for unrealistic or unimportant combinations of policies are not calculated.

countries to make an embargo threat is the unequal distribution of gain from the international trade, as indicated by the pay-off in Case (A). Sequential retaliatory actions lead to the worst situation for the importing country, as shown by the pay-off in Case (C). In order to avoid this worst situation, the importing country should take an initial move to transfer approximately 30 percent of its gain in Case (A) to the exporting countries. This action will prevent the latter countries' embargo threat by inducing them and the importing country itself to the situation in Case (D). Of course, Case (D) is much better for the importing country compared to Case (C), and at the same time, maximum world gain from the international trade is preserved.

CONCLUSION

In the preceding sections, a heuristic discussion which leads to a possible way of resolving the mutual loss conflict initiated with an embargo threat, has been developed. The final calculation of the amount of initial transfer necessary to prevent the worst situation, of course, depends upon the specific values of the parameters given in the text, but the general principle of logic remains the same with different cases.

The most important point in this analysis is that both parties should analyze the outcome of alternative combinations of different policies adopted by themselves *beforehand*, and should start the process of negotiation before the adoption of any retaliative action and not after it. The hypothetical pay-off matrix approach described earlier would be, I think, very indicative as a datum for such a negotiation.

REFERENCES

Nordhaus, W.D. 1974. "The 1974 Report of the President's Council of Economic Advisors; Energy in the Economic Report." *American Economic Review* 64: 558–565.

Tolley, G.S., and J.D. Wilman. 1977. "The Foreign Dependence Question." *Journal of Political Economy* 85: 323–346.

Environment and Planning A, London, Vol. 15 (1983) 1175-1184

Evaluation of regional development policy—an alternative approach†

N Sakashita
Institute of Socio-Economic Planning, University of Tsukuba, Ibaraki, Japan
Received 9 March 1982; in revised form 16 November 1982

Abstract. As a theoretical basis for the evaluation of regional development policies which include capital subsidy in the form of low interest rate financing, we have the famous Borts's criteria. Borts's criteria, however, presuppose the existence of an immobile labor force as an idle resource in a specific region, and this assumption makes the criteria practically inapplicable to the situation of present-day Japan, where the interregional mobility of the labor force is extremely high. The only way to justify the meaningfulness of regional development policies which use subsidy in Japan is to take the nationwide dispersion of population as a supreme social-policy objective and to evaluate the relative cost-effectiveness of alternative economic policies instead of using the cost-benefit approach of Borts's criteria. In the present paper, different intervention policies to attain a desired distribution of population between two regions are compared from the point of view of social cost as well as from that of the amount of subsidy (or tax) needed.

1 Introduction

As a method of efficient evaluation of alternative tax-subsidy programs for the purpose of regional development, there is the famous and clear-cut analysis by Borts (1966). The criteria which were developed in his analysis were scrutinized by the present author (Sakashita, 1970), and recently they were extended to the case in which the cost of interregional migration was taken into account (Boadway and Flatters, 1981).

In all the cases cited above, however, the theoretical prerequisite of the analysis was the existence of an immobile factor of production (usually the labor force) in a specific region of the nation. In Japan nowadays, however, we have extremely high mobility of the labor force among regions, and this makes the straightforward application of Borts's criteria to the situation in Japan impractical if not impossible. Notwithstanding the strong mobility factor, we still observe extensive use of subsidizing policies by the government to promote regional development in Japan.

It is my opinion that such a situation can be theoretically justified only in terms of a supreme social-policy objective which denies, at least partially, the desirability of a population (labor force) distribution resulting from the working of the market mechanism. Therefore, if we have a desired pattern of population distribution among regions, our analysis should be focused on the effectiveness of alternative policies of market intervention in the attainment of the desired pattern. In this sense, the method of analysis should be changed from that of cost-benefit as in the case of the Borts criteria to that of cost-effectiveness in our case (or in the case of Japan).

In the next section, a simple two-region model of production and distribution is developed to compare the relative effectiveness of alternative tax-subsidy policies. Using a numerical example we compare in section 3 the capital- or price-subsidy (or tax) policy with the wage-subsidy (or tax) policy from the aspect of the social cost involved. The fourth section explores directions for an extension of the analysis.

† The original draft of this paper was presented at the Second World Regional Development and Planning Conference at the University of Tsukuba, Ibaraki, Japan, 10-12 August 1981.

2 Policy intervention in a two-region model

In the first place, I define the following symbols:

X_i is the (net) output in region i, $i = 1, 2$ ($i = 1, 2$ throughout the paper),
K_i is the capital input in region i,
N_i is the labor input in region i,
$\overline{K}$ is the capital endowment in the nation (given level),
$\overline{N}$ is the labor endowment in the nation (given level),
$\overline{k}$, $\overline{k} = \overline{K}/\overline{N}$ is the national capital/labor ratio (given level),
k_i, $k_i = K_i/N_i$ is the capital/labor ratio in region i (variable),
ρ_i is the net rental in region i,
w_i is the net wage rate in region i,
x_i, $x_i = X_i/N_i$ is the per capita (net) output in region i,
n_i, $n_i = N_i/\overline{N}$ is the share of the labor force in region i.

Second, I define a specific and well-behaved linear homogeneous production function for each region, that is,

$$X_i = F_i(K_i, N_i) . \tag{1}$$

By the assumption of well-behaved linear homogeneity[(1)], we can deduce a productivity function for each region, that is,

$$x_i = f_i(k_i) , \quad f_i(k_i) = F_i(k_i, 1) , \quad \frac{\mathrm{d}f_i}{\mathrm{d}k_i} > 0 , \quad \frac{\mathrm{d}^2 f_i}{\mathrm{d}k_i^2} < 0 . \tag{2}$$

General conditions of resource constraint which hold in any equilibrium are:

$$K_1 + K_2 = \overline{K} , \qquad N_1 + N_2 = \overline{N} . \tag{3}$$

In a free market, we have the following additional equilibrium conditions[(2)]

$$\frac{\partial F_1}{\partial K_1} = \frac{\partial F_2}{\partial K_2} , \tag{4}$$

$$\frac{\partial F_1}{\partial N_1} = \frac{\partial F_2}{\partial N_2} . \tag{5}$$

In terms of ratio variables, equations (3), (4), and (5) are transformed into:

$$\frac{\mathrm{d}f_1(k_1)}{\mathrm{d}k_1} = \frac{\mathrm{d}f_2(k_2)}{\mathrm{d}k_2} , \tag{6}$$

$$f_1(k_1) - k_1 \frac{\mathrm{d}f_1(k_1)}{\mathrm{d}k_1} = f_2(k_2) - K_2 \frac{\mathrm{d}f_2(k_2)}{\mathrm{d}k_2} , \quad \text{market solution,} \tag{7}$$

$$n_1 k_1 + n_2 k_2 = \overline{k} , \tag{8}$$

$$n_1 + n_2 \equiv 1 , \tag{9}$$

for four unknowns, k_1, k_2, n_1, and n_2.

For this market solution, notice that the choice of production techniques is determined by equations (6) and (7) *independently* of the value of $\overline{k}$, the national capital/labor ratio, as far as there exists an interior solution. I symbolize this solution as $\hat{k}_1$, $\hat{k}_2$, $\hat{n}_1$, and $\hat{n}_2$.

Now we leave the world of the free market with no intervention, and we assume that there is a preassigned value of n_1, that is, $\overline{n}_1$ as a supreme policy objective

(1) A well-behavedness condition $\mathrm{d}^2 f_i/\mathrm{d}k_i^2 < 0$ excludes the possibility of a negative cross derivative in the original production function F_i, because $\partial^2 F_i/\partial K_i \partial N_i = (-K_i/N_i^2)\,\mathrm{d}^2 f_i/\mathrm{d}k_i^2$.

(2) Here we are assuming the existence of an 'interior' solution.

(needless to say, $\bar{n}_2 \equiv 1-\bar{n}_1$). Then we have a predetermined relation for k_1 and k_2:

$$\bar{n}_1 k_1 + (1-\bar{n}_1)k_2 = \bar{k}\,. \tag{10}$$

Therefore, there is only one degree of freedom for k_1 and k_2 in this case. The problem of regional development policy now becomes that of choosing another relation between k_1 and k_2 according to some 'suboptimizing' criterion.

Consider the following suboptimizing problem:

$$\text{maximize } x = \bar{n}_1 f_1(k_1) + (1-\bar{n}_1) f_2(k_2)\,, \tag{11}$$

subject to constraint (10), where x is the national average of per capita output. It is easily shown that the optimizing conditions for problem (11) are given by the combination of:

$$\left.\begin{aligned} &\bar{n}_1 k_1 + (1-\bar{n}_1)k_2 = \bar{k}\,, && (10)\\ &\frac{\mathrm{d}f_1(k_1)}{\mathrm{d}k_1} = \frac{\mathrm{d}f_2(k_2)}{\mathrm{d}k_2}\,. && (12)\end{aligned}\right\} \text{ wage-intervention solution.}$$

The reason I call this combination the wage-intervention solution is that it prohibits any policy intervention in the capital market, as shown by equation (12) which has the same form as equation (6). Instead, equation (7) must be violated for the solution of k_1 and k_2 in equations (10) and (12), and that means the necessity of some wage-intervention program for one or both regions.

In other words, the combination of equations (10) and (12) is nothing other than a proof of the fact that wage intervention is the best policy to achieve a *given* goal of interregional labor (population) distribution. In comparison with the market solution given by equations (6)–(9), the wage-intervention solution can be taken as the second-best solution in the sense that it minimizes the loss of national output induced by a compulsory goal of labor-force distribution. The loss can be considered as a social cost which is brought about by such a social goal.

Now let us assume that region 1 is less productive than region 2 in the market solution:

$$f_2(\hat{k}_2) > f_1(\hat{k}_1)\,, \qquad \hat{k}_2 > \hat{k}_1 \tag{13}$$

for the solutions $\hat{k}_1$ and $\hat{k}_2$ of equations (6)–(9). Under the circumstances, a *self-financing* market intervention by the government which aims at a higher $\bar{n}_1$ than $\hat{n}_1$ will be expressed as:

$$(1+s_p)\frac{\mathrm{d}f_1(k_1)}{\mathrm{d}k_1} = (1-t_p)\frac{\mathrm{d}f_2(k_2)}{\mathrm{d}k_2}\,, \tag{14}$$

$$(1+s_w)\left[f_1(k_1) - k_1\frac{\mathrm{d}f_1(k_1)}{\mathrm{d}k_1}\right] = (1-t_w)\left[f_2(k_2) - k_2\frac{\mathrm{d}f_2(k_2)}{\mathrm{d}k_2}\right], \tag{15}$$

$$\begin{aligned}&\left\{s_p\frac{\mathrm{d}f_1(k_1)}{\mathrm{d}k_1}k_1 + s_w\left[f_1(k_1) - k_1\frac{\mathrm{d}f_1(k_1)}{\mathrm{d}k_1}\right]\right\}\bar{n}_1\\ &\quad = \left\{t_p\frac{\mathrm{d}f_2(k_2)}{\mathrm{d}k_2}k_2 + t_w\left[f_2(k_2) - k_2\frac{\mathrm{d}f_2(k_2)}{\mathrm{d}k_2}\right]\right\}(1-\bar{n}_1)\,.\end{aligned} \tag{16}$$

where

s_p is the rate of capital subsidy in region 1,
s_w is the rate of wage subsidy in region 1,
t_p is the rate of capital tax in region 2,
t_w is the rate of wage tax in region 2.

Apparently, equation (16) implies a balance between subsidy expenditure and tax revenue procured by the government.

Let us prove that the additional constraint of equation (16) *does not* change the solution of suboptimizing problem (11). For that purpose we formulate the following Lagrangian form:

$$\phi = [\bar{n}_1 f_1 + (1-\bar{n}_1)f_2] + \lambda[\bar{k} - \bar{n}_1 k_1 - (1-\bar{n}_1)k_2] + \mu\left[(1+s_p)\frac{df_1}{dk_1} - (1-t_p)\frac{df_2}{dk_2}\right]$$
$$+\nu\left[(1+s_w)\left(f_1 - k_1\frac{df_1}{dk_1}\right) - (1-t_w)\left(f_2 - k_2\frac{df_2}{dk_2}\right)\right]$$
$$+\theta\left\{\left[s_p\frac{df_1}{dk_1}k_1 + s_w\left(f_1 - k_1\frac{df_1}{dk_1}\right)\right]\bar{n}_1 - \left[t_p\frac{df_2}{dk_2}k_2 + t_w\left(f_2 - k_2\frac{df_2}{dk_2}\right)\right](1-\bar{n}_1)\right\}, \tag{17}$$

which contains all of the constraints of equations (10), (14), (15), and (16).

By partial differentiation, we have:

$$\frac{\partial\phi}{\partial s_p} = \mu\frac{df_1}{dk_1} + \theta\frac{df_1}{dk_1}k_1\bar{n}_1 = 0, \tag{18}$$

$$\frac{\partial\phi}{\partial t_p} = \mu\frac{df_2}{dk_2} - \theta\frac{df_2}{dk_2}k_2(1-\bar{n}_1) = 0, \tag{19}$$

$$\frac{\partial\phi}{\partial s_w} = \nu\left(f_1 - k_1\frac{df_1}{dk_1}\right) + \theta\left(f_1 - k_1\frac{df_1}{dk_1}\right)\bar{n}_1 = 0, \tag{20}$$

$$\frac{\partial\phi}{\partial t_w} = \nu\left(f_2 - k_2\frac{df_2}{dk_2}\right) - \theta\left(f_2 - k_2\frac{df_2}{dk_2}\right)(1-\bar{n}_1) = 0. \tag{21}$$

It is easily shown that $\nu = \theta = 0$ by equations (20) and (21), and hence $\mu = 0$ by equation (18) or (19). The constraints imposed by equations (14), (15), and (16) are, therefore, ineffective in the formulation of equation (17), and we have the original suboptimizing problem of (11). This completes the proof.

As a matter of fact, after solving for the values of k_i $(= \tilde{k}_i)$ for equations (10) and (12), we can calculate the values of s_w and t_w for this self-financing wage-intervention problem by the equations:

$$(1+s_w)\tilde{w}_1 = (1-t_w)\tilde{w}_2, \tag{22}$$

$$s_w\tilde{w}_1\bar{n}_1 = t_w\tilde{w}_2(1-\bar{n}_1), \tag{23}$$

$$\tilde{w}_i = f_i(\tilde{k}_i) - \tilde{k}_i\frac{df_1}{dk_1}(\tilde{k}_i), \qquad i = 1, 2 \tag{24}$$

where the tilde indicates the solution to equations (10) and (12).

Calculated values of s_w and t_w are(3):

$$s_w = \frac{(1-\bar{n}_1)(\tilde{w}_2 - \tilde{w}_1)}{\tilde{w}_1}, \tag{25}$$

$$t_w = \frac{\bar{n}_1(\tilde{w}_2 - \tilde{w}_1)}{\tilde{w}_2}. \tag{26}$$

In the case of self-financing intervention, there is little incentive for the government to economize on the amount of tax or subsidy. But, if the subsidy is financed by common funds without specific tax, or if the tax is imposed on the 'rich' region without

(3) This method of solving for s and t can be also used with a little modification for the capital-market-intervention policy and for the price-intervention policy discussed later.

subsidizing the 'poor' region, there will be a strong incentive for the government to minimize the amount of such a subsidy or tax.

From this point of view, we now formulate the following subsidy-minimizing problem:

$$\text{minimize } s = \left[\left(\frac{\mathrm{d}f_2}{\mathrm{d}k_2}-\frac{\mathrm{d}f_1}{\mathrm{d}k_1}\right)k_1+\left(f_2-k_2\frac{\mathrm{d}f_2}{\mathrm{d}k_2}\right)-\left(f_1-k_1\frac{\mathrm{d}f_1}{\mathrm{d}k_1}\right)\right]\bar{n}_1\,, \tag{27}$$

subject to constraint (10). To analyze this problem, let us express a general subsidizing (taxing) program as follows:

$$\bar{n}_1k_1+(1-\bar{n}_1)k_2 = \bar{k}\,, \tag{10}$$

$$\frac{\mathrm{d}f_2}{\mathrm{d}k_2}-\frac{\mathrm{d}f_1}{\mathrm{d}k_1} = g\,, \tag{28}$$

in which g is an instrumental variable showing the gap between the marginal productivities of capital in the two regions. Then we have:

$$\frac{\mathrm{d}k_1}{\mathrm{d}g} = -\frac{(1-\bar{n}_1)}{\Delta} > 0\,, \tag{29}$$

$$\frac{\mathrm{d}k_2}{\mathrm{d}g} = \frac{\bar{n}_1}{\Delta} < 0\,, \tag{30}$$

in which

$$\Delta = \bar{n}_1\frac{\mathrm{d}^2f_2}{\mathrm{d}k_2^2}+(1-\bar{n}_1)\frac{\mathrm{d}^2f_1}{\mathrm{d}k_1^2} < 0\,.$$

Using equations (29) and (30), we can show that:

$$\frac{\mathrm{d}s}{\mathrm{d}g} = \frac{\bar{n}_1}{\Delta}\left[-\bar{n}_1\frac{\mathrm{d}^2f_2}{\mathrm{d}k_2^2}(k_2-k_1)-(1-\bar{n}_1)g\right]. \tag{31}$$

Starting from $g \approx 0$, first we have a phase of $\mathrm{d}s/\mathrm{d}g < 0$ by equation (31), then for larger values of g we have a smaller gap between k_2 and k_1 by equations (29) and (30) so that we will see a phase of $\mathrm{d}s/\mathrm{d}g > 0$ later. We can, therefore, safely say that the minimum amount of subsidy will be attained at the point where $\mathrm{d}s/\mathrm{d}g = 0$. The minimizing condition is:

$$\left.\begin{aligned} &\bar{n}_1k_1+(1-\bar{n}_1)k_2 = \bar{k}\,, && (10)\\ &\left[-\frac{\mathrm{d}^2f_2}{\mathrm{d}k_2^2}(k_2-k_1)\right]\Big/\left(\frac{\mathrm{d}f_2}{\mathrm{d}k_2}-\frac{\mathrm{d}f_1}{\mathrm{d}k_1}\right) = \frac{1-\bar{n}_1}{\bar{n}_1}\,. && (32)\end{aligned}\right\}\ \text{minimum-subsidy solution.}$$

This solution should be a mixture of wage and capital subsidies.

Also we can formulate a tax-minimizing problem as follows:

$$\text{minimize } t = \left[\left(\frac{\mathrm{d}f_2}{\mathrm{d}k_2}-\frac{\mathrm{d}f_1}{\mathrm{d}k_1}\right)k_2+\left(f_2-k_2\frac{\mathrm{d}f_2}{\mathrm{d}k_2}\right)-\left(f_1-k_1\frac{\mathrm{d}f_1}{\mathrm{d}k_1}\right)\right](1-\bar{n}_1)\,, \tag{33}$$

subject to constraint (10). In this case, we will have:

$$\frac{\mathrm{d}t}{\mathrm{d}g} = \frac{(1-\bar{n}_1)}{\Delta}\left[(1-\bar{n}_1)\frac{\mathrm{d}^2f_1}{\mathrm{d}k_1^2}(k_2-k_1)+\bar{n}_1g\right], \tag{34}$$

so that $\mathrm{d}t/\mathrm{d}g > 0$ when $g \approx 0$, and $\mathrm{d}t/\mathrm{d}g < 0$ for larger values of g. Thus we cannot have an 'interior' minimum for this problem. An exclusively wage-tax solution ($g = 0$) or a mixed-tax solution or an exclusively capital-tax solution (g takes the maximum possible in both of the last two cases) will be the minimizing solution.

The relative desirability between the minimum-subsidy program and the minimum-tax program depends on the values of $\bar{n}_1$ and $(1-\bar{n}_1)$ as is easily seen by the definitions of s and t. If $\bar{n}_1$ is rather large, the tax program will be preferred, and vice versa.

To turn to other forms of intervention policy, two popular schemes are:

$$\left.\begin{aligned} &\bar{n}_1 k_1 + (1-\bar{n}_1)k_2 = \bar{k}\,, && (10)\\ &f_1 - k_1\frac{\mathrm{d}f_1}{\mathrm{d}k_1} = f_2 - k_2\frac{\mathrm{d}f_2}{\mathrm{d}k_2}\,, && (35)\end{aligned}\right\}\ \text{capital-market-intervention solution,}$$

and

$$\left.\begin{aligned} &\bar{n}_1 k_1 + (1-\bar{n}_1)k_2 = \bar{k}\,, && (10)\\ &p\frac{\mathrm{d}f_1}{\mathrm{d}k_1} = \frac{\mathrm{d}f_2}{\mathrm{d}k_2}\,, && (36)\\ &p\left(f_1 - k_1\frac{\mathrm{d}f_1}{\mathrm{d}k_1}\right) = f_2 - k_2\frac{\mathrm{d}f_2}{\mathrm{d}k_2}\,, && (37)\end{aligned}\right\}\ \text{price-intervention solution,}$$

where p is an additional endogenous variable which embodies the level of intervention. The inferiority of these solutions to the wage-intervention solution from the point of view of efficient (or least inefficient) resource allocation is already proved. We can say that price intervention is somewhere between wage intervention and capital-market intervention from this aspect, as shown by numerical examples in the next section.

To return to the wage-intervention solution, the effect of a small change in the assigned value of $\bar{n}_1$ can be calculated by the method of comparative statics, and we have:

$$\frac{\mathrm{d}k_1}{\mathrm{d}\bar{n}_1} = (k_2-k_1)\frac{\mathrm{d}^2 f_2}{\mathrm{d}k_2^2}\Bigg/\left[\bar{n}_1\frac{\mathrm{d}^2 f_2}{\mathrm{d}k_2^2} + (1-\bar{n}_1)\frac{\mathrm{d}^2 f_1}{\mathrm{d}k_1^2}\right], \tag{38}$$

$$\frac{\mathrm{d}k_2}{\mathrm{d}\bar{n}_1} = (k_2-k_1)\frac{\mathrm{d}^2 f_1}{\mathrm{d}k_1^2}\Bigg/\left[\bar{n}_1\frac{\mathrm{d}^2 f_2}{\mathrm{d}k_2^2} + (1-\bar{n}_1)\frac{\mathrm{d}^2 f_1}{\mathrm{d}k_1^2}\right], \tag{39}$$

$$\frac{\mathrm{d}x}{\mathrm{d}\bar{n}_1} = \left(f_1 - k_1\frac{\mathrm{d}f_1}{\mathrm{d}k_1}\right) - \left(f_2 - k_2\frac{\mathrm{d}f_2}{\mathrm{d}k_2}\right) = w_1 - w_2\,. \tag{40}$$

If we assume that the wage-intervention solution is not very different from the market solution and that $\hat{k}_2 > \hat{k}_1$ for the latter [see relation (13)], we can safely say that:

$$\frac{\mathrm{d}k_1}{\mathrm{d}\bar{n}_1} > 0\,, \qquad \frac{\mathrm{d}k_2}{\mathrm{d}\bar{n}_2} > 0\,. \tag{41}$$

In addition, if we assume that region 1 is wage-subsidized, we have the following relations:

$$\bar{n}_1 > \hat{n}_1\,, \tag{42}$$

where $\hat{n}_1$ is the market solution,

$$w_1 < w_2\,. \tag{43}$$

Here w_i denotes, of course, the wage rate in region i *net of* subsidy. Wage rates are equated between regions with wage-subsidy programs.

It is clear from equations (40) and (43) that, if one wishes to further increase the share of the labor force in region 1, which is already wage-subsidized, the national average per capita output decreases further, that is, there will be additional social cost involved in an increase in $\bar{n}_1$.

If the initial value of $\bar{n}_1$ is equal to $\hat{n}_1$, the market solution, then obviously we have $(\mathrm{d}\bar{x}/\mathrm{d}\bar{n}_1)_{\bar{n}_1=\hat{n}_1} = 0$, because of equation (7). We can, however, show that:

$$\left(\frac{\mathrm{d}^2x}{\mathrm{d}\bar{n}_1^2}\right)_{\bar{n}_1=\hat{n}_1} = (k_2-k_1)^2\frac{\mathrm{d}^2f_1}{\mathrm{d}k_1^2}\frac{\mathrm{d}^2f_2}{\mathrm{d}k_2^2}\bigg/\left[\bar{n}_1\frac{\mathrm{d}^2f_2}{\mathrm{d}k_2^2}+(1-\bar{n}_1)\frac{\mathrm{d}^2f_1}{\mathrm{d}k_1^2}\right] < 0\,, \tag{44}$$

which implies that national productivity always decreases when $\bar{n}_1$ departs from $\hat{n}_1$ in either direction. Equation (44) also implies that $\mathrm{d}(w_1-w_2)/\mathrm{d}\bar{n}_1 < 0$, so that as $\bar{n}_1$ becomes larger than $\hat{n}_1$ then the discrepancy between w_1 and w_2 also becomes larger, so that a greater amount of wage subsidy is needed.

Finally, let us consider the case of capital subsidy. As counterparts to equations (38), (39), and (40), we now have:

$$\frac{\mathrm{d}k_1}{\mathrm{d}\bar{n}_1} = (k_2-k_1)k_2\frac{\mathrm{d}^2f_2}{\mathrm{d}k_2^2}\bigg/\left[\bar{n}_1k_2\frac{\mathrm{d}^2f_2}{\mathrm{d}k_2^2}+(1-\bar{n}_1)k_1\frac{\mathrm{d}^2f_1}{\mathrm{d}k_1^2}\right] \tag{45}$$

$$\frac{\mathrm{d}k_2}{\mathrm{d}\bar{n}_1} = (k_2-k_1)k_1\frac{\mathrm{d}^2f_1}{\mathrm{d}k_1^2}\bigg/\left[\bar{n}_1k_2\frac{\mathrm{d}^2f_2}{\mathrm{d}k_2^2}+(1-\bar{n}_1)k_1\frac{\mathrm{d}^2f_1}{\mathrm{d}k_1^2}\right] \tag{46}$$

$$\left.\right\} > 0 \quad \text{if} \quad \bar{n}_1 \approx \hat{n}_1, \quad \text{and} \quad \hat{k}_2 > \hat{k}_1$$

$$\frac{\mathrm{d}x}{\mathrm{d}\bar{n}_1} = \left\{\left[\bar{n}_1k_2^2\frac{\mathrm{d}^2f_2}{\mathrm{d}k_2^2}+(1-\bar{n}_1)k_1^2\frac{\mathrm{d}^2f_1}{\mathrm{d}k_1^2}\right]\bigg/\left[\bar{n}_1k_2\frac{\mathrm{d}^2f_2}{\mathrm{d}k_2^2}+(1-\bar{n}_1)k_1\frac{\mathrm{d}^2f_1}{\mathrm{d}k_1^2}\right]\right\}\left(\frac{\mathrm{d}f_1}{\mathrm{d}k_1}-\frac{\mathrm{d}f_2}{\mathrm{d}k_2}\right)$$

$$= k^*(\rho_1-\rho_2)\,, \tag{47}$$

where k^* is a weighted average of k_1 and k_2. Obviously $\mathrm{d}x/\mathrm{d}\bar{n}_1 = 0$, when $\bar{n}_1 = \hat{n}_1$, but $\mathrm{d}x/\mathrm{d}\bar{n}_1 < 0$, when $\bar{n}_1 > \hat{n}_1$, and therefore, $\rho_1 < \rho_2$, where ρ_i is the rental in region i *net of* subsidy.

It is not easy to obtain the second derivative of x with respect to $\bar{n}_1$, but if we can assume that k^* in equation (47) is approximately constant, we have:

$$\left(\frac{\mathrm{d}^2x}{\mathrm{d}\bar{n}_1^2}\right)_{\bar{n}_1=\hat{n}_1} \approx k^*(k_2-k_1)^2\frac{\mathrm{d}^2f_1}{\mathrm{d}k_1^2}\frac{\mathrm{d}^2f_2}{\mathrm{d}k_2^2}\bigg/\left[\bar{n}_1k_2\frac{\mathrm{d}^2f_2}{\mathrm{d}k_2^2}+(1-\bar{n}_1)k_1\frac{\mathrm{d}^2f_1}{\mathrm{d}k_1^2}\right] < 0\,, \tag{48}$$

which is analogous to equation (44).

3 Numerical examples and a comparison of different intervention policies

In this section, I give numerical examples of wage-, capital-market-, and price-intervention policies using Cobb–Douglas production functions. As Borts emphasized in his paper, since tax collection and/or subsidy expenditure are merely a matter of income redistribution and are not related to the efficiency of resource allocation, the most important point in the comparison of different policies is the amount of the national average of per capita output (x) which reflects the real social cost of the intervention policies.

For the numerical examples, we specify the productivity functions of two regions and national capital/labor ratio by:

$$x_1 = Ak_1^{\alpha_1}\,, \qquad x_2 = k_2^{\alpha_2}\,, \tag{49}$$

where $A = 1.25$, $\alpha_1 = 0.4$, $\alpha_2 = 0.6$;

$$\bar{k} = 3.0\,. \tag{50}$$

With this specification, interregional equilibrium under the particular intervention scheme is given by:

Wage-intervention scheme

$$\bar{n}_1 k_1 + (1-\bar{n}_1)k_2 = \bar{k}, \tag{51a}$$

$$\alpha_1 A k_1^{\alpha_1 - 1} = \alpha_2 k_2^{\alpha_2 - 1}, \tag{51b}$$

$$x = \bar{n}_1 A k_1^{\alpha_1} + (1-\bar{n}_1)k_2^{\alpha_2}. \tag{51c}$$

Capital-market-intervention scheme

$$\bar{n}_1 k_1 + (1-\bar{n}_1)k_2 = \bar{k}, \tag{52a}$$

$$(1-\alpha_1)A k_1^{\alpha_1} = (1-\alpha_2)k_2^{\alpha_2}, \tag{52b}$$

$$x = \bar{n}_1 A k_1^{\alpha_1} + (1-\bar{n}_1)k_2^{\alpha_2}, \tag{52c}$$

Price-intervention scheme

$$\bar{n}_1 k_1 + (1-\bar{n}_1)k_2 = \bar{k}, \tag{53a}$$

$$p\alpha_1 A k_1^{\alpha_1 - 1} = \alpha_2 k_2^{\alpha_2 - 1}, \tag{53b}$$

$$p(1-\alpha_1)A k_1^{\alpha_1} = (1-\alpha_2)k_2^{\alpha_2}, \tag{53c}$$

$$x = \bar{n}_1 A k_1^{\alpha_1} + (1-\bar{n}_1)k_2^{\alpha_2}, \tag{53d}$$

In table 1, the solution of the wage-intervention scheme is given for each preassigned value of $\bar{n}_1$. The national average of the per capita output, x, attains its maximum when $\bar{n}_1 = 0.62035$, which is equivalent to the free-market equilibrium, and, in the seventh column of the table, indices of x relative to this maximum are given. These indices can be taken as indicators of real social cost of intervention.

In table 2, the solution of the capital-market-intervention scheme is given in the same manner. Comparison of the seventh column of table 2 with that of table 1 shows (marginal) inferiority of this intervention to the suboptimal wage-intervention.

In table 3, the solution of the price-intervention scheme is shown with the value of the price-intervention level (p) in the second column. Again $\bar{n}_1 = 0.62035$ gives the maximum value of x and this value is equal to that for the market solution, and in this case $p = 1$. The eighth column shows the values of 'nominal' per capita output, x^*, for the calculation of which the value of p is taken into consideration. The ninth column of this table shows the intermediate character of this intervention compared with the seventh columns of tables 1 and 2.

Table 1. The solution of the wage-intervention scheme for preassigned values of $\bar{n}_1$.

$\bar{n}_1$	k_1	k_2	x_1	x_2	x	$(x/x_{max}) \times 100$
0.0		3.0		1.93318	1.93318	97.8
0.1	1.58808	3.15688	1.50404	1.99322	1.94430	98.4
0.2	1.64823	3.33794	1.52657	2.06104	1.95415	98.9
0.3	1.71723	3.54976	1.55182	2.13855	1.96253	99.3
0.4	1.79755	3.80164	1.58045	2.22834	1.96919	99.7
0.5	1.89265	4.10735	1.61339	2.33419	1.97379	99.9
0.6	2.00789	4.48816	1.65199	2.46173	1.97589	100.0
0.62035	2.03451	4.57764	1.66071	2.49106	1.97595	100.0
0.7	2.15179	4.97915	1.69836	2.61995	1.97484	100.0
0.8	2.33915	5.64340	1.75604	2.82439	1.96971	99.7
0.9	2.59897	6.61925	1.83160	3.10521	1.95896	99.1
1.0	3.0		1.93981		1.93981	98.2

The remarkably small difference between the outcomes of these three tables implies the extra technological flexibility of the Cobb–Douglas production function which adjusts itself smoothly to the conditions of different types of intervention. Probably we should not expect such strong flexibility in the real world.

Table 2. The solution of the capital-market-intervention scheme for preassigned values of $\bar{n}_1$.

$\bar{n}_1$	k_1	k_2	x_1	x_2	x	$(x/x_{max}) \times 100$
0.0		3.0		1.93318	1.93318	97.8
0.1	1.18975	3.20114	1.33996	2.00994	1.94294	98.3
0.2	1.31460	3.42135	1.39453	2.09179	1.95234	98.8
0.3	1.45564	3.66187	1.45255	2.17882	1.96094	99.2
0.4	1.61450	3.92367	1.51400	2.27099	1.96819	99.6
0.5	1.79269	4.20731	1.57875	2.36812	1.97343	99.9
0.6	1.99145	4.51282	1.64656	2.46984	1.97587	100.0
0.62035	2.03451	4.57764	1.66071	2.49106	1.97595	100.0
0.7	2.21161	4.83957	1.71709	2.57563	1.97465	99.9
0.8	2.45343	5.18626	1.78986	2.68481	1.96885	99.6
0.9	2.71658	5.55079	1.86431	2.79649	1.95753	99.1
1.0	3.0		1.93981		1.93981	98.2

Table 3. The solution of the price-intervention scheme for preassigned values of $\bar{n}_1$.

$\bar{n}_1$	p	k_1	k_2	x_1	x_2	x	$x^{*\,a}$	$(x/x_{max}) \times 100$
0.0			3.0		1.93318	1.93318		97.8
0.1	0.929524	1.41176	3.17647	1.43488	2.00063	1.94406	1.93394	98.4
0.2	0.940863	1.50000	3.37500	1.47010	2.07474	1.95381	1.93643	98.9
0.3	0.953086	1.60000	3.6	1.50854	2.15666	1.96222	1.94099	99.3
0.4	0.966329	1.71429	3.85714	1.55076	2.24781	1.96899	1.94810	99.6
0.5	0.980758	1.84615	4.15385	1.59741	2.35001	1.97371	1.95834	99.9
0.6	0.996585	2.00000	4.5	1.64939	2.46563	1.97588	1.97250	100.0
0.62035	1.000000	2.03451	4.57764	1.66071	2.49106	1.97595	1.97595	100.0
0.7	1.01408	2.18182	4.90909	1.70786	2.59777	1.97479	1.99162	99.9
0.8	1.03360	2.40000	5.4	1.77417	2.75066	1.96947	2.01715	99.7
0.9	1.05561	2.66667	6.0	1.85054	2.93016	1.95850	2.05111	99.1
1.0		3.0		1.93981		1.93981		98.2

[a] $x^* = p\bar{n}_1 x_1 + (1-\bar{n}_1)x_2$.

4 Conclusion

In the preceding two sections, we discussed the relative advantages and disadvantages of different intervention policies as a measure of attaining a desired pattern of interregional population (labor force) distribution. The superiority of wage intervention from the point of view of lesser social cost is almost unchallenged, but it is not a policy which, in general, gives the minimum amount of subsidy.

As a further investigation, regional allocation of public investment can be also taken as a form of preferential regional policy, and the effectiveness of this policy should be studied very carefully. Furthermore, a combined policy of public investment and wage intervention or capital intervention can be studied from a similar point of view (see Sakashita, 1982).

Another aspect of regional policy is the difference in the speeds of interregional movement of capital and labor. No subsidizing policy can expect an instantaneous effect if there is a certain stickiness in the interregional mobility of factors. Therefore, we should distinguish long-run effects from short-run effects in such a case. The cost of short-run adjustments may make the desirable regional policy infeasible. We should proceed to this sort of dynamic analysis.

In any case, the approach adopted in this paper can be understood as a necessary and important procedure to give a scientific basis to the analysis of regional development policy.

Acknowledgement. The author wishes to thank an anonymous referee for valuable comments. However, the author is solely responsible for remaining errors.

References

Boadway R, Flatters F, 1981, "The efficiency basis for regional employment policy" *The Canadian Journal of Economics* **14**(1) 58–135

Borts G H, 1966, "Criteria for the evaluation of regional development programs" in *Regional Accounts for Policy Decisions* Ed. W Z Hirsch (Johns Hopkins University Press, Baltimore, MD) pp 183–218

Sakashita N, 1970, "Efficiency evaluation of regional development policy" *Papers and Proceedings of the Eighth Congress of Econometrics at Kobe*, Kansai Economic Research Centre, Osaka; in Japanese, pp 363–392

Sakashita N, 1982, "Population dispersion and regional economic policy" in *Essays in Honor of Professor Yasuhiko Oishi* Eds T Neghishi, Y Okano; in Japanese (forthcoming)

Human Behaviour in Geographical Space, ed. by J.H. Paelinck, Aldershot (1986) 45–61

Location quotients, export industries and shift-share analysis

N. SAKASHITA

1. Introduction

Identification of export industries and forecasting growth potentials of those industries for a specific region are the most important procedures in the empirical analysis of a regional economy. If we have sufficient data of input-output relations as in the case of quite a number of regions (states) in Japan, the identification of export industries is not a formidable task at all. However if we turn to the smaller units of regions, e.g. cities or towns, such data become out of our reach even for the data-conscious municipalities in Japan.

As a more intuitive indicator of exportability, regional economists favoured the concept of location quotients especially because they are easily calculated with a modest degree of data requirement. Let the share of the employment of industry i in region j in the total employment of the same region be λ_i^j, and the national counterpart of the share be λ_i^o, then the location quotient of industry i in region j, q_i^j, is simply defined by

$$q_i^j = \lambda_i^j / \lambda_i^o \tag{1.1}$$

If the value of q_i^j is larger than unity, it may indicate that region j is more or less specialised in industry i so that we can safely conjecture that industry i may be an export industry for region j. So far so simple and so clear.

The above statement is, however, totally dependent on an intuitive conjecture and is not based on any rigorous economic theory. Regional economists were well aware of this weakness of the concept of location quotients, but they carefully avoided the discussion of the theoretical foundation of the concept, perhaps being afraid to lose this all-round convenient tool of empirical analysis under certain conditions where it is not justifiable to use the concept.

In 1975, Mayer and Pleeter bravely broke the silence and examined the conditions under which a more-than-unity value of the location quotient for an industry actually meant that the industry was an export-oriented one, using a neoclassical two-region model with three industries. In their analysis one of the industries was supposed to be producing a non-tradable commodity. Their problem consciousness and their method of approach can be highly appreciated, but there is a methodological drawback in their analysis: they applied a mathematical technique of total differentiation in analysing cross-sectional differences among regions, but that method is only justifiable for an extreme case in which an almost infinite number of regions are scattered as a continuous spectrum of regional characteristics, but this is certainly not applicable to the case of the discrete two-region economy which they formulated.

In this chapter we adopt a simpler two-region two-industry model to analyse the relations among the exogenous conditions, the exporting or importing property of particular industry in a particular region, and the relevant value of the location quotient without methodological difficulties. Our two-industry assumption can be justified in an advanced economy where almost all commodities (even services) are tradable given the high technologies of transportation and communication.

In addition we discuss the relation between location quotient analysis and shift-share analysis by a somewhat more specific mode in a dynamic setting. Shift-share analysis is another intuitive tool used in dynamic regional economics. Some efforts to establish a theoretical background to the shift-share analysis have already been made (e.g. Sakashita, 1973), but so far were not so successful. The present chapter could be a first step to its further theoretical elaboration.

2. Assumptions and symbols

We postulate the following eight assumptions regarding our theoretical model.

1 The national economy consists of two regions, and two factors of production, capital and labour, are immobile between regions at least in the short run.
2 Both regions produce two types of final commodities by the same technologies (i.e. by a common production function for each of the final commodities) and consume them. The interregional movement of final commodities and the intraregional interindustry movement of factors of production are completely free.
3 The national economy itself is a closed one so that there is no international import or export.
4 Labour employment as a factor of production and the size of population are proportional to each other by a fixed and interregionally common ratio so that they can be treated as a single variable.
5 Each region has a specific factor endowment in the short run so that regional ratios of factor endowment are exogenously fixed at least in that short run.
6 As for the mobile commodities or factors, perfect competition prevails interregionally and intraregionally so that there is a full employment or full utilisation of factors.
7 The production function of each industry is linear homogeneous, twice continuously differentiable, and strictly quasi-concave; in addition there will be no reversal of factor intensities between two industries.
8 The per capita demand function for each final commodity is the same among regions except for a shift parameter, and the arguments of the per capita demand function are the relative price of two commodities and per capita income.

The above assumptions are of course restrictive in their nature but none of them are particularly purposeful, and altogether they describe an ordinary world of neoclassical economy.

Symbols in our model, except for the already defined λ_i^j, λ_i^o and q_i^j, are defined as follows using *a* and *b* as regional superfixes and 1 and 2 as industrial suffixes:

k_i = capital – labour ratio of industry i (no regional difference), i = 1, 2;

$f_i(k_i)$ = average labour productivity function of industry i;

p_i = price of the final commodity produced by industry i ($p_1 = 1$ as the numeraire);

$\bar{k}^j$ = factor endowment (regional capital – labour) ratio of region j, j = *a*, *b*;

x_i^j = per capita output of final commodity i in region j;

y^j = per capita income in region j in terms of the first final commodity;

d_i^j = per capita demand for final commodity i in region j;

e_i^j = $x_i^j - d_i^j$ = per capita export of final commodity i from region j;

$\bar{n}^j$ = proportion of the national population in region j; $(\bar{n}^a + \bar{n}^b \equiv 1)$;

f_i' = $\frac{df_i}{dk_i}$

α^j = a shift parameter in the demand function of region j.

Henceforth we shall call final commodities simply commodities, and factors of production simply factors.

3. Interregional general equilibrium

Under the set of assumptions given in the previous section, we can formulate an interregional general equilibrium by the following equations. First of all, we have the marginal productivity relations between two industries which are common for the two regions by assumptions 2, 6 and 7.

$$f_1' = p_2 f_2' \quad \text{: determination of rent} \tag{3.1}$$

$$f_1 - k_1 f_1' = p_2 (f_2 - k_2 f_2') \quad \text{: determination of wage} \tag{3.2}$$

When p_2 is given as a common relative price for both regions, equations (3.1) and (3.2) determine k_1 and k_2 which are also common to both regions. This is the simplest case of the well-known factor-price-equalisation theorem in international economics. The uniqueness of the values of k_1 and k_2 for any specific value of p_2 is assured by the non-reversibility of factor intensities in assumption 7.

Next, we have the following two equations by the definition of λ_i^j $(i = 1, 2; j = a, b)$:

$$\lambda_1^j + \lambda_2^j \equiv 1, j = a, b \tag{3.3}$$

$$\lambda_1^j k_1 + \lambda_2^j k_2 = \bar{k}^j, j = a, b \tag{3.4}$$

Since k_1 and k_2 are predetermined in the sense that they are given functions of given p_2, equations (3.3) and (3.4) suffice to determine λ_1^j and λ_2^j in each region ($j = a, b$) as functions of p_2 too.

As a third step, the x_i^j ($i = 1, 2$; $j = a, b$) are determined by the following (four) equations again as functions of p_2:

$$x_i^j = \lambda_i^j f_i(k_i), \quad i = 1, 2; j = a, b \tag{3.5}$$

These equations also determine the supply side of commodities.

Per capita income of each region in terms of the first commodity is defined by:

$$y^j = x_1^j + p_2 x_2^j, \quad j = a, b \tag{3.6}$$

and finally per capita demand for each commodity in each region is determined by the following equation owing to assumption 8:

$$d_i^j = d_i\,(p_2, y^j; \alpha^j), \quad i = 1, 2; j = a, b \tag{3.7}$$

In this and the next sections, it will be assumed that $\alpha^a = \alpha^b = \alpha$, so that provisionally we have completely identical per capita demand functions for the two regions.

By equations (3.1) to (3.7), all endogenous variables except p_2 itself are determined as functions of p_2, so that our final step is to determine p_2 by either of the following two equations of supply–demand balance:

$$\bar{n}^a x_i^a + \bar{n}^b x_i^b = \bar{n}^a d_i^a + \bar{n}^b d_i^b, \quad i = 1, 2 \tag{3.8}$$

Actually since one of the two equations in (3.8) is derived from the other by using equation (3.6) and an implicit relation:

$$y^j = d_1^j + p_2 d_2^j, \quad j = a, b \tag{3.9}$$

behind equations (3.7), there is no equation redundancy (an example of the Walrasian Law).

The determination of p_2 by one of the equations in (3.8) completes our system of interregional general equilibrium in which the regional equilibrium for either of the regions *a* and *b* is determined separately to a certain extent by taking p_2, k_1, and k_2 as 'quasi-exogenous' variables for the region.

Now let us fix j for a particular region and consider the seven equations of (3.3) to (3.7) simultaneously. They form a system of simultaneous equations for seven regional endogenous variables, λ_1^j, λ_2^j, x_1^j, x_2^j, y^j, d_1^j, and d_2^j, and the latter variables are determined as functions of exogenous and quasi-exogenous variables, $\bar{k}^j$, p_2, k_1, and k_2. However, all functions in that system are common to both regions on the additional assumption of $\alpha^a = \alpha^b$ so that if $\bar{k}^a = \bar{k}^b$, by coincidence we have the same set of solutions to the seven regional endogenous variables.

Under this circumstance of *twin* regions, we have the following two consequences. First, since $\lambda_i^a = \lambda_i^b = \lambda_i$ (i = 1, 2), by the definition of equation (1.1) all four location quotients become unity, i.e.

$$q_i^j = \frac{\lambda_i^j}{\bar{n}^a \lambda_i^a + \bar{n}^b \lambda_i^b} = \frac{\lambda_i}{(\bar{n}^a + \bar{n}^b)\lambda_i} = 1, \quad i = 1, 2; j = a, b \tag{3.10}$$

Secondly, by equations (3.8) it is obvious that

$$x_i^a = x_i^b = x_i = d_i^a = d_i^b = d_i, \quad i = 1, 2 \tag{3.11}$$

so that by the definition of e_i^j we will have

$$e_i^j = 0, \qquad i = 1, 2; j = a, b \tag{3.12}$$

Equation (3.12) tell us that there will be no interregional trade of commodities (more exactly no need for it) under the circumstance of twin regions. These conclusions are by no means of much interest to us, but they form a starting point of our analysis in the following sections.

Before going on, we now define symbols for the values of variables *after* the change:

$$\tilde{q}_1^a = q_1^a(\bar{k}^a) + \Delta q_1^a(\Delta \bar{k}^a) \tag{3.13}$$

$$\tilde{q}_1^b = \tilde{q}_1^b(\bar{k}^a) + \Delta q_1^b(\Delta \bar{k}^a) \tag{3.14}$$

$$\tilde{e}_1^a = e_1^a(\bar{k}^a) + \Delta e_1^a(\Delta \bar{k}^a) \tag{3.15}$$

$$\tilde{e}_1^b = \tilde{e}_1^b(\bar{k}^a) + \Delta_1^b(\Delta \bar{k}^a), \text{etc.} \tag{3.16}$$

$$\tilde{y}^a = y^a(\bar{k}^a) + \Delta y^a(\Delta \bar{k}^a) \tag{3.17}$$

$$\tilde{y}^b = y^b(\bar{k}^a) + \Delta y^a(\Delta \bar{k}^a) \tag{3.18}$$

$$\approx e_1^a = e_1^a(\alpha^a) + \Delta e_1^a(\Delta \alpha^a) \tag{3.19}$$

$$\tilde{\tilde{e}}_1^{b} = e_1^b(\alpha^a) + \Delta e_1^b(\Delta\alpha^b), \text{ etc.} \tag{3.20}$$

4. Effect of a change in factor endowment

Starting from the initial state of twin regions, now let us assume that only $\bar{k}^a$ increases marginally; by differentiation of both sides of equations (3.3) and (3.4), we have

$$(k_1 - k_2)\frac{d\lambda_1^a}{d\bar{k}^a} = 1 - \lambda_1^a \frac{dk_1}{d\bar{k}^a} - (1 - \lambda_1^a)\frac{dk_2}{d\bar{k}^a} \tag{4.1}$$

$$(k_1 - k_2)\frac{d\lambda_1^b}{d\bar{k}^a} = -\lambda_1^b \frac{dk_1}{d\bar{k}^a} - (1 - \lambda_1^b)\frac{dk_2}{d\bar{k}^a} \tag{4.2}$$

Since $\lambda_1^a = \lambda_1^b$ at the initial state, we can derive

$$\frac{d_1\ (\lambda_1^a - \lambda_1^b)}{d\bar{k}^a} = \frac{1}{k_1 - k_2} \tag{4.3}$$

from equations (4.1) and (4.2).

If we assume that always $k_1 > k_2$ on assumption 7 and without loss of generality, equation (4.3) implies that

$$\frac{d(\lambda_1^a - \lambda_1^b)}{d\bar{k}^a} > 0 \tag{4.4}$$

By the definition of location quotients, it is obvious that sign $(q_1^a - q_1^b)$ = sign $(\lambda_1^a - \lambda_1^b)$ and that it is impossible to have $(1 - q_1^a)(1 - q_1^b) > 0$ so that relations (3.10) and (4.4) mean that

$$\tilde{q}_1^a > 1 > \tilde{q}_1^b \tag{4.5}$$

after the change in $\bar{k}^a$. It is also clear that we have $\tilde{q}_2^a < 1 < \tilde{q}_2^b$. In words this means that if region *a* becomes relatively more capital-abundant than region *b*, region *a* will be more or less specialised in more capital-intensive industry 1 and it will have a more-than-unity location quotient for industry 1 and a less-than-unity location quotient for industry 2 under this specific circumstance.

On the other hand, the effect of a change in $\bar{k}^a$ on e_i^j is derived as follows; from equations (3.3) and (3.5) to (3.7) e_1^j is expressed as:

$$e_1^j = \lambda_1^j f_1(k_1) - d_1 \left\{ p_2, \lambda_1^j f_1(k_1) + p_2(1-\lambda_1^j) f_2(k_2), \alpha \right\} \tag{4.6}$$

$$j = a, b$$

By total differentiation of both sides of equation (4.6) with respect to $\bar{k}^a$, we have:

$$\frac{de_1^j}{d\bar{k}^a} = \frac{d\lambda_1^j}{d\bar{k}^a} f_1 + \lambda_1^j f_1' \frac{dk_1}{d\bar{k}^a} - \left(\frac{\partial d_1}{\partial p_2}\right)^j \frac{dp_2}{d\bar{k}^a}$$

$$- \frac{\partial d_1}{\partial y^j} \left\{ \frac{d\lambda_1^j}{d\bar{k}^a} f_1 + \lambda_1^j f_1' \frac{dk_1}{d\bar{k}^a} + \frac{dp_2}{d\bar{k}^a} (1 - \lambda_1^j) f_2 \right.$$

$$\left. - p_2 \frac{d\lambda_1^j}{d\bar{k}^a} f_2 - p_2 (1 - \lambda_1^j) f_2' \frac{dk_2}{d\bar{k}^a} \right\}, \quad j = a, b \tag{4.7}$$

At the initial state of $\bar{k}^a = \bar{k}^b$, we know that $\lambda_1^a = \lambda_1^b$, $\left(\frac{\partial d_1}{\partial p_2}\right)^a = \left(\frac{\partial d_1}{\partial p_2}\right)^b$ and $\left(\frac{\partial d_1}{\partial y^a}\right) = \left(\frac{\partial d_1}{\partial y_1^b}\right)$ therefore, the deduction of equation (4.7) for *b* from the same equation for *a* gives us:

$$\frac{d(e_1^a - e_1^b)}{d\bar{k}^a} = \left\{ f_1\left(1 - \frac{\partial d_1}{\partial y}\right) + p_2 f_2 \frac{\partial d_1}{\partial y} \quad \frac{d(\lambda_1^a - \lambda_1^b)}{d\bar{k}^a} \right\} \tag{4.8}$$

We can safely assume that neither of two commodities is an inferior commodity in consumption so that $0 < \frac{\partial d_1}{\partial y} < 1$. With this additional assumption and relation (4.4), it is obvious that:

$$\text{sign}\left\{\frac{d(e_1^a - e_1^b)}{d\bar{k}^a}\right\} = \text{sign}\left\{\frac{d(\lambda_1^a - \lambda_1^b)}{d\bar{k}^a}\right\} = \text{positive} \tag{4.9}$$

By a similar discussion as in the case of q_1^a and q_1^b, we can say that:

$$\tilde{e}_1^a > 0 > \tilde{e}_1^b \tag{4.10}$$

as well as $\tilde{e}_2^a < 0 < \tilde{e}_2^b$ after the change. In words, capital-abundant region *a* exports capital-intensive commodity 1 and this exactly corresponds to the more-than-unity location quotient for industry 1 in region *a* under this specific circumstance; the opposite situation emerges in labour-abundant region *b* and the situation in that region is easy to spell out.

It is important to notice that we have the following equation concomitantly in the process of deduction concerning equation (4.7):

$$\frac{d(y^a - y^b)}{d\bar{k}^a} = (f_1 - p_2 f_2)\frac{d(\lambda_1^a - \lambda_1^b)}{d\bar{k}^a}$$
$$= (k_1 - k_2) f_1' \frac{d(\lambda_1^a - \lambda_1^b)}{d\bar{k}^a} > 0 \tag{4.11}$$

using equations (3.1) and (3.2). Apparently, therefore, $\tilde{y}^a > \tilde{y}^b$ after the change in $\bar{k}^a$, i.e. capital-abundant region *a* will now have a larger amount of per capita (per unit of labour) income than labour-abundant region *b*.

In this section we have seen that, in a setting of twin regions as the starting point, if the export of commodity 1 from region *a* is initiated by a change of the factor-endowment ratio in the same region, this 'exportability' exactly corresponds to a more-than-unity location quotient of industry 1 in region *a*, as the 'exportability' of commodity 2 from region *b* does to more-than-unity location quotient of industry 2 in region *b*. By our analysis (particularly by relation (4.9)), it has been clarified that the value of the location quotient for an industry in a region and the exportability of the commodity produced by that industry for the same region do not have any *direct causal* relationship, but they are simultaneous outcomes of changes in the common exogenous factors which determine the interregional equilibrium. We will see, therefore, a different set of outcomes for a change in different causes.

5. Effect of a change in taste

Returning to the initial state of twin regions, we analyse the effect of a marginal change in α^a from its common value α with α^b. First of all we should recall that:

$$\frac{\partial d_1}{\partial \alpha^a} = -p_2 \frac{\partial d_2}{\partial \alpha^a} \tag{5.1}$$

as an outcome of consistent consumer behaviour because of an implicit relation of (3.9), and in addition we assume that $\frac{\partial d_1}{\partial \alpha^a} < 0$.
for all y and p_2

By a similar discussion as in the beginning of the previous section we have this time:

$$\frac{d(\lambda_1^a - \lambda_1^b)}{d\alpha^a} = 0 \tag{5.2}$$

i.e. λ_1^a and λ_1^b change in the same direction and in the same amount so that all location quotients will not change from the value of unity.

On the other hand, the effects of a change in α^a on e_1^j can be analysed in a similar manner as done in the previous section and the result will be:

$$\frac{d(e_1^a - e_1^b)}{d\alpha^a} = \left\{ f_1 \left(1 - \frac{\partial d_1}{\partial y}\right) + p_2 f_2 \frac{\partial d_1}{\partial y} \right\} \frac{d(\lambda_1^a - \lambda_1^b)}{d\alpha^a}$$

$$- \frac{\partial d_1}{\partial d^a} = - \frac{\partial d_1}{\partial \alpha^a} > 0 \tag{5.3}$$

Therefore we shall have $\tilde{\tilde{e}}_1^a > 0 > \tilde{\tilde{e}}_1^b$ as well as $\tilde{\tilde{e}}_2^a < 0 < \tilde{\tilde{e}}_2^b$ after the change, and there is no correspondence between the value of the location quotient and the exportability of a particular industry in a particular region. In addition y^a and y^b remain equal in this case although both of them may change in the same direction and to the same amount (since commodity 1 loses some of the demand for it by assumption, p_2 may rise and y^a and y^b in terms of commodity 1 may increase).

6. Interregional general equilibrium for specific functions

Our analysis in the previous three sections was heavily dependent on the initial setting of twin regions; if instead we have different values of $\bar{k}^a$ and $\bar{k}^b$ the comparative-statics calculation becomes formidable even if we assume completely identical per capita demand functions in the two regions. Because of this difficulty, we introduce specific functional forms regarding production functions and demand functions to analyse a more general case of non-twin regions.

As for the production side, we introduce fixed input coefficients instead of the flexible production functions in assumption 7; m_i is the capital input coefficient and n_i is the labour input coefficient for industry i. The capital–labour ratio of each industry becomes a fixed coefficient in this case, i.e.:

$$k_i = \frac{m_i}{n_i}, \quad i = 1, 2 \tag{6.1}$$

and we again assume that:

$$k_1 > k_2 \tag{6.2}$$

without loss of generality.

As for the demand functions, we basically assume a log-linear utility function with allocation coefficients α and $(1 - \alpha)$ for commodities 1 and 2.

Now instead of equations (3.1) and (3.2), we have:

$$rm_1 + wn_1 = 1 \tag{6.3}$$

$$rm_2 + wn_2 = p_2 \tag{6.4}$$

in which r and w are rent and wage in terms of commodity 1 respectively. Solutions for r and w are:

$$r = s(n_2 - n_1 p_2) \tag{6.5}$$

$$w = s(m_1 p_2 - m_2) \tag{6.6}$$

in which $s = (m_1 n_2 - m_2 n_1)^{-1} > 0$. We need special conditions regarding k_1 and k_2, and the national factor endowment ratio, $\bar{k}$, to assure non-negativity of r and w. We shall come back to this point later.

By equations (3.3) and (3.4), we have the following solutions for λ_i^j which are independent from p_2 in this case:

$$\lambda_1^j = \frac{\bar{k}^j - k_2}{k_1 - k_2} \quad , \quad j = a \ , \ b \tag{6.7}$$

$$\lambda_2^j = \frac{k_1 - \bar{k}^j}{k_1 - k_2} \quad , \quad j = a \ , \ b \tag{6.8}$$

Here we assume $k_1 > \bar{k}^j > k_2$ for both regions. Solutions to x_i^j, y^j, and d_i^j are straightforwardly calculated by equations (3.5), (3.6) and (3.7) with the additional assumption of this section.

$$x_1^j = \frac{1}{n_1} \left(\frac{\bar{k}^j - k_2}{k_1 - k_2}\right) \ , \ j = a \ , \ b \tag{6.9}$$

$$x_2^j = \frac{1}{n_2} \left(\frac{k_1 - \bar{k}^j}{k_1 - k_2}\right) \ , \ j = a \ , \ b \tag{6.10}$$

$$y^j = \frac{1}{k_1 - k_2} \left\{ \frac{1}{n_1} (\bar{k}^j - k_2) + \frac{1}{n_2} (k_1 - \bar{k}^j) \ p_2 \right\} \ , \ j = a \ , \ b \tag{6.11}$$

$$d_1^j = \alpha \ y^j, \qquad j = a \ , \ b \tag{6.12}$$

$$d_2^j = \frac{(1 - \alpha) \ y^j}{p_2} \ , \qquad j = a \ , \ b \tag{6.13}$$

We are now in a position to carry out the calculation of equation (3.8) to obtain an explicit solution for p_2; the solution becomes surprisingly simple as:

$$p_2 = \frac{1 - \alpha}{\alpha} \ \frac{n_2}{n_1} \ \frac{\bar{k} - k_2}{k_1 - \bar{k}} \tag{6.14}$$

in which $\bar{k}$ is the national factor endowment ratio defined by

$$\bar{k} = \bar{n}^a \ \bar{k}^a + \bar{n}^b \bar{k}^b \tag{6.15}$$

Equation (6.14) implies that the relative price of commodities is independent from the interregional allocation of factors in this model. $\bar{k}$ is also defined as a doubly weighted average of k_1 and k_2 so that we can safely say that $k_1 - \bar{k} > 0$ and $\bar{k} - k_2 > 0$. [1]

Coming back to (6.5) and (6.6), we need:

$$\alpha k_1 + (1 - \alpha) k_2 > \bar{k} \tag{6.16}$$

for the non-negativity of r, and:

$$\frac{\alpha}{k_1} + \frac{1-\alpha}{k_2} > \frac{1}{\bar{k}} \tag{6.17}$$

for that of w. These rather delicate conditions are met, for the set $k_1 = 5, k_2 = 2, \bar{k} = 4$, and $\alpha = 0.8$.

Substituting equation (6.14) into equations (6.11) and (6.12), we finally obtain:

$$e_1^a = x_1^a - d_1^a = \frac{1-\alpha}{n_1} \quad \frac{\bar{k}^a - \bar{k}}{k_1 - \bar{k}} \tag{6.18}$$

which is comparable with

$$\lambda_1^a - \lambda_1^b = \frac{\bar{k}^a - \bar{k}^b}{k_1 - k_2} \tag{6.19}$$

Considering equations (6.18) and (6.19) under the condition of $\bar{k}^a > \bar{k}^b$ for instance, we reach a conclusion that exportability of commodity 1 in region *a* exactly corresponds to the more-than-unity value of the location quotient for industry 1 in the same region for the model of this section. We can say, almost in general, that location quotients may be taken as the indicators of exportability if the latter reflects the difference in factor endowment ratios between two regions.

As an additional proposition, we have

$$y^a - y^b = \frac{\bar{k}^a - \bar{k}^b}{\alpha n_1 (k_1 - k_2)(k_1 - \bar{k})} [\{ \alpha k_1 + (1 - \alpha) k_2 \} - \bar{k}] > 0 \tag{6.20}$$

if $\bar{k}^a > \bar{k}^b$ and condition (6.16) is met; again we find that the difference in per capita incomes between the two regions corresponds to the difference in factor endowment ratios.

7. Shift-share analysis

So far we have assumed that $\bar{n}^j$ and $\bar{k}^j$ are fixed exogenous variables (or parameters). The labour force, however, has an incentive to move interregionally in the long run because the levels of per capita income are not equal among regions. Of course we are assuming here that all of the produced income in a region is distributed *within* the same region and therefore there is no transfer of incomes between the two regions. If there is an interregional movement of labour force, it implies changes in the amounts of employment of the respective industries in the respective regions, and that is certainly a situation which shift-share analysis is eager to deal with.

In this section we attempt to formulate a shift-share analysis on the basis of the non-twin-regions model developed in the previous section. For that purpose, we first introduce some absolute-level variables with related assumptions:

1 $\bar{K}^j$ = capital endowment in region j which is fixed, $j = a,b$

2 N_i^j = employment in industry i in region j which is changeable in the long run, $i = 1, 2; j = a, b$

3 $N = \sum_i \sum_j N_i^j$ = total amount of employment in the nation (fixed)

4 $N_i = \sum_j N_i^j$ = total employment in industry i, $i = 1, 2$

5 $N^j = \sum_i N_i^j$ = total employment in region j, $j = a, b$

We also define a general symbol for the instantaneous growth rate of a variable X as:

6 $X^* = \dfrac{dX}{dt} / X$

Now let us assume that at a short run equilibrium described in the previous section we observe $\bar{n}^{a*} > 0$ up to the next short run equilibrium, because $y^a > y^b$ owing to $\bar{k}^a > \bar{k}^b$. According to the new assumptions 1 and 3 (actually capital has no incentive to move because there is no interregional difference in rents), $\bar{k}^a$ and $\bar{n}^a$ are in a reciprocal relation so that we can show that:

$$\bar{k}^a{}_* = -\bar{n}^a{}_* \tag{7.1}$$

On the other hand, by equations (3.3) and (3.4) which were also used for the model in the previous section we have:

$$\lambda_1^{a}* = \left(\frac{\bar{k}^a}{\bar{k}^a - k_2}\right) \bar{k}^{a}* \tag{7.2}$$

$$\lambda_2^{a}* = \left(-\frac{\bar{k}^a}{k_1 - \bar{k}^a}\right) \bar{k}^{a*} \tag{7.3}$$

Since $N_1^a = \lambda_1^a \bar{n}^a N$, using (7.1), (7.2) and (7.3) with the new assumption 3, we finally have the following growth (or decline) formula:

$$N_1^{a}* = -\frac{k_2}{\bar{k}^a - k_2} \bar{n}^{a}* \tag{7.4}$$

$$N_2^{a}* = \frac{k_1}{k_1 - \bar{k}^a} \bar{n}^{a}* \tag{7.5}$$

Symmetrically we have

$$N_1^{b}* = \left(\frac{k_2}{\bar{k}^b - k_2}\right) \frac{\bar{n}^a}{\bar{n}^b} \bar{n}^{a}* \tag{7.6}$$

$$N_2^{b}* = -\left(\frac{k_1}{k_1 - \bar{k}^b}\right) \frac{\bar{n}^a}{\bar{n}^b} \bar{n}^{a}* \tag{7.7}$$

for region *b*, and from these four equations finally we see that:

$$N_i* = 0, \qquad i = 1, 2 \tag{7.8}$$

implying that there will be no change in employment in each industry as a whole; there will be just an across-the-border-type movement of labour from industry 2 in region *b* to the same industry in region *a* and some inter-industry reshuffle of employment within each region.

A shift-share decomposition of regional employment growth is something like: 145

$$\begin{aligned} &\text{– shift factor –} \\ N^{j*} = &\left\{ \sum_i \lambda_i^j \left(N_i^{j*} - N_i^*\right) \right\} \\ &\text{– share factor –} \\ &+ \left\{ \sum_i \lambda_i^j N_i^* \right\}, \qquad j = a, b \end{aligned} \tag{7.9}$$

In our case equation (7.9) takes a very special form of:

$$N^{a*} = \left\{ \frac{\bar{k}^a - k_2}{k_1 - k_2} \left(- \frac{k_2}{\bar{k}^a - k_2} \bar{n}^{a*} \right) + \frac{k_1 - \bar{k}^a}{k_1 - k_2} \left(\frac{k_1}{k_1 - \bar{k}^a} \bar{n}^{a*} \right) \right\} \tag{7.10}$$

$$+ \left\{ 0 + 0 \right\} = \bar{n}^{a*}$$

for region *a*. Apparently the share factor is zero and the shift factor is composed of a negative and a positive element which together produce positive growth of total employment in region *a*.

In this section we have examined consequences of the labour force movement from region *b* to region *a* caused by the difference in per capita income between the two regions, and we have achieved a shift-share expression of interrelated changes. It is important to see that there are specific internal relationships among the different industrial elements that construct the shift factor. By the labour-force movement which initiates the shift-share changes, the factor-endowment ratios of the two regions, $\bar{k}^a$ and $\bar{k}^b$, will ultimately be converged to a common value $\bar{k}$ and the twin-region model emerges again.

8. Conclusion

In this chapter, we first examined the relationship between the exportability of a specific industry in a region and the value of the location quotient of an industry in a given region using a two-region, two-industry neoclassical model in a special setting of initially twin regions. We have found that the existence or non-existence of exact correspondence between the two characteristics (exportability and location quotient) depends on what causes initiated interregional trade.

In the section 'Interregional general equilibrium for specific functions' we formulated an operational general equilibrium model with specific forms of production and demand functions but in a more general setting of non-twin regions. For this model we have established unambiguous relationships among exportability, location quotients, regional factor endowment ratios, and interregional differentials in per capita incomes. Finally in the previous section we explored a relation between our preceding analysis and so-called shift-share analysis and established a theoretically informative expression of the latter.

In the light of our analysis in the earlier sections the conclusions which were reached by Mayer and Pleeter in 1975 can be considered generally correct for their three-industry two-region model in spite of a conceptual difficulty in their analysis. This means that the mathematical operations in their paper must be interpreted differently from their own interpretation with some additional mathematical rigour. Reformulation of a three-industry two-region model in that direction and some further study of comparative statics (concerning the behaviour of the relative price, for example) on our own model may be our next task.

Note

1 For a general case where region b has allocation coefficients β and $(1-\beta)$ distinct from region a, however, (6.14) changes into

$$p_2 = \frac{n_2}{n_1}\left\{\frac{(1-\alpha)(\bar{k}-k_2) + (\alpha-\beta)\,\bar{n}^b\,(\bar{k}^b - k_2)}{\alpha\,(k_1 - \bar{k}) + (\beta-\alpha)\,\bar{n}^b\,(k_1 - \bar{k}^b)}\right\} \qquad (6.14)$$

which is dependent on the interregional allocation of factors.

References

Mayer, Wolfgang and Pleeter, Saul (1975), A Theoretical Justification for the Use of Location Quotients, *Regional Science and Urban Economics*, vol. 5, pp.343–55.

Sakashita, N. (1973), An Axiomatic Approach to Shift-and-Share Analysis, *Regional and Urban Economics*, vol. 3, no. 3, pp.263–72.

[11]

Journal of Regional Science, Arizona, Vol. 27 (1987) 1–12

OPTIMUM LOCATION OF PUBLIC FACILITIES UNDER THE INFLUENCE OF THE LAND MARKET*

Noboru Sakashita†

ABSTRACT. This paper discusses the problem of the optimal location of public facility(ies) in a long narrow city, especially taking into consideration the externality-internalizing effect of the land market. It shows a systematic approach to dealing with the land market mechanism in first a one-facility and then a two-facility case. The analysis assures the importance of posing the location-optimizing problem even under the influence of the land market.

1. INTRODUCTION

Let us suppose a very narrow rectangular city of length D in the sense that the width of the city is negligible in contrast with D for analytical purposes, as in the famous Solow and Vickrey (1971) model. The local authority is now planning the construction of a new public facility such as a public hospital or a fire station within the city. The extent of benefit which a resident of the city receives from this facility usually depends on the distance between the location of the facility and that of his(her) residence, that is, on his(her) accessibility to the facility.

This sort of spatial character of the externality which emerges from public facilities was systematically analyzed by Feldman (1974) and Jurion (1983). However, there is a strong argument for the countervailing power of the land market which reequilibrates the welfare distribution among the residents of the city. In other words, the rent profile within a city will reflect the spatial distribution of the externality very quickly and will make the welfare of any resident indifferent to the location of the facility. We may call this function of the land market its externality-internalizing effect. See Walter (1974).

The purpose of this paper is to discuss the observation that the aforementioned externality-internalizing effect of the land market does not make the selection of the optimal public facility location meaningless and that, on the

*After being presented at the Fifteenth European Congress of the Regional Science Association at Budapest in August 1975, this paper has been hidden in a drawer of my desk for more than eight years. Perhaps I wished to generalize the analysis in various directions and then forgot it because of my interests in other subjects. Now I decided to expect such generalizations to be done by other young and more productive scholars and to submit the paper to this journal as is. Concerning this decision I owe thanks to Professor Masahisa Fujita of the University of Pennsylvania. Although the paper itself is not revised from its original version, the reference list on the subjects of linear city models and of the locational problem of public facilities has been brought up to date. This work of updating was, however, mainly done by Professor Fujita and Professor Komei Sasaki of Tohoku University. I wish to thank them very much for their efforts. I also wish to thank the editors of this journal for their kind treatment of the present paper.

†Professor of Economics, Institute of Socio-Economic Planning, University of Tsukuba, Japan.

Received February, 1984; accepted March, 1984; received in revised form June, 1984 and October, 1986.

contrary, we need delicate consideration of the conditions which determine the optimal location under the influence of the land market. In the following section, we present the general setting of our model. In Section 3, the basic methodology of our analysis will be given. The simplest one-facility case will be discussed in Sections 4 and 5. The final section will be devoted to the two-facilities case with an agglomeration effect, and some tentative conclusions will follow.

2. ASSUMPTIONS

(i) As indicated at the outset of the paper, we assume a long narrow city the width of which is negligible when we measure the distance between two points in the city. In short we assume a "linear" city. The length of the city is denoted as D.

(ii) The distribution of population within the city is already given as a uniform one.

(iii) Each resident of the city has the same monetary income y before paying the land rent which depends on the location of his(her) residence.

(iv) Each resident also has the same utility function which has the following two arguments: (a) the monetary income after paying the land rent $r(x)$ in which x is a variable indicating the resident's location, (b) the external-economy-like benefit which the resident receives from the public facility(ies) $z(x)$ also depending on his(her) residential location.

(v) The size of benefit which a resident receives from a public facility depends on the distance between the location of the facility (x_0) and that of his(her) residence (x). Therefore we can express it as $z(x) = z_0 - \gamma \mid x - x_0 \mid$, where $\gamma > 0$.

(vi) The housing space available in this city is redundant relative to its population so that the minimum land rent within the city is zero.

By Assumptions (iii), (iv), and (v), the (indirect) utility function of a citizen in our model can be expressed as

$$u = u[y - r(x), z_0 - \gamma \mid x - x_0 \mid] \tag{1}$$

3. BASIC PROCEDURE OF OPTIMIZATION

An important conclusion which is derived from Assumptions (iii) and (iv) is that the utility function of each resident described by (1) takes the same level regardless of his(her) residential location, that is

$$u[y - r(x), z_0 - \gamma \mid x - x_0 \mid] = \overline{u} \tag{2}$$

for any relevant x. We can then reduce the rent profile within the city which realizes (2) with an unknown constant c that reflects $\overline{u}$:

$$r = r^*[x, x_0, c(\overline{u})] \tag{3}$$

Under the usual assumption of an increasing and concave utility function, it is easy to show that r^* is a decreasing and convex function of the distance $\mid x - x_0 \mid$. Therefore, the zero rent of Assumption (vi) realizes itself at the farthest place from x_0. Denoting this place by $\hat{x}$, the unknown constant $c(\overline{u})$ is determined by the relation

$$0 = r^*[\hat{x}, x_0, c(\overline{u})] \tag{4}$$

and the form of r^* is completely determined by (3) and (4). Replacing $r(x)$ in (2) by (3), we can determine the realized utility function as a function of y and x_0:

$$\begin{aligned} \hat{u} &= u[y - r^*(x, x_0), z_0 - \gamma | x - x_0 |] \\ &= \phi(y, x_0) \end{aligned} \tag{5}$$

The final step of the optimization is to maximize $\phi(y, x_0)$ with respect to x_0 in order to find the optimal location of the public facility. However, we should not expect an interior maximum of ϕ in general because it is fairly probable that ϕ is not a well-behaved function of x_0.

4. ONE-FACILITY CASE—A COLUMBUS' EGG

Let us assume the following utility function as an example of (1):

$$u = \log [y - r(x)] + \beta[z_0 - \gamma(x - x_0)] \qquad (x_0 \leqq x \leqq D) \tag{6}$$

taking the case of one public facility. Since the left-hand side of x_0 where the facility is located is a mirror image of its right-hand side, we can concentrate our attention on the latter (see Figure 1).

From (6) we can deduce the rent profile within the city as

$$r^*(x) = y - Ae^{\beta\gamma x} \qquad (x_0 \leqq x \leqq D) \tag{7}$$

in which A is a constant that reflects the common utility level $\bar{u}$. We may treat the subcases (I) $x_0 \leqq D/2$ and (II) $x_0 > D/2$ since the farthest place from x_0 is different according to each subcase.

(I) If $x_0 \leqq D/2$, then the farthest place is $x = D$. Therefore, Assumption (vi) enables us to calculate A by

$$r^*(D) = y - Ae^{\beta\gamma D} = 0 \rightarrow A = ye^{-\beta\gamma D} \tag{8}$$

and we have the solution of $r^*(x)$ as

$$r^*(x) = y[1 - e^{\beta\gamma(x-D)}] \qquad (x_0 \leqq x \leqq D) \tag{9}$$

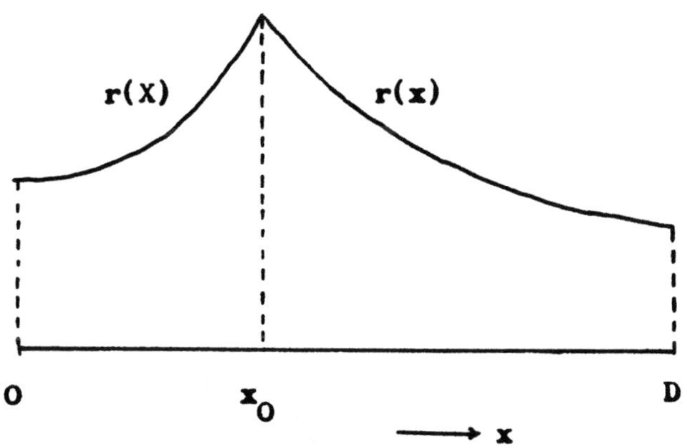

FIGURE 1: One-Facility Case.

The realized utility in this subcase is

$$\begin{aligned}\hat{u}(x_0) &= \log y + \beta\gamma(x - D) + \beta[z_0 - \gamma(x - x_0)] \\ &= \log y + \beta\gamma(x_0 - D) + \beta z_0\end{aligned} \tag{10}$$

(II) If $x_0 > D/2$, then the farthest place is $x = 0$ on the left-hand side of x_0 and the mirror image of $x = 0$ on the right-hand side is $x = 2x_0$ beyond the border of the city. Therefore, A can be calculated by

$$r^*(2x_0) = y - Ae^{2\beta\gamma x_0} = 0 \rightarrow A = ye^{-2\beta\gamma x_0} \tag{11}$$

and $r^*(x)$ becomes

$$r^*(x) = y[1 - e^{\beta\gamma(x-2x_0)}] \qquad (x_0 \leqq x \leqq D) \tag{12}$$

The realized utility is now

$$\begin{aligned}\hat{u}(x_0) &= \log y + \beta\gamma(x - 2x_0) + \beta[z_0 - \gamma(x - x_0)] \\ &= \log y - \beta\gamma x_0 + \beta z_0\end{aligned} \tag{13}$$

Combining (10) and (13), we can visualize the behavior of the realized utility as a function of x_0, i.e., location of the public facility, as is shown in Figure 2.

The final conclusion for the one-facility case is made very clear by this diagram. The optimal location of the facility is

$$x_0^* = \frac{1}{2}D \tag{14}$$

i.e., the middle point of the city. This conclusion is intuitively so clear that one may take it as self-evident without any analysis. The optimal location of the public facility(ies) is, however, not so self-evident for slightly more general cases, and we need more complicated analyses to solve these cases. The present one-facility case is only a starting point for such analyses. In this sense, the present case is nothing but a tiny Columbus' egg.

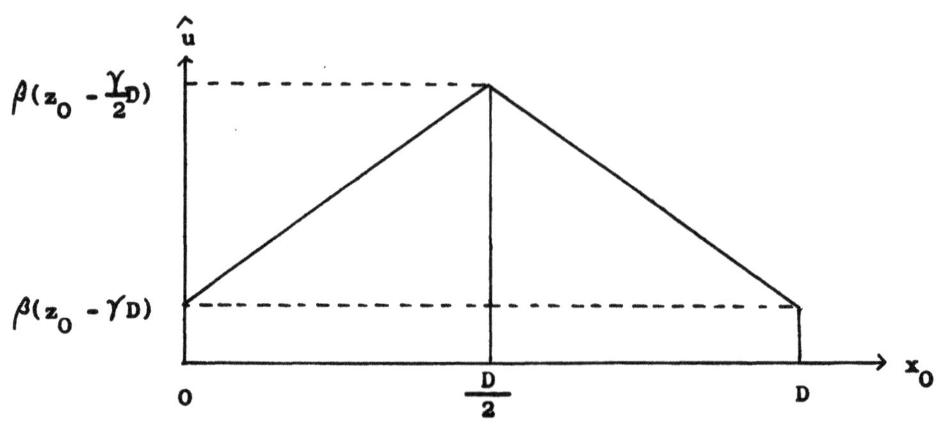

FIGURE 2: Realized Utility as a Function of x_0.

5. SOME DISCUSSION OF THE ONE-FACILITY CASE

Even a Columbus' egg needs some additional discussion before being cooked. Firstly, let us discuss a kind of total condition in the sense of Hicks (1939) concerning the introduction of the facility itself into the city. For the optimal solution of (14), the realized utility level is

$$\hat{u}(x_0^*) = \log y + \beta\left(z_0 - \frac{\gamma}{2}D\right) \tag{15}$$

It is clear by (15) that the introduction of the facility can obtain a consensus of all citizens only when $z_0 - \gamma(D/2) > 0$, i.e., it brings forth some positive utility at the farthest place from its optimal location. If not, the initial state of no facility and no rent will be maintained. This is another very plausible conclusion.

Secondly, let us consider the total rent revenue within the city with an additional simplifying assumption of unit population density, i.e., we observe one household within a unit distance $\Delta x = 1$. The rent profile associated with the optimal solution is

$$r^*(x) = \begin{cases} y(1 - e^{-\beta\gamma x}) & \text{for } 0 \leqq x \leqq \frac{1}{2}D \\ y[1 - e^{\beta\gamma(x-D)}] & \text{for } \frac{1}{2}D < x \leqq D \end{cases} \tag{16}$$

so that the total rent revenue in the city is calculated as

$$\begin{aligned} R(x_0^*) &= 2\int_0^{1/2D} y(1 - e^{-\beta\gamma x})dx \\ &= y\left[D - \frac{2}{\beta\gamma}(1 - e^{-(1/2)\beta\gamma D})\right] \end{aligned} \tag{17}$$

The rent revenue $R(x_0^*)$ may be used to cover the current expenses of the public facility, but there is no guarantee that the revenue covers the expenses completely. If there is any deficit, it must be financed by, say, a poll tax imposed on each resident. In this case the total condition must be explained by comparing

$$\hat{u}(x_0^*) = \log(y - t) + \beta\left(z_0 - \frac{\gamma}{2}D\right) \tag{18}$$

in which t is the level of poll tax, with $u = \log y$, instead of considering (15).

Thirdly, the rent revenue for a general (nonoptimal) case can be calculated as

$$\begin{aligned} R(x_0) &= \int_{x_0}^{D} y[1 - e^{\beta\gamma(x-D)}]dx + \int_{x_0}^{2x_0} y[1 - e^{\beta\gamma(x-D)}]dx \\ &= y\left\{D - \frac{1}{\beta\gamma}[1 + e^{\beta\gamma(2x_0-D)} - 2e^{\beta\gamma(x_0-D)}]\right\} \end{aligned} \tag{19}$$

for x_0 between 0 and $1/2D$. It is easily seen by (19) that $dR/dx_0 < 0$ and $d^2R/dx_0^2 < 0$ for $0 \leqq x_0 \leqq 1/2D$. The rent revenue function is depicted in Figure 3 and we can see

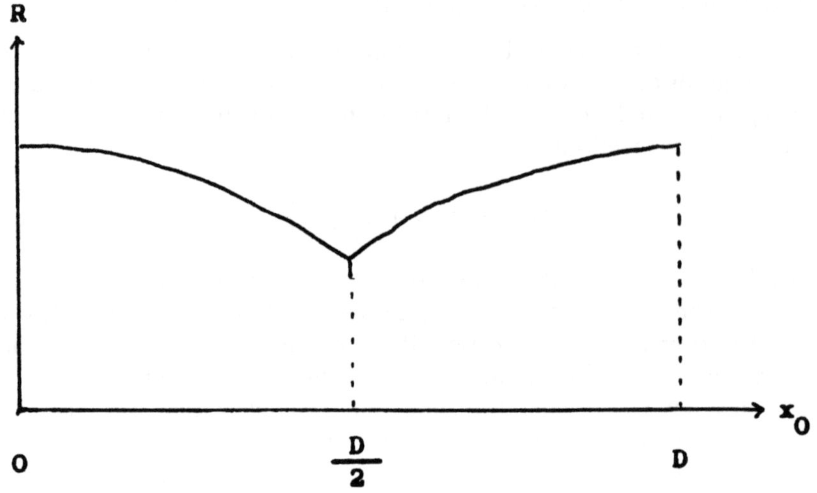

FIGURE 3: Rent Revenue as a Function of x_0.

that it is maximized at an endpoint $x_0 = 0$ or $x_0 = D$. If the current cost of the facility is financed by the rent revenue, there might be a strong incentive for the local government to locate the facility at the place where the revenue is maximized.[1] This decision is, however, contradictory to the welfare maximum location of the middle point. Therefore, the residents of the city must be very cautious in watching the behavior of the local authority.

Finally, let us suppose for a moment that β in (6) is negative. This is the case of a facility such as a garbage collection unit, which gives negative externality to the residents. All the arguments proceed as in Section 4 except having a V-shaped curve instead of the curve in Figure 2. Therefore, the endpoint location is desirable in this case, and it is a very reasonable solution too.

6. TWO-FACILITIES CASE

In this section, we assume that the construction of two similar facilities is possible and that the uniform utility function of the resident is expressed as

$$(20)\quad u = \log\,[y - r(x)] + \beta\{z_0 - \gamma[\mathrm{Min}\,(|\,x - x_1\,|, |\,x - x_2|)]\} - \delta(x_1 - x_2)^2$$

in which x_1 and x_2 represent the locations of the two facilities and the third term expresses an agglomeration effect that the two facilities produce by their mutual accessibility. This kind of agglomeration effect is easily seen, particularly in the case of hospitals, police stations, or information centers.

As a simplifying assumption, we postulate that

$$\text{(vii)}\qquad \beta\gamma < 2\delta D.$$

The meaning of this assumption becomes clear later.

[1]This sort of solution is fairly possible in practice for a private developer who wishes to obtain maximum profit from the land or housing rent.

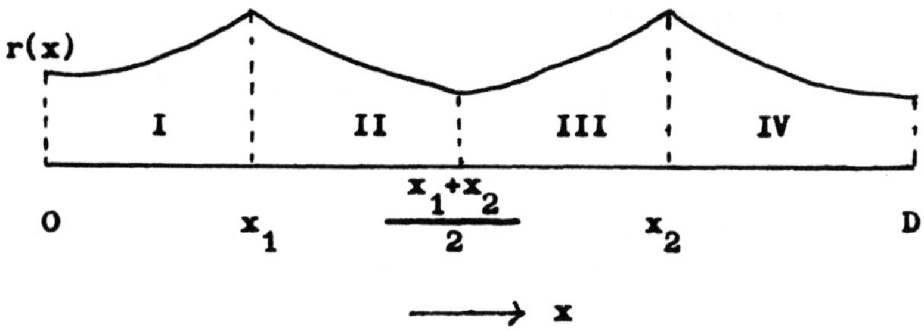

FIGURE 4: Regions within City and Rent Profile.

This two-facilities case is much more complicated than the previous one-facility case, so that we must be very systematic in its treatment. For fixed location points of the facilities, x_1 and x_2, the city area will be divided into four regions from the viewpoint of the rent profile, as shown in Figure 4.

In each region the following utility function is realized

$$\text{(21)}\quad \begin{aligned} &\text{I. } \hat{u} = \log[y - r(x)] + \beta[z_0 - \gamma(x_1 - x)] - \delta(x_1 - x_2)^2 \\ &\text{II. } \hat{u} = \log[y - r(x)] + \beta[z_0 - \gamma(x - x_1)] - \delta(x_1 - x_2)^2 \\ &\text{III. } \hat{u} = \log[y - r(x)] + \beta[z_0 - \gamma(x_2 - x)] - \delta(x_1 - x_2)^2 \\ &\text{IV. } \hat{u} = \log[y - r(x)] + \beta[z_0 - \gamma(x - x_2)] - \delta(x_1 - x_2)^2 \end{aligned}$$

and resulting rent profiles are

$$\text{(22)}\quad \begin{aligned} &\text{I. } r = y - A_I e^{-\beta\gamma x} && (0 \leqq x \leqq x_1) \\ &\text{II. } r = y - A_{II} e^{\beta\gamma x} && \left(x_1 < x \leqq \frac{x_1 + x_2}{2}\right) \\ &\text{III. } r = y - A_{III} e^{-\beta\gamma x} && \left(\frac{x_1 + x_2}{2} < x \leqq x_2\right) \\ &\text{IV. } r = y - A_{IV} e^{\beta\gamma x} && (x_2 < x \leqq D) \end{aligned}$$

with unknown constants $A_I, \ldots, A_{IV}$.

If we denote the rent at $x = 0$ as $r(0) = r_0$, the four functions in (22) are expressed as follows:

$$\text{(23)}\quad \begin{aligned} &\text{I. } r = y - (y - r_0)e^{-\beta\gamma x} \\ &\text{II. } r = y - (y - r_0)e^{-\beta\gamma(2x_1 - x)} \\ &\text{III. } r = y - (y - r_0)e^{-\beta\gamma(x_1 - x_2 + x)} \\ &\text{IV. } r = y - (y - r_0)e^{-\beta\gamma(x_1 + x_2 - x)} \end{aligned}$$

Our next step is to find the minimal rent point in view of Assumption (vi) in Section 1. We have three candidates for the minimal rent point, $x = 0$, $x = (x_1 + x_2)/2$, and $x = D$, and corresponding rents are

$$r = r_0 \text{ at } x = 0$$

(24)
$$r = r_m = y - (y - r_0)e^{-(\beta\gamma/2)(3x_1 - x_2)} \text{ at } x = \frac{x_1 + x_2}{2}$$

$$r = r_d = y - (y - r_0)e^{-\beta\gamma(x_1 + x_2 - D)} \text{ at } x = D$$

Therefore, we should find the minimum of (r_0, r_m, r_d) for every set of (x_1, x_2) in which $0 \leqq x_1 \leqq x_2 \leqq D$. Apparently there is the following correspondence:

(25)
$$\text{Min}\,(r_0, r_m, r_d) \Longrightarrow \text{Max}\,(y - r_0, y - r_m, y - r_d)$$
$$\Longrightarrow \text{Min}\left[0, \frac{\beta\gamma}{2}(3x_1 - x_2), \beta\gamma(x_1 + x_2 - D)\right]$$

and we can visualize positive and negative areas of the following three equations on the half plane of $\{x_1, x_2 \mid 0 \leqq x_1 \leqq x_2 \leqq D\}$:

(26)
$$\text{(a)}\quad 3x_1 - x_2 = 0$$
$$\text{(b)}\quad x_1 + x_2 - D = 0$$
$$\text{(c)}\quad \frac{\beta\gamma}{2}(3x_1 - x_2) - [\beta\gamma(x_1 + x_2 - D)] = 0$$

The relevant half plane is divided into three areas by Equations (a), (b), and (c) of (26) as shown in Figure 5.[2] Area M is in the negative area of (a) and (c) so that r_m takes the minimal value of (r_0, r_m, r_d) in this area. Area D is in the positive area of (c) and in the negative area of (b) so that r_d is the minimum. Finally, Area O is in the positive areas of (a) and (b) so that r_0 is the minimum.

In Area O we have the realized utility function

(27)
$$\hat{u} = \log y + \beta(z_0 - \gamma x_1) - \delta(x_1 - x_2)^2$$

because $r_0 = 0$, and the first derivatives are

(28)
$$\frac{\partial \hat{u}}{\partial x_1} = -\beta\gamma - 2\delta(x_1 - x_2)$$

(29)
$$\frac{\partial \hat{u}}{\partial x_2} = 2\delta(x_1 - x_2) \qquad (\leqq 0 \text{ for } x_1 \leqq x_2)$$

By (29) it is clear that the maximum $\hat{u}$ of (27) is attained on $\overline{EF}$ or on $\overline{FH}$. On $\overline{FH}$ it is obvious that $d\hat{u}/dx_1 < 0$, but on $\overline{EF}$ (27) becomes

(27′)
$$\hat{u} = \log y + \beta(z_0 - \gamma x_1) - \delta(2x_1 - D)^2$$

and it attains an interior maximum at $x_1 = (4\delta D - \beta\gamma)/8\delta$ that is bigger than $D/4$ by Assumption (vii). The corresponding value of x_2 is $x_2 = (4\delta D + \beta\gamma)/8\delta$ and the realized maximal utility level is

(30)
$$\hat{u}_0^* = \log y + \beta\left(z_0 - \frac{\gamma D}{2}\right) + \frac{\beta^2\gamma^2}{16\delta}$$

[2]There is no loss of generality in assuming $x_2 \geqq x_1$.

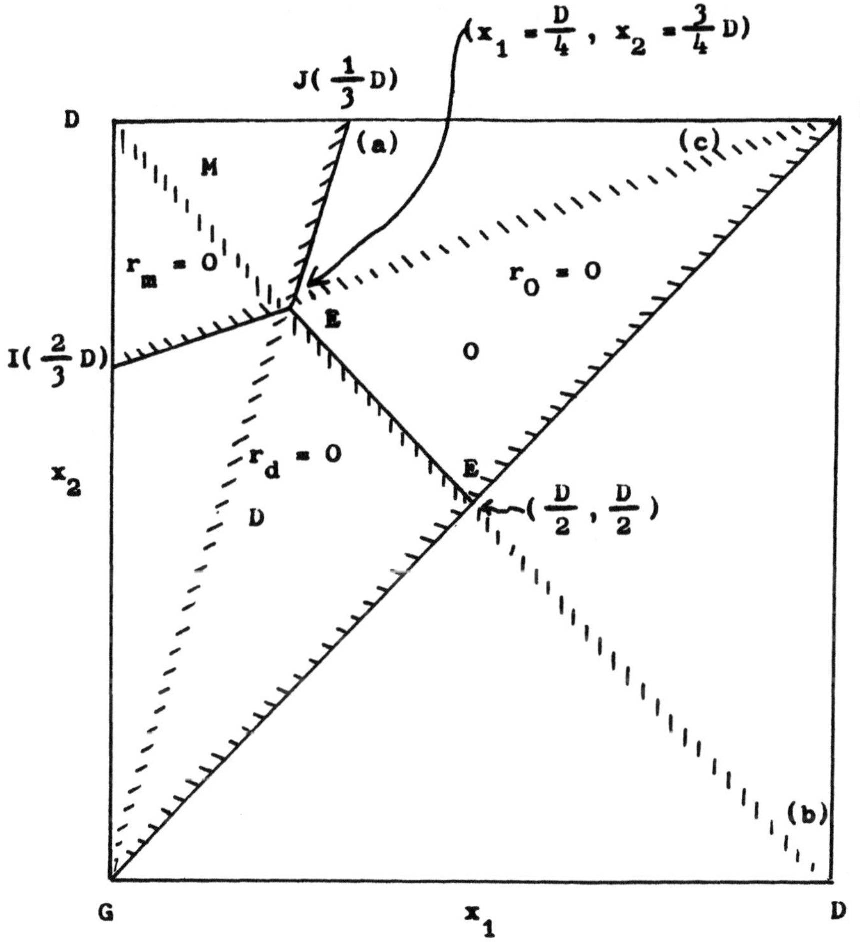

FIGURE 5: Areas on the x_1-x_2 Plane.

In Area D, the realized utility function is

(31) $$\hat{u} = \log y + \beta\gamma(x_1 + x_2 - D) + \beta(z_0 - \gamma x_1) - \delta(x_1 - x_2)^2$$

because $r_d = 0$ so that $y - r_0 = ye^{\beta\gamma(x_1+x_2-D)}$. The first derivatives are

(32) $$\frac{\partial\hat{u}}{\partial x_1} = -2\delta(x_1 - x_2) \qquad (\geqq 0 \text{ for } x_1 \leqq x_2)$$

(33) $$\frac{\partial\hat{u}}{\partial x_2} = \beta\gamma + 2\delta(x_1 - x_2)$$

and we have the maximum $\hat{u}$ of (31) on $\overline{EF}$ or on $\overline{GF}$. On $\overline{GF}$ it is clear that $d\hat{u}/dx_1 > 0$, but on $\overline{EF}$ (31) becomes the same as (27′) and has the same interior maximum as (30) with $[x_1 = (4\delta D - \beta\gamma)/8\delta,\ x_2 = (4\delta D + \beta\gamma)/8\delta]$.

Finally, in Area M, $r_m = 0$; then $r_0 = y[1 - e^{(\beta\gamma/2)(3x_1 - x_2)}]$ and the realized unity function is

(34) $$\hat{u} = \log y + \frac{\beta\gamma}{2}(3x_1 - x_2) + \beta(z_0 - \gamma x_1) - \delta(x_1 - x_2)^2$$

The first derivatives are

(35) $$\frac{\partial \hat{u}}{\partial x_1} = \frac{\beta\gamma}{2} - 2\delta(x_1 - x_2) \qquad (>0 \text{ for } x_1 \leqq x_2)$$

(36) $$\frac{\partial \hat{u}}{\partial x_2} = -\frac{\beta\gamma}{2} + 2\delta(x_1 - x_2) \qquad (<0 \text{ for } x_1 \leqq x_2)$$

and we have the maximum of $\hat{u}$ of (34) on $\overline{IE}$ or on $\overline{EJ}$. It is clear that $d\hat{u}/dx_1 < 0$ on $\overline{EJ}$ but $d\hat{u}/dx_1 > 0$ on $\overline{IE}$ by (26). Therefore, the maximum of (34) is attained at the intersection of (a) and (c), i.e. ($x_1 = D/4$, $x_2 = 3/4D$) with the realized utility level of

(37) $$\hat{u}_M^* = \log y + \beta\left(z_0 - \frac{\gamma D}{2}\right) + \frac{D}{4}\left(\beta\gamma - \delta D\right)$$

The final comparison must be made between (30) and (37) to determine the maximum maximoram. However, we can show that

(38) $$\frac{\beta^2\gamma^2}{16\delta} - \frac{D}{4}(\beta\gamma - \delta D) = \frac{1}{16\delta}[\beta^2\gamma^2 - 4\delta D(\beta\gamma - \delta D)] = \frac{1}{16\delta}(\beta\gamma - 2\delta D)^2 > 0$$

by Assumption (vii) so that it is very clear that

(39) $$u_0^* > \hat{u}_M^*$$

and the location of the facilities at

(40) $$x_1^* = \frac{4\delta D - \beta\gamma}{8\delta}, \; x_2^* = \frac{4\delta D + \beta\gamma}{8\delta}$$

gives the true optimal solution to the problem.

A slight reflection on the whole procedure of this section enables us to deduce the following extreme cases that are intuitively plausible.

(A) If $\delta = 0$, then the optimal location will be

(41) $$x_1^* = \frac{1}{4}D, \; x_2^* = \frac{3}{4}D$$

(B) If $\delta = \infty$, then the optimal location will be

(42) $$x_1^* = \frac{D}{2}, \; x_2^* = \frac{D}{2}$$

 (duplication of facilities).

Tiebout (1956), Oates (1969), and Negishi (1972) discussed the optimal character of an equilibrium that was brought about by intercity migration of people among different municipalities which offered different sets of environmental factors including public facilities. This kind of adjustment, however, usually takes a long time to reach an equilibrium. A local government needs day to day guidance to decide the optimal location of public facilities taking the residential distribution of people as given. The present paper is a tentative attempt to solve this sort of practical problem.

REFERENCES

Arnott, Richard J. and J. E. Stiglitz. "Aggregate Land Rents, Expenditure on Public Goods, and Optimal City Size," *Quarterly Journal of Economics,* 93 (1979), 471–500.

Beckmann, Martin J. "Equilibrium Models of Residential Land Use," *Regional Science and Urban Economics,* 3 (1973), 361–368.

——. "On Optimal Spacing under Exponential Distance Effect," in J.-F. Thisse and H. G. Zoller (eds.), *Locational Analysis of Public Facilities.* Amsterdam: North-Holland, 1983.

Feldman, Stephen. "Income Redistribution and Externalities in Urban Space," Paper presented at the Third Advanced Studies Institute in Regional Science, Karlsruhe, 1974.

Fisch, Oscar. "Spatial Equilibrium with Local Public Goods: Urban Land Rent, Optimal City Size and the Tiebout Hypothesis," in G. J. Papageorgiou (ed.), *Mathematical Land Use Theory.* Lexington, MA: Lexington Books, 1976.

Fujita, Masahisa. "Optimal Location of Public Facilities: A Columbus' Egg Revisited," Paper presented at the Second World Regional Science Congress, Rotterdam, 1984.

Fujita, Masahisa and H. Ogawa. "Multiple Equilibria and Structural Transition of Non-Monocentric Urban Configurations," *Regional Science and Urban Economics,* 12 (1982), 161–196.

Hansen, P., D. Peeters, and J.-F. Thisse. "Public Facility Location Models: A Selected Survey," in J.-F. Thisse and H. G. Zoller (eds.), *Locational Analysis of Public Facilities.* Amsterdam: North Holland, 1983.

Helpman, E. and D. Pines. "Optimal Public Investment and Dispersion Policy in a System of Open Cities," *American Economic Review,* 70 (1980), 507–514.

Helpman, E., D. Pines, and E. Borukhov. "The Interaction between Local Government and Urban Residential Location: Comment," *American Economic Review,* 66 (1976), 961–967.

Hicks, John R. "The Foundations of Welfare Economics," *Economic Journal,* 49 (1939), 696–712.

Jurion, B. J. "A Theory of Public Services with Distance-Sensitive Utility," in J.-F. Thisse and H. G. Zoller (eds.), *Locational Analysis of Public Facilities.* Amsterdam: North-Holland, 1983.

Kanemoto, Y. *Theories of Urban Externalities.* Amsterdam: North-Holland, 1980, Chap. III.

Lea, A. C. "Public Facility Location Models and the Theory of Impure Public Goods," *Sistemi Urbani,* 3 (1981), 345–390.

Negishi, T. "Public Expenditure Determined by Voting with One's Feet and Fiscal Profitability," *Swedish Journal of Economics,* 74 (1972), 452–458.

Oates, W. E. "The Effects of Property Taxes and Local Public Spending on Property Values: An Empirical Study of Tax Capitalization and the Tiebout Hypothesis," *Journal of Political Economy,* 77 (1969), 957–971.

Ogawa, H. and Masahisa Fujita. "Equilibrium in Land Use Patterns in a Non-Monocentric City," *Journal of Regional Science,* 20 (1980), 455–475.

Paroush, J. and C. S. Tapiero. "Optimal Location of a Polluting Plant on a Line under Uncertainty," *Journal of Regional Science,* 16 (1976), 365–374.

Pines, D. and Y. Weiss. "Land Improvements Projects and Land Values: An Addendum," *Journal of Urban Economics,* 11 (1982), 199–204.

Romanos, M. C. "Household Location in a Linear Multi-Center Metropolitan Area," *Regional Science and Urban Economics,* 7 (1977), 233–250.

Schuler, Richard. "The Interaction between Local Government and Urban Residential Location," *American Economic Review,* 64 (1974), 682–696.

Solow, R. M. and W. S. Vickrey. "Land Use in a Long Narrow City," *Journal of Economic Theory,* 3 (1971), 430–447.
Tapiero, C. S. "The Probable Demand for Two Facilities Located on a Line," *Regional Science and Urban Economics,* 5 (1975), 335–341.
Tapiero, C. S. and M. Desplas. "Optimal Location of Two Competing Facilities under Uncertainty," in J.-F. Thisse and H. G. Zoller (eds.), *Locational Analysis of Public Facilities.* Amsterdam: North-Holland, 1983.
Thisse, Jacques-Francois and H. G. Zoller. *Locational Analysis of Public Facilities.* Amsterdam: North-Holland, 1983.
Tiebout, C. M. "A Pure Theory of Local Expenditures," *Journal of Political Economy,* 64 (1956), 416–424.
Walter, Gerald. "Towards a Theory of Urban Investment in a Monocentric City," Paper presented at the Third Advanced Studies Institute in Regional Science, Karlsruhe, 1974.
Yang, C. H. and Masahisa, Fujita. "Urban Spatial Structure with Open Spaces," *Environment and Planning A,* 15 (1983), 67–84.
Yellin, J. "Urban Population Distribution, Family Income, and Social Prejudice, 1: The Long Narrow City," *Journal of Urban Economics,* 1 (1974), 21–47.

Papers of the Regional Science Association, Arizona, Vol. 67 (1989) 1–11

PRESIDENTIAL ADDRESS:

SPATIAL INTERDEPENDENCE AND EXTERNALITIES

Noboru Sakashita
Institute of Socio-Economic Planning
University of Tsukuba
Tsukuba, Ibaraki 305, Japan

ABSTRACT Pecuniary externalities in a two-region economy are examined from several aspects. The analysis includes fiscal externality, inefficiency of free migration, and inefficiency of autarky non-wage income sharing. Measures to restore the productive efficiency that is lacking in the multiregion economy with local public goods are discussed. Finally, a new aspect of the interregional allocation of residential activities is analyzed as the economics of multi-habitation.

1. INTRODUCTION

In his historic paper of 1954, Tibor Scitovsky discussed the concepts of technological external economies and pecuniary external economies. Both of these concepts are especially relevant to the spatial economy in which direct interdependence of economic activities is by no means an exceptional phenomenon.

The concept of technological externalities in space is comprehensively discussed in a recent publication by Kanemoto (1987); in this paper I wish to concentrate my discussion on the concept of pecuniary externalities in a spatial economy. Inequivalence among the productive efficiency (equality of marginal productivities), the social optimum, and the market equilibrium in a multiregion economy, which is a symptom of the existence of externalities, has been discussed previously using several models *without* a local public good (see, e.g., Sakashita 1984, 1989). Here I wish to discuss "fiscal externality," inefficiency of free migration, and the role of commuting costs between different regions as examples of pecuniary externalities in a spatial economy *with* a local public good. Through these analyses I wish to reveal the essence of pecuniary externalities in a spatial setting and also wish to explore measures to *overcome* these externalities.

2. FISCAL EXTERNALITIES AND THE INEFFICIENCY OF LOCAL AUTONOMY

In this section I discuss a model of a two-region economy with the supply of local public good financed by local taxation, and I reveal the source of locational inefficiency characterized as "fiscal externality," which is the direct consequence of local autonomy uncontrolled by the central government.

The model used is an extremely simplified version of David Wildasin's more general model (Wildasin 1986, Chapter 2). Consider an economy which consists of two regions. In each region i, a resident enjoys utility U_i by the consumption of a private good C_i and a public good G_i, i.e., $U_i = U_i(C_i, G_i)$. Region i's productive capacity is expressed by its specific production function F_i, the sole input of which is the residents' labor, L_i. The total economy's population is fixed as $\bar{L}$ and is the sum of L_1 and L_2. U_i, F_i, and $\bar{L}$ complete the description of the environment in which this two-region economy operates.

First I consider the problem for a social planner who wishes to maximize the level of utility under the following three constraints: (i) a supply and demand balance of production and consumption, (ii) a resource constraint, and (iii) an equal utility constraint between the two regions (free locational choice with costless mobility). As the optimizing conditions for this problem, there will be one Samuelsonian condition for the supply of (local) public good in each of the two regions and a *social net benefit condition of migration* which states that the gap between marginal productivity of labor (F'_i) and per capita consumption (C_i) takes the same value in each region. Together with the aforementioned three constraints, we have six equations for six unknowns, L_i, C_i, and G_i, $i = 1, 2$ (see Appendix 1).

Now I turn to the description of market equilibrium with free migration and optimizing behavior of *each* local government. Firstly we need to specify the distributive pattern of non-wage income in the economy. Following Wildasin, here I adopt a realistic institutional setup called the "uniform national dividend scheme (UNDS)" in which each individual (labor unit) receives an equal share of the national nonwage income regardless of his (her) locational choice (Sakashita 1989). Secondly I assume that the local government in each region determines the level of head tax (t_i) and uses the resultant tax revenue for the supply of local public good to maximize the utility of individual residents, *taking the size of population in its region as given.* In this sense, the behavior of the local government is myopic. Since the size of population is fixed and people are completely homogeneous in a region, there is no need to distinguish between head tax and income tax in this case.

Under the above circumstances, there will be ten conditions for the ten unknowns in this two-region market equilibrium: (i) definition of per capita consumption in each region, (ii) equality of wage income (w_i) and marginal productivity of labor (F'_i) in each region, (iii) equality of the supply of local public good and the tax revenue in each region, (iv) one Samuelsonian condition for each region, (v) equal utility among regions, and (vi) fixed total (labor) population. The ten unknowns are L_i, C_i, G_i, w_i, and t_i, $i = 1, 2$.

The market equilibrium satisfies almost all conditions of the social optimum *except* the social net benefit condition of migration. We can see this by noticing that the gap between marginal productivity of labor (F'_i) and per capita consumption (C_i) in each region equals the gap between the rate of head tax (t_i) and uniform nonwage income (say, I). When the rates of head tax are different, we cannot have a market equilibrium which is equivalent to the social optimum. This is the content of "fiscal externality" and it reveals inefficiency of the local autonomy which does not obey control imposed by the central government. Looking at the market equilibrium from a different viewpoint, the term which is equalized among regions is not $(F'_i - C_i)$ but $(F'_i - C_i - t_i)$, $i = 1, 2$. People decide their locational choice taking local tax rates into consideration in addition to the per capita surplus $(F'_i + I - C_i)$ they produce in a particular region and this behavior imposes an inefficiency on the economy as a whole. This is a typical case of distortion introduced by an uncoordinated tax system (see Appendix 2).

The local governments, however, do not decide tax rates arbitrarily; rather they set them to maximize welfare in each region. Nevertheless their behavior may contradict the objective of national efficiency. The "central" government should coordinate policies taken by the different local governments and achieve equivalence between the market equilibrium and the social optimum via a system of interregional income transfer in the scheme of market equilibrium. Letting the per capita "subsidy" (positive or negative) given to individuals in region i by the central government be s_i, the term equalized changes to $(F_i' - C_i - t_i + s_i)$ from $(F_i' - C_i - t_i)$. The social net benefit condition of migration will be established if the interregional difference in s_i offsets the difference in t_i. In addition, a clearance condition of $s_1 L_1 + s_2 L_2 = 0$ must be introduced so that equality of numbers of conditions and unknowns will be maintained. Equilibrium values of all variables including L_i will be changed by the introduction of intervention by the central government.

The analysis thus far does not change essentially when we introduce a congestion effect into the consumption of the local public good although there will be fairly complicated conditions in that case.

Finally I wish to point out that even in the social optimum in which there is no fiscal externality we do not have productive efficiency in the sense of equality of marginal productivities among regions which corresponds to the maximum national output. This result comes from the regional residents' *dual* character as labor force (a factor of production) and as utility-enjoyers. These dual aspects of the residents in a specific region cannot be separated from each other. No individual can be a laborer in one region and a utility-enjoyer in the other region at the same time. In my opinion this inseparability is the fundamental cause of spatial pecuniary externalities. I shall come back to this point later.

3. INEFFICIENCY OF FREE MIGRATION UNDER AUTARKY

Boadway and Flatters (1982) discussed the inefficiency of free migration under autarky when there is no spatial interdependence between two regions *except* an equal utility condition between the two regions. The local government in each region will try to maximize a representative resident's utility taking the region's population as given, although the population itself will change depending on the policy adopted by the local government. In that sense the local government's behavior can be again taken as myopic.

The above situation can be, however, formulated as a trivial maximizing problem with the following constraints: (i) a supply and demand balance of production and consumption for each region, (ii) a resource constraint, and (iii) an equal utility constraint between the two regions. Derived optimizing conditions are two Samuelsonian conditions, one for each region. These two conditions with the above four constraints are sufficient to determine the values of six unknowns, C_i, G_i, and L_i, $i = 1, 2$. Here we do not have the social net benefit condition of migration, but instead we have equalization of the gap between marginal productivity of labor and per capita consumption multiplied by the shadow price of supply and demand balance in each region. This condition is trivial but it will give some additional insight in the improved situation to be discussed later (see Appendix 3).

The inefficiency of free migration reveals itself when we calculate the change of social welfare in region i when one migrant enters. The change is equal to the per capita gap between expenditure in the local public good and nonwage income in that region multiplied by the marginal utility of the private good in the same region. Denoting this change as MBL_i, $(MBL_1 - MBL_2)$ expresses the net increase of social benefit gained by migration of a resident. This amount could be positive or negative but could not be zero except fortuitously so that the social welfare can certainly be improved by one (or more) resident's migration in one direction or the other. Of course the situation after the above migration does not satisfy the equal utility condition so that it cannot be said to be a market equilibrium with free migration. However, it could be the social optimum with a Benthamite social welfare function which is the population-weighted sum of per capita utilities in the two regions (Hartwick 1980).

The inefficiency discussed above can be lessened by the introduction of the *UNDS* defined in the preceding section *or* by some interregional income transfer system. I discuss the latter first. Add transfer variable S in the supply-demand condition for the first region and subtract the same from the corresponding condition for the second region. The marginal contribution of ΔS to the social welfare is the gap between the shadow price of the supply-demand condition for the first region and the second region. By making ΔS positive (transfer from the second to the first) when the gap is positive or by making ΔS negative (transfer in the opposite direction) when it is negative we can increase the social welfare in any case. The social optimum defined in the last section can be obtained by making the two shadow prices equal with an appropriate amount of S that is equivalent to the joint supply and demand constraint. At the same time we have the social net benefit condition of migration by these equalized shadow prices (see Appendix 4).

Next I introduce a partial *UNDS* to the autarky system. Assume that 100 α percent of nonwage income in each region is poured into the *UNDS* and $100(1 - \alpha)$ percent is retained within the region. Now we have complicated supply-demand constraints in this system. However, two Samuelsonian conditions and four constraints together determine six unknowns, C_i, G_i, and L_i, $i = 1, 2$, as before. In addition we have an interesting expression for the marginal contribution of $\Delta\alpha$ to the social welfare. It is proportional to the product of the gap between the two shadow prices of the supply-demand conditions and the gap between per capita nonwage incomes in the two regions. The condition that attains the social optimum in this situation is equality of the two shadow prices. This equality again combines two separate supply-demand constraints into one, and reduces the present problem to that of social optimization in the last section (see Appendix 5).

In this section we have observed that an autarky system with free migration can be transformed into the social optimum *either* by partial introduction of *UNDS or* by appropriate interregional income transfer. By these measures we may eliminate the inefficiency of free migration under autarky but we cannot eliminate the productive inefficiency. Finally I wish to emphasize that any of the three optimizing systems discussed above may be attained as a market equilibrium with adequate interventions by local *and* central governments.

4. TWO UNORTHODOX APPROACHES TO RESTORING PRODUCTIVE EFFICIENCY

When there is either a supply of local public good or the existence of any region-specific factors in a two-region economy, the productive efficiency is never reached except in very fortuitous cases (Sakashita 1989). A natural question is whether there is any opportunity for optimizing models in which productive efficiency (equalization of marginal productivities between regions) is restored. In this section, I wish to discuss two rather unorthodox approaches to this question. One is the case of *producers' sovereignty* in which national output is taken as the objective to be maximized with appropriate constraints. An example is the Japanese interregional economy during the period of very rapid growth, say, from 1960 to 1973. The other is the case of *low-cost commuting between regions,* in which inseparability of working site and residential site can be overcome to some extent. This could be a raison d'etre of the so-called linear motor car technology for high speed railway networks in advanced and urbanized economies.

Producers' Sovereignty

A rapidly growing economy might have as its objective the maximization of annual saving instead of per capita utility. In that case the central government must first determine the allocation of labor (population) to maximize the national output. There is then equalization of marginal productivities of labor between the two regions and the resultant maximized national output. This national output will be distributed between the two regions by the following two principles: (i) equal utility between the two regions, and (ii) one Samuelsonian condition for each region.

When we interpret the above procedure as a two-stage maximization problem, we may deduce the change of equalized utility in response to the marginal change of labor allocation by applying the envelope theorem to the second stage maximization. The change is proportional to the difference of per capita consumption between the two regions ($[C_2 - C_1]$ or $[C_1 - C_2]$). Therefore, we always can make this change positive by choosing the direction of labor shift correctly. This expresses the sacrifice of utility caused by the principle of producers' sovereignty (see Appendix 6). This sacrifice could be justified in many cases since it is necessary for rapid capital accumulation. However, we can measure the social inefficiency of producers' sovereignty by the gap in per capita consumption between the two regions. If C_2 exceeds C_1 labor must be shifted from region 2 to region 1 and vice versa from the viewpoint of utility maximization.

Interregional Commuting

If we can separate work and residential sites, then the possible range of policy variables will be very much greater and we can open a new dimension for the interregional economy. Let L_{ij} be the number of people who reside in region i and work in region j, i.e., commuting from region i to region j. Then $(L_{11} + L_{21})$ is the amount of labor input in region 1 and $(L_{12} + L_{22})$ is the same in region 2. On the other hand, $[C_1(L_{11} + L_{12}) + G_1]$ is the total consumption of private and public goods in region 1 and $[C_2(L_{22} + L_{21}) + G_2]$ is the same in region 2.

Commuting itself needs social resources so that $\theta(L_{12} + L_{21})$ must be deducted from the national output in which θ is the unit transport cost. Under these circumstances we may clearly define the optimizing problem of a social planner and easily derive the related optimizing conditions. First, it is obvious that there will be no "cross-hauling" of people between the regions. That is, at least one of L_{12} and L_{21} must be zero; otherwise we will have a contradiction among optimizing conditions. Secondly, we have the net social benefit condition of migration in this case too, but the gaps in marginal productivities and in per capita consumption of private good between the two regions are both equal to the per capita transport cost, θ. Thirdly, the impact of reduction in the unit transport cost is equal to the product of marginal utility of private good averaged between the two regions and the ratio of commuters (L_{12} or L_{21}) to total population ($\bar{L}$) (see Appendix 7).

If we consider an extreme case in which the unit transport cost becomes zero, there occurs an extraordinary situation. First, there will be concentration of residential area in one of the two regions, i.e., one of L_1 (= $L_{11} + L_{12}$) and

L_2 ($= L_{21} + L_{22}$) must become zero; otherwise we shall have overdetermination among optimizing conditions. This is because there is fiscal economy of scale in the consumption of the local public good. If we introduce a congestion effect in that consumption, the above concentration may disappear. Secondly, we have the condition of productive efficiency ($F_1' = F_2'$) at last in this case and it may easily be interpreted. People will reside in one region where the living amenity is better and some of them also work in the same region. But other people will commute to the other region and work there to avoid the declining effect of marginal productivity. Such phenomena are actually observed in many dormitory towns near Tokyo, for instance, where rapid transit systems are very well developed. At least we can say that the development of efficient interregional transit systems (e.g., linear motor car system) is indispensable for the revival of productive efficiency.

5. ECONOMICS OF MULTI-HABITATION

In the fourth comprehensive regional development plan of Japan (Yonzensoh), worked out in 1987, there was suggested the idea of multi-habitation. In this penultimate section I wish to touch upon a model of multi-habitation in which the optimal allocation of time for each individual is analyzed. Every year each individual spends $100p$ percent of time in region 1 and $100(1\text{-}p)$ percent in region 2. If the total population $\bar{L}$ is large enough, region 1 can maintain labor input of approximately $p\bar{L}$ always and region 2 can maintain $(1\text{-}p)\bar{L}$. Per capita consumption is a p- and $(1\text{-}p)$-weighted average of C_1 and C_2, respectively. Maximizing the p- and $(1\text{-}p)$-weighted average of U_1 and U_2, we have the following five conditions: (i) one Samuelsonian condition for each region, (ii) equalization of marginal utilities of private good consumption between the two regions, and (iii) social net benefit condition of multi-habitation (see Appendix 8). Together with the supply-demand constraint, five equations are sufficient to determine the five unknowns (C_i, G_i, i = 1, 2, and p).

It is easily shown that the average utility maximized in this multi-habitation model is larger than the utility at the social optimum of single habitation. Therefore the multi-habitation policy in Yonzensoh has some practical merit which the policymakers probably did not realize.

6. CONCLUDING REMARKS

In the latter part of this paper, I concentrated my attention on optimizing models. Any of them, however, may be attained as a market equilibrium with appropriate intervention by the central government. I wish to emphasize this point again.

By the discussion of these various models I clarified the working of pecuniary externalities in a spatial setting that do not exist in the traditional one-point economy without spatial separation. Externalities come from the difficulty in overcoming distance between regions. In that sense, externalities can be said to be the outcome of "tyranny of distance," which was the title of the late Professor William Warntz's presidential address at the St. Louis meeting of the Regional Science Association in 1966.

Owing to the development of rapid transit systems, the power of our tyrant is being weakened day by day. However it will take a very long time for us to overcome the hurdle of distance completely so that there are still many subjects which we, regional scientists, must attack and clear up.

APPENDIX 1
Social Planner's Problem
Maximize $U_1(C_1, G_1)$
w.r.t. $C_i, G_i, L_i, \quad i = 1, 2$
subject to:

$$U_2(C_2, G_2) - U_1(C_1, G_1) = 0.$$
$$F_1(L_1) + F_2(L_2) - C_1L_1 - C_2L_2 - G_1 - G_2 = 0.$$
$$\bar{L} - L_1 - L_2 = 0.$$

Optimizing conditions: $\dfrac{\partial U_i}{\partial C_i} = \dfrac{\partial U_i}{\partial G_i} L_i, \quad i = 1, 2.$
(the social optimum)

$$F'_1 - C_1 = F'_2 - C_2 \tag{1}$$

(social net benefit condition of migration).

APPENDIX 2
UNDS Market Equilibrium

$$w_i + I - C_i - t_i = 0, \quad i = 1, 2. \tag{2}$$

$$\left(I = \frac{\sum_{i=1}^{2}(F_i - w_iL_i)}{\bar{L}}\right., \text{ uniform per capita non-wage income).}$$

$$w_i = F'_i, \quad i = 1, 2. \tag{3}$$

$$G_i = t_iL_i, \quad i = 1, 2.$$

$$\frac{\partial U_i}{\partial C_i} = \frac{\partial U_i}{\partial G_i} L_i, \quad i = 1, 2.$$

$$U_1(C_1, G_1) = U_2(C_2, G_2).$$

$$\bar{L} = L_1 + L_2.$$

$$(2), (3) \rightarrow F'_1 - C_1 - t_1 = F'_2 - C_2 - t_2, \text{ instead of (1).}$$

Possible intervention by the central government

$$F'_i + I - C_i - t_i + s_i = 0, \text{ instead of (2), (3).}$$
$$s_1 - s_2 = t_1 - t_2.$$
$$s_1L_1 + s_2L_2 = 0.$$
$$\rightarrow F'_1 - C_1 = F'_2 - C_2 \text{ (1).}$$

APPENDIX 3
Autarky Market Equilibrium

$$F_i - C_iL_i - G_i = 0, \quad i = 1, 2. \tag{4}$$

$$\frac{\partial U_i}{\partial C_i} = \frac{\partial U_i}{\partial G_i} L_i, \quad i = 1, 2.$$

$$U_1(C_1, G_1) = U_2(C_2, G_2).$$

$$\overline{L} = L_1 + L_2.$$

$$(4) \rightarrow F_1' + \frac{R_1}{L_1} - C_1 - \frac{G_1}{L_1} = F_2' + \frac{R_2}{L_2} - C_2 - \frac{G_2}{L_2},$$

instead of (1)

$$(R_i = F_i - F_i' L_i, \quad i = 1, 2 \text{ non-wage income}).$$

Inefficiency of free migration

Optimizing behavior of local government, $i = 1, 2$:

Max $[\Phi_i = U_i(C_i, G_i) + \lambda_i\{F_i(\overline{L}_i) - C_i\overline{L}_i - G_i\}]$
w.r.t. C_i, G_i

$$\frac{\partial U_i}{\partial C_i} - \lambda_i\overline{L}_i = 0, \qquad \frac{\partial U_i}{\partial G_i} - \lambda_i = 0.$$

By the Envelope Theorem, $\dfrac{d\Phi_i}{dL_i} = \dfrac{\partial \Phi_i}{\partial L_i} = \lambda_i(F_i' - C_i)$

$$= \frac{\frac{\partial U_i}{\partial C_i}}{\overline{L}_i}\left(F_i' - \frac{F_i - G_i}{\overline{L}_i}\right)$$

$$MBL_1 - MBL_2 = \overline{L}_1 \frac{\partial \Phi_1}{\partial L_1} - \overline{L}_2 \frac{\partial \Phi_2}{\partial L_2} = \frac{\partial U_1}{\partial C_1}\left(\frac{G_1 - R_1}{\overline{L}_1}\right) - \frac{\partial U_2}{\partial C_2}\left(\frac{G_2 - R_2}{\overline{L}_2}\right) \neq 0.$$

APPENDIX 4
Interregional Income Transfer

Formulation as a maximizing problem:

$$\begin{aligned} &\text{Max } [\Phi = U_1(C_1, G_1) + \lambda\ \{U_2(C_2, G_2) - U_1(C_1, G_1)\} \\ &\text{w.r.t. } C_i, G_i, L_i, \ i = 1, 2, \quad + \mu_1\ \{F_1(L_1) - C_1L_1 - G_1 + S\} \\ &\quad (S) \qquad\qquad\qquad\quad + \mu_2\ \{F_2(L_2) - C_2L_2 - G_2 - S\} \\ &\qquad\qquad\qquad\qquad\qquad + \nu\ (\overline{L} - L_1 - L_2)]. \end{aligned}$$

$S = 0 \rightarrow$ Autarky Market Equilibrium

$$\left(\frac{\partial \Phi_i}{\partial L_i} = \mu_i(F_i' - C_i) - \nu = 0, \qquad i = 1, 2\right).$$

By the Envelope Theorem, $\dfrac{d\Phi}{dS} = \dfrac{\partial \Phi}{\partial S} = \mu_1 - \mu_2.$

At the optimum, $\dfrac{\partial \Phi}{\partial S} = 0 \rightarrow F_1' - C_1 = F_2' - C_2$ (1).

APPENDIX 5

Partial UNDS Market Equilibrium

$$\begin{aligned}
&\text{Max } [\Phi = U_1(C_1, G_1) + \lambda \{U_2(C_2, G_2) - U_1(C_1, G_1)\} \\
&\text{w.r.t. } C_i, G_i, L_i,\ i = 1, 2, (\alpha) \qquad + \sum_{i=1}^{2} \mu_i \{F_i' L_i + (1 - \alpha)(F_i - F_i' L_i) \\
&\qquad + \frac{\sum_{k=1}^{2} \alpha (F_k - F_k' L_k)}{\overline{L}} L_i - C_i L_i - G_i\} \\
&\qquad + \nu (\overline{L} - L_1 - L_2)].
\end{aligned}$$

By the Envelope Theorem, $\dfrac{d\Phi}{d\alpha} = \dfrac{\partial\Phi}{\partial\alpha} = \dfrac{L_1 L_2}{\overline{L}_1} (\mu_1 - \mu_2)\left(\dfrac{R_2}{L_2} - \dfrac{R_1}{L_1}\right).$

At the optimum, $\dfrac{d\Phi}{d\alpha} = 0 \rightarrow \mu_1 = \mu_2,$

and two constraints become one constraint
→ social optimum.

APPENDIX 6

Producers' Sovereignty

1st stage: Max $\{F_1(L_1) + F_2(L_2)\}$
w.r.t. L_1, L_2
subject to $\overline{L} - L_1 - L_2 = 0.$
Maximizing condition $F_1' = F_2' \rightarrow L_1^*, L_2^*.$

2nd stage:

$$\begin{aligned}
&\text{Max } [\Phi = U_1(C_1, G_1) + \lambda \{U_2(C_2, G_2) - U_1(C_1, G_1)\} \\
&\text{w.r.t. } C_i, G_i\ \ i = 1, 2 \qquad + \mu \{F_1(L_1^*) + F_2(L_2^*) \\
&\qquad - C_1 L_1^* - C_2 L_2^* - G_1 - G_2\}].
\end{aligned}$$

By the Envelope Theorem,
$$\frac{d\Phi}{dL_1^*} - \frac{d\Phi}{dL_2^*} = \mu(F_1'^* - F_2'^* - C_1 + C_2) = \mu(C_1 - C_2) \neq 0.$$

APPENDIX 7

Interregional Commuting

$$\begin{aligned}
&\text{Max } [\Phi = U_1(C_1, G_1) + \lambda \{U_2(C_2, G_2) - U_1(C_1, G_1)\} \\
&\text{w.r.t. } C_i, G_i L_{ij}\ \ i = 1, 2; j = 1, 2 \qquad + \mu \{F_1(L_{11} + L_{21}) + F_2(L_{12} + L_{22}) \\
&\qquad - C_1(L_{11} + L_{21}) - C_2(L_{12} + L_{22}) \\
&\qquad - G_1 - G_2 - \theta(L_{12} + L_{21})\}].
\end{aligned}$$

$$\left.\begin{aligned}
&\frac{\partial\Phi}{\partial C_1} : (1 - \lambda) \frac{\partial U_1}{\partial C_1} - \mu(L_{11} + L_{12}) = 0 \qquad (5)\\
&\frac{\partial\Phi}{\partial G_1} : (1 - \lambda) \frac{\partial U_1}{\partial G_1} - \mu = 0 \\
&\frac{\partial\Phi}{\partial C_2} : \lambda \frac{\partial U_2}{\partial C_2} - \mu(L_{22} + L_{21}) = 0 \qquad (6)\\
&\frac{\partial\Phi}{\partial G_2} : \lambda \frac{\partial U_2}{\partial G_2} - \mu = 0
\end{aligned}\right\} \text{Samuelsonian conditions}$$

$$\frac{\partial \Phi}{\partial L_{11}} : [\mu(F'_1 - C_1) - \nu]\, L_{11} = 0.$$

$$\frac{\partial \Phi}{\partial L_{21}} : [\mu(F'_1 - C_2 - \theta) - \nu]\, L_{21} = 0.$$

$$\frac{\partial \Phi}{\partial L_{12}} : [\mu(F'_2 - C_1 - \theta) - \nu]\, L_{12} = 0.$$

$$\frac{\partial \Phi}{\partial L_{22}} : [\mu(F'_2 - C_2) - \nu] = 0.$$

Propositions: (i) No cross hauling: L_{21} or L_{12} must be zero.

(ii) Social net benefit condition of migration is satisfied: $F'_1 - C_1 = F'_2 - C_2$.

(iii) Wage and consumption gaps are equal to unit transport cost: $F'_2 = F'_1 + \theta$ and $C_2 = C'_2 + \theta$ if $L_{12} > 0$.

(iv) Impact of reduction in θ:

$$\frac{d\Phi}{d\theta} = \frac{\partial \Phi}{\partial \theta} = -\mu(L_{12} + L_{21})$$

$$= \left[(1 - \lambda)\frac{\partial U_1}{\partial C_1} + \lambda \frac{\partial U_2}{\partial C_2}\right] \frac{L_{12} + L_{21}}{\bar{L}};$$

by (5) and (6),

Net Social Benefit $\equiv$ Direct Users' Benefit.

Extreme case of $\theta = 0$.

Propositions: (i) Residential concentration, i.e., $L_{11} > 0$, $L_{12} > 0$, $L_{21} = L_{22} = 0$ for instance. (Otherwise some contradiction occurs among optimizing conditions).

(ii) Productive efficiency is established finally, i.e., $F'_1 = F'_2$.

APPENDIX 8

Economics of Multi-habitation

$$\begin{aligned} \text{Max } \Phi = {} & pU_1(C_1, G_1) + (1 - p)\, U_2(C_2, G_2) \\ \text{w.r.t. } p, C_i, G_i \quad i = 1, 2 \quad & + \mu\, \{F_1(p\bar{L}) + F_2\, [(1 - p)\bar{L}] \\ & - [pC_1 + (1 - p)C_2]\, \bar{L} - G_1 - G_2\}. \end{aligned}$$

$$\left.\begin{aligned} \frac{\partial \Phi}{\partial C_1} &: \quad p\frac{\partial U_1}{\partial C_1} - \mu p \bar{L} = 0 \\ \frac{\partial \Phi}{\partial G_1} &: \quad p\frac{\partial U_1}{\partial G_1} - \mu = 0 \\ \frac{\partial \Phi}{\partial C_2} &: (1 - p)\frac{\partial U_2}{\partial C_2} - \mu(1 - p)\,\bar{L} = 0 \\ \frac{\partial \Phi}{\partial G_2} &: (1 - p)\frac{\partial U_2}{\partial G_2} - \mu = 0 \end{aligned}\right\}$$

Samuelsonian conditions

$$\frac{\partial U_1}{\partial C_1} = \frac{\partial U_1}{\partial G_1}(p\bar{L})$$

$$\frac{\partial U_2}{\partial C_2} = \frac{\partial U_2}{\partial G_2}((1 - p)\bar{L})$$

and

$$\frac{\partial U_1}{\partial C_1} = \frac{\partial U_2}{\partial C_2}\ (= \mu\bar{L}).$$

$$\frac{\partial \Phi}{\partial p} : U_1 + \frac{\partial U_1}{\partial C_1}(F'_1 - C_1) = U_2 + \frac{\partial U_2}{\partial C_2}(F'_2 - C_2)$$

(Social net benefit condition of multi-habitation).

Superiority of multi-habitation over single-habitation

Max $\hat{\Phi} = \Phi + \lambda[U_2(C_2, G_2) - U_1(C_1, G_1) + \varepsilon]$, for given ε.

w.r.t. p, C_i, G_i

$\varepsilon = 0 \rightarrow$ social planner's problem (Appendix 1).

$$\frac{d\hat{\Phi}}{d\varepsilon} = \frac{\partial\hat{\Phi}}{\partial\varepsilon} = \lambda \neq 0, \left[\frac{d\hat{\Phi}}{d\varepsilon}(\Delta\varepsilon) = \lambda\,(\Delta\varepsilon)\right] \text{ can be made positive}$$

by $\Delta\varepsilon > 0$ or by $\Delta\varepsilon < 0$.

(Social optimum without equal utility constraint is better than the same with it).

REFERENCES

Boadway, R. and Flatters, F. 1982. Efficiency and equalization payments in a federal system of government: a synthesis and extension of recent results. *Canadian Journal of Economics,* 15, 4: 613–33.

Hartwick, J. M. 1980. The Henry George rule, optimal population, and interregional equity. *Canadian Journal of Economics,* 13, 4: 695–700.

Kanemoto, Y. 1987. Externalities in space. In *Urban dynamics and urban externalities,* eds. T. Miyao and Y. Kanemoto, pp. 43–103. Chur, Switzerland: Harwood Academic Publishers.

Sakashita, N. 1984. Market equilibrium and social optimum in a two-region economy. University of Tsukuba, Tsukuba: Institute of Socio-Economic Planning, Discussion Paper No. 242.

Sakashita, N. 1989. Market equilibrium and optimum social welfare in a two-region economy. In *Developments in Japanese economics,* eds. R. Sato and T. Negishi, pp. 43–58. Tokyo: Harcourt Brace Jovanovich.

Scitovsky, T. 1954. Two concepts of external economies. *Journal of Political Economy,* 17: 143–51.

Wildasin, D. E. 1986. *Urban public finance.* New York: Harwood Academic Publishers.

Does Economic Space Matter? ed. by J.F. Thisse and H. Ohta,
New York (1993) 165–184

Optimal Utilization of the Central Business District with Economy and Diseconomy of Agglomeration

Noboru Sakashita*

9.1 INTRODUCTION

The central business district (CBD) of big cities like Tokyo is constantly suffering from congestion phenomenon for the consumption of services generated by the urban infrastructures (transport, communication, water, sewage, and so on). A typical example is dangerously crowded peak-time commuting trips into the CBD of Tokyo.

The best way to control such congestion phenomenon is, needless to say, to impose an appropriate congestion charge for the consumption of *each* infrastructural service. In the case of commuting trips by railways, for example, an extremely high peak-load pricing should be introduced in order to encourage, say, flexible work-hours. Politically, however, it is extremely difficult to adopt such a policy of marginal social cost pricing particularly because there are too many kinds of such infrastructural services and also because some consideration from the viewpoint of income distribution is unavoidable.

In my opinion, the second-best policy to control this situation is the imposition of an *overall* special business tax on the enterprises which operate in the CBD. This policy was once suggested as a form of the office dispersal policy by Rhodes and Kan (1971, pp. 85–6). In fact, a tax of this type was planned when the Japanese Government (specifically its National Land Agency) formulated *The Fourth Nationwide Comprehensive Regional Development Plan* (*Yonzensoh* in Japanese)

* The author is thankful to Professors H. Inamura, H. Ohta, J. M. Quigley and J.-F. Thisse for their valuable comments on an earlier version of the present chapter.

in 1987 (see Sakashira, 1987). However, this plan was quickly abandoned under the pressure of strong opposition from the business world and the Tokyo Metropolitan Government.

On the other hand, it is argued that there still exists agglomeration economy for concentration of business offices in the CBD. It can be discussed, therefore, that some form of subsidy is desirable for this aspect of concentration (see Hatta and Ohkawara, 1991, for example).

In this chapter I wish to demonstrate a theoretical background for this type of special business tax and to explore the extent to which this tax can be a substitute for the marginal social cost pricing policy. At the same time, the possibility of agglomeration economy subsidy is also considered.

In Section 9.2, a model of non-intervention market equilibrium is introduced and analyzed. In Section 9.3, conditions for the social optimum are derived and compared with those for the market equilibrium. The possibility of a special business tax for the second-best social optimum is analyzed in Section 9.4. In Section 9.5, an illustrative analysis with specific functions and a numerical simulation are performed in order to give some intuitive understanding. Concluding remarks are given in Section 9.6.

9.2 MODEL OF MARKET EQUILIBRIUM

Consider identical firms producing office services with a production function of the following form:

$$x = \phi(n) f(z, l, k, h) \tag{9.1}$$

in which x is the output of a firm, z is the input of an infrastructural service (hereafter simply called 'service'), and l, k, and h are the inputs of labour, capital, and land. It is assumed that the function $f(\cdot)$ is of a decreasing return to scale for larger values of output.[1] The n is the number of identical firms, and $\phi(n)$ expresses agglomeration economy caused by concentration of offices in the CBD. It is assumed that $\phi' > 0$ and $\phi'' < 0$. The average cost of the service is expressed as $c(nz)$, and it is assumed that $c' > 0$ and $c'' \gtreqless 0$. Finally, the area of the CBD is assumed to be fixed as H.

Denoting price of the output p, wage of the labour w, rate of return of the capital ρ, and rent of the land r, the behaviour of a firm is formulated as follows:

$$\max_{\langle z, l, k, h \rangle}[\Pi = p \cdot \phi(n)f(z, l, k, h) - c(nz)z - wl - \rho k - rh]$$

Here one may assume that the individual firm ignores its impact on $c(nz)$ to z since n is relatively large and exogenous to the firm. By the same token, the firm is not aware of the fact that the cause of productivity change is n, the number of identical firms. In addition, the wage w and the rate of capital return ρ are exogenously given for this CBD economy.

As individual profit-maximizing conditions, we have

$$p\phi(n)f_z - c(nz) = 0 \tag{9.2}$$

$$p\phi(n)f_l - w = 0 \tag{9.3}$$

$$p\phi(n)f_k - \rho = 0 \tag{9.4}$$

$$p\phi(n)f_h - r = 0 \tag{9.5}$$

in which the rent r is exogenously given to each firm although it is an endogenous variable for the CBD as a whole, and $f_z = \partial f/\partial z$ and so on.

For the market equilibrium, there are two additional conditions:

$$\Pi = p \cdot \phi(n)f(z, l, k, h) - c(nz)z - wl - \rho k - rh = 0 \tag{9.6}$$

$$nh = H \tag{9.7}$$

Equation (9.6) implies free entry and perfect competition among identical firms, and equation (9.7) shows the demand-and-supply balance of the land in the CBD. Equations (9.2)–(9.7) are sufficient to determine the equilibrium values of six unknowns, that is, n, z, l, k, h, and r.

Putting equations (9.2)–(9.5) into equation (9.6), we have

$$p\phi(f - f_z z - f_l l - f_k k - f_h h) = 0 \tag{9.8}$$

which implies a linear homogeneous property at the equilibrium.

9.3 SOCIAL OPTIMUM

The social optimum in this situation is defined as the state in which the social surplus *including land rent* is maximized under the constraint. The task of a social planner is, therefore, formulated as:

$$\max_{\langle z, l, k, h, n \rangle}[L = n\{p \cdot \phi(n)f(z, l, k, h) - c(nz)z - wl - \rho k\} + \lambda (H - nh)]$$

Optimizing conditions are:

$$p\phi(n)f_z - (c + c'\, nz) = 0 \tag{9.9}$$

$$p\phi(n)f_l - w = 0 \tag{9.10}$$

$$p\phi(n)f_k - \rho = 0 \tag{9.11}$$

$$p\phi(n)f_h - \lambda = 0 \tag{9.12}$$

$$\{p \cdot \phi(n)f - cz - wl - \rho k\} + n\{p\phi' f - c'\, z^2\} - \lambda h = 0 \tag{9.13}$$

Putting equations (9.9)–(9.12) into equation (9.13), we have

$$p\phi\{(1 + e_\phi)f - f_z z - f_l l - f_k k - f_h h\} = 0 \tag{9.14}$$

in which $e_\phi = n\phi'/\phi$, that is, elasticity of the ϕ-function.

Contrast between the equation system (9.2)–(9.5), (9.8) and the equation system (9.9)–(9.12), (9.14) is clear-cut. Difference appears only between equation (9.2) and equation (9.9), and between equation (9.8) and equation (9.14). Roughly speaking, the free market overuses infrastructural services by ignoring the external diseconomy part ($c'\, nz$) of increasing average cost. On the other hand, the free market gives a smaller number of firms than the social optimum does by ignoring the elasticity part (e_ϕ) of equation (9.14).

Under the circumstances, a well-organized system of taxes and subsidies can convert a market equilibrium into the social optimum.

In order to adjust the number of firms, a lump-sum *bonus* (b) to each firm is effective, and a form of *congestion charge* (t) is appropriate for saving the use of services. By the latter device equation (9.2) is modified as

$$p\phi f_z - (c + t) = 0, \qquad t = c' nz \tag{9.2a}$$

On the other hand, a lump-sum bonus changes equation (9.6) into

$$(p\phi f + b) - (c + t)z - wl - \rho k - rh = 0 \tag{9.6a}$$

Putting equations (9.2a), (9.3), (9.4) and (9.5) into equation (9.6a), we have

$$p\phi \left\{ \left(1 + \frac{b}{p\phi f}\right) f - f_z z - f_l l - f_k k - f_h h \right\} \tag{9.8a}$$

and if we can set b at the level of

$$b = e_\phi p\phi f \tag{9.15}$$

the optimizing condition (9.14) is realized.

The modified system of equations (9.2a), (9.3)–(9.15), (9.8a), (9.15) is perfectly equivalent to the optimizing conditions (9.9)–(9.12), (9.14) so that realization of the social optimum *through* market equilibrium with moderate public intervention seems to be easily implementable. The actual number of infrastructural services is, however, quite large, not only one as in our model, and it might be very difficult to implement social marginal cost pricing to *each* of those services.

9.4 MARKET EQUILIBRIUM WITH SPECIAL BUSINESS TAX

The introduction of a special business tax changes the price of output faced by the firms from p to $p(1 - s)$ in which s is the rate of the special business tax. We have, therefore, the following conditions in this case:

$$p(1-s)\phi(n)f_z - c(nz) = 0 \tag{9.16}$$

$$p(1-s)\phi(n)f_l - w = 0 \tag{9.17}$$

$$p(1-s)\phi(n)f_k - \rho = 0 \tag{9.18}$$

$$p(1-s)\phi(n)f_h - r = 0 \tag{9.19}$$

$$p(1-s)\phi(n)f(z, l, k, h) - c(nz)z - wl - \rho k - rh = 0 \tag{9.20}$$

$$nh = H \tag{9.21}$$

Comparative statics

In order to make the analysis manageable we set a drastic assumption that the function $f(\cdot)$ is separable. Total differentiation of equations (9.16)–(9.21) by s with this assumption gives us the following:

$$\{p(1-s)\phi' f_z - c'z\}\frac{dn}{ds} + \{p(1-s)\phi f_{zz} - c'n\}\frac{dz}{ds} = p\phi f_z \tag{9.22}$$

$$\phi' f_l \frac{dn}{ds} + \phi f_{ll}\frac{dl}{ds} = \frac{\phi f_l}{1-s} \tag{9.23}$$

$$\phi' f_k \frac{dn}{ds} + \phi f_{kk}\frac{dk}{ds} = \frac{\phi f_k}{1-s} \tag{9.24}$$

$$p(1-s)\phi' f_h \frac{dn}{ds} + p(1-s)\phi f_{hh}\frac{dh}{ds} - \frac{dr}{ds} = p\phi f_h \tag{9.25}$$

$$\{p(1-s)\phi' f - c'z^2\}\frac{dn}{ds} - c'nz\frac{dz}{ds} - h\frac{dr}{ds} = p\phi f \tag{9.26}$$

$$h\frac{dn}{ds} + n\frac{dh}{ds} = 0 \tag{9.27}$$

In deriving equation (9.26) we utilize the optimizing conditions of equations (9.16)–(9.19). In addition, we can eliminate dh/ds in equation (9.25) by use of equation (9.27) and this gives us

$$p(1-s)\left(\phi' f_h - \frac{h}{n}\phi f_{hh}\right)\frac{dn}{ds} - \frac{dr}{ds} = p\phi f_h \tag{9.25a}$$

Now we have three equations (9.22), (9.25a) and (9.26) for dn/ds, dz/ds, and dr/ds so that we can obtain the following solutions:

$$\frac{dn}{ds} = \frac{N_n}{D}, \qquad \frac{dz}{ds} = \frac{N_z}{D}, \qquad \frac{dr}{ds} = \frac{N_r}{D} \tag{9.28}$$

$$D \triangleq -cc'ze_\phi + p(1-s)\{p(1-s)\phi f_{zz} - c'n\}$$
$$\left\{\phi'(f_h h - f) - \frac{\phi}{n} f'_{hh} h^2\right\} + p(1-s)\phi f_{zz} c' z^2 \tag{9.29}$$

$$N_n \triangleq p\phi[\{p(1-s)\phi f_{zz}\}(f_h h - f) + c'n(f - f_h h - f_z z)] \tag{9.30}$$

$$N_z \triangleq \frac{p\phi c}{n}(e_\phi - e_c)(f - f_h h) - \{p(1-s)\phi' f - c'z^2\}p\phi f_z$$
$$+ h\left\{p(1-s)\left(\phi' f_h - \frac{h}{n}\phi f_{hh}\right)\right\}p\phi f \tag{9.31}$$

$$N_r \triangleq \frac{cc'nzp\phi f_h}{n}(e_\phi - e_c)$$
$$+ p^2(1-s)\phi\left(\phi' f_h - \frac{h}{n}\phi f_{hh}\right)[c'n(f - f_z z) - p(1-s)\phi f f_{zz}]$$
$$+ \{p(1-s)\phi f_{zz} - c'n\}\{p(1-s)\phi' f - c'z^2\}p\phi f_h \tag{9.32}$$

in which $e_c = c'nz/c$ and $e_\phi = n_\phi'/\phi$, that is, e_c is elasticity of average service cost function with respect to per firm service input and e_ϕ is elasticity of agglomeration effect with respect to the number of firms.

If the value of $\{\phi'(f_h h - f) - (\phi/n)f_{hh}h_2\}$ in equation (9.29) is positive, D becomes unambiguously negative. On the other hand, equations (9.30) and (9.8) imply that

$$N_n > 0 \tag{9.33}$$

We have, therefore,

$$\frac{dn}{ds} < 0 \tag{9.34}$$

in this case.

Deduction of other comparative statics results is not so conclusive, but it becomes much easier when we assume some specific forms for related functions.

Evaluation of welfare change

Now we are in a position to calculate the change in social surplus by the introduction of a special business tax. Since the social surplus W is expressed by $n(p\phi f - cz - wl - \rho k)$, resultant change is calculated as follows:

$$\begin{aligned}
\left.\frac{dW}{ds}\right|_{s=0} &= \frac{dn}{ds}(p\phi f - cz - wl - \rho k) \\
&\quad + n\left\{ p\phi' f\frac{dn}{ds} + p\phi\left(f_z\frac{dz}{ds} + f_l\frac{dl}{ds} + f_k\frac{dk}{ds} + f_h\frac{dh}{ds}\right)\right. \\
&\quad \left. - c'\left(\frac{dn}{ds}z + n\frac{dz}{ds}\right)z - c\frac{dz}{ds} - w\frac{dl}{ds} - \rho\frac{dk}{ds}\right\} \\
&= \left(rh\frac{dn}{ds} + np\phi f_h\frac{dh}{ds}\right) + n\left\{ p\phi' f\frac{dn}{ds} - c'\left(\frac{dn}{ds}z + n\frac{dz}{ds}\right)z\right\} \\
&= 0 + n\left\{ (p\phi' f - c'z^2)\frac{dn}{ds} - c'nz\frac{dz}{ds}\right\} \qquad \text{(by (9.27))} \\
&= n\left[\{p\phi'(f - f_z z) + (p\phi' f_z - c'z)z\}\frac{dn}{ds} - c'nz\frac{dz}{ds}\right] \\
&= n\left[p\phi'(f - f_z z)\frac{dn}{ds} + \frac{cz}{n}(e_\phi - e_c)\frac{dn}{ds} - c'nz\frac{dz}{ds}\right]
\end{aligned} \tag{9.35}$$

If both of (dn/ds) and (dz/ds) are negative as usually expected and if e_c is much bigger than e_ϕ, it is very likely that

$$\left.\frac{dW}{ds}\right|_{s=0} > 0$$

by equation (9.35). This point will be confirmed for a case of specific functions in the next section.

9.5 ILLUSTRATIVE ANALYSIS WITH SPECIFIC FUNCTIONS

In order to obtain intuitive insight into the present model, let us analyze a case with specific functional forms. First, the production function is assumed to be the following simplified form:

$$x = \max[0, n^g(\alpha \log z + \beta \log h)],\ g, \alpha, \beta > 0,$$
$$g < 1,\ \alpha g < \beta \tag{9.36}$$

Second, the average cost function of services is assumed to be:

$$c(nz) = \lambda(nz)^\mu,\ \lambda, \mu > 0,\ g < \mu < 1 \tag{9.37}$$

Social optimum

The social planner faces the following problem in this case with the constraint of available land, that is, $nh = H$:

$$\max_{\langle z, n\rangle} W = pn \cdot n^g \left(\alpha \log z + \beta \log\frac{H}{n}\right) - n\lambda\,(nz)^\mu z \tag{9.38}$$

The first-order conditions give us the following two equations:

$$\alpha\, pn^g = \lambda\,(1 + g)\,(nz)^\mu z \tag{9.39}$$

$$pn^g[(1 + g)\,\{\alpha \log z + \beta\,(\log H - \log n)\} - \beta]$$
$$= \lambda\,(1 + \beta)\,(nz)^\mu z \tag{9.40}$$

From equations (9.39) and (9.40) we obtain an equation:

$$\alpha \log z - \beta \log n = P, \qquad P = \log\left\{ exp\left(\frac{\alpha + \beta}{1 + g}\right) / H^{\beta} \right\} \quad (9.41)$$

By taking logarithms of both sides of equation (9.39), we have

$$(1 + \mu)\log z + (\mu - g)\log n = Q, \; Q = \log\left\{\frac{\alpha p}{\lambda\,(1 + \mu)}\right\} \quad (9.42)$$

The solution of equations (9.41) and (9.42) is as follows:

$$\log z^{*} = \frac{1}{\Omega}\, \{(\mu - g)P + \beta Q\} \quad (9.43)$$

$$\log n^{*} = \frac{1}{\Omega}\, \{\alpha Q - (1 + \mu)P\} \quad (9.44)$$

$$\Omega = (\alpha + \beta)\,\mu + (\beta - \alpha g) > 0 \quad (9.45)$$

Apparently z^{*} is a decreasing function of H and increasing function of p, and n^{*} is an increasing function of H and p.

It is not difficult to see that the second-order conditions for the local maximum are satisfied.

Market equilibrium with special business tax

In this case, profit-maximizing behaviour of the individual firm gives us the following:

$$(1 + \mu)\log z + (\mu - g)\log n = \tilde{Q}(s),$$

$$\tilde{Q}(s) = \log\left\{\frac{\alpha p(1 - s)}{\lambda}\right\} \quad (9.46)$$

$$\log r = \log\{\beta p(1 - s)\} + g \log n - \log h \quad (9.47)$$

Equation (9.20) in this case becomes

182 $$\alpha \log z + \beta \log h = \alpha + \beta \quad (9.48)[2]$$

and this equation with equation (9.21) gives us the following:

$$\alpha \log z - \beta \log n = \widetilde{P}, \ \widetilde{P} = \log\{e^{(\alpha + \beta)}/H^{\beta}\} \tag{9.49}$$

Obviously $\widetilde{P} > P$ and $\widetilde{Q}(0) > Q$ and the solution is

$$\log\{\widetilde{z}(s)\} = \frac{1}{\Omega} \{(\mu - g)\widetilde{P} + \beta\widetilde{Q}(s)\} \tag{9.50}$$

$$\log\{\widetilde{n}(s)\} = \frac{1}{\Omega} \{(\alpha\widetilde{Q}(s) - (1 + \mu)\widetilde{P}\} \tag{9.51}$$

It is obvious that $\widetilde{z}(0) > z^*$ but the sign of $\{\widetilde{n}(0) - n^*\}$ is indefinite. Therefore, there is excess use of services at the market equilibrium without tax, but the number of firms could be less than or more than the same at the social optimum. By setting s as $(1 - s)(1 + \mu) = 1(\widetilde{Q}(s) = Q)$, we can neutralize the effect of μ (increasing average cost of the service) but it fails to offset the effect of g (agglomeration economy).

On the other hand, it is easily seen that

$$\frac{d\widetilde{z}}{ds} = -\frac{\beta}{\Omega(1 - s)} \widetilde{z} < 0 \tag{9.52}$$

$$\frac{d\widetilde{n}}{ds} = -\frac{\alpha}{\Omega(1 - s)} \widetilde{n} < 0 \tag{9.53}$$

$$\frac{d\widetilde{r}}{ds} = -\frac{\alpha}{\Omega(1 - s)} \widetilde{r} < 0 \tag{9.54}$$

Numerical example

Let us specify the values of parameters as follows:

$$\alpha = 0.2, \ \beta = 1, \ g = 0.2, \ \lambda = 1, \ \mu = 0.8,$$
$$H = 100, \ p = 100, \ (\Omega = 1.92) \tag{9.55}$$

Then we have the following values of variables by equations (9.43), (9.44), (9.50) and (9.51):

$$z^* = 1.133, \qquad n^* \cong 38 \tag{9.56}$$

$$\tilde{z}(0) = 1.645, \qquad \tilde{n}(0) \cong 33 \tag{9.57}$$

In this case, therefore, we have a larger amount of service input and a smaller number of firms at the market equilibrium than at the social optimum.

Values of social welfare are calculated as follows:

$$W^* = 6934 \tag{9.58}$$

$$\tilde{W}(0) = 6704 \tag{9.59}$$

Since it is given that

$$\frac{\partial W}{\partial z} = p\alpha n^{1+g} z^{-1} - \lambda(1+\mu) n^{1+\mu} z^{\mu} \tag{9.60}$$

$$\frac{\partial W}{\partial n} = p(1+g)n^{g}\{\alpha \log z + \beta(\log H - \log n)\} - p\beta n^{g} - \lambda(1+\mu)n^{\mu}z^{1+\mu} \tag{9.61}$$

in general, dW/ds at $s = 0$ is calculated as:

$$\frac{d\tilde{W}(0)}{ds} = \frac{\partial \tilde{W}(0)}{\partial z}\frac{dz}{ds} + \frac{\partial \tilde{W}(0)}{\partial n}\frac{dn}{ds} \tag{9.62}$$

Actually it is shown that

$$\frac{d\tilde{W}(0)}{ds} \cong (-648.1) \times (-0.8568) + (17.37) \times (-3.448) = 495.4 > 0 \tag{9.63}$$

In this case, therefore, introduction of a special business tax certainly raises the level of welfare.

Conjectures

Comparison between (9.56) and (9.57) encourages us to make some conjectures concerning the role of a special business tax. It seems obvious that the free market brings an excess use of infrastructural services and a less-than-optimum number of firms. The special business tax can improve the former defect of the free market but it fails to remedy the latter defect as shown by equations (9.52) and (9.53). Nevertheless it is possible to improve the level of welfare to some extent by the introduction of a special business tax (s) as shown by equation (9.63). It is not impossible to calculate the (second-best) optimal level of s in a numerical model.[3]

9.6 CONCLUDING REMARKS

In this chapter we analyzed the gap between social optimum and market equilibrium for the office service activities in the CBD under a situation of increasing average cost of infrastructural services and agglomeration economy caused by a cluster of firms. If we can utilize *both* congestion charge on the use of infrastructural services *and* lump-sum subsidy to each firm for entering the office service market, the social optimum can be achieved as a modified market equilibrium.

If available policy instruments are limited to one device, say, a special business tax, its effect on the market equilibrium is very much complicated. We can, however, conclude that a special business tax can improve the level of welfare under certain conditions and it would be better than nothing. The tax may also reduce the land price as shown by equation (9.54).

Sometimes it is asserted that a combination of entrance subsidy and congestion charges is much better than any regulation on office service activities in the CBD, including a special business tax on the firms in the CBD. However, the political feasibility of such a policy mix is rather doubtful and we may encounter much less resistance to the introduction of a special business tax.

Appendix: Expositions with specific functions

We take up the following forms of production function and average cost function:

$$x = \max[0, n^g(\alpha \log z + \beta \log h)],\ g, \alpha, \beta > 0,\quad g < 1,\ \alpha g < \beta \qquad \text{(A9.1)} \rangle (9.36) \rangle$$

$$c(nz) = \lambda (nz)^\mu,\ \lambda, \mu > 0,\ g < \mu < 1 \qquad \text{(A9.2)} \langle (9.37) \rangle$$

1. *No economy – no diseconomy case*

In this case $g = 0$ and $\mu = 0$.

Behaviour of individual firm:

$$\max_{\langle z, h \rangle}[\Pi = p(\alpha \log z + \beta \log h) - (\lambda z + rh)]$$

Derived demand functions: $z = \frac{\alpha}{\lambda} p, \quad h = \frac{\beta}{r} p$ (A9.3)

Demand–supply balance of land: $nh = H$ (A9.4) ⟨ (9.7) ⟩

Indirect profit function:

$$\Pi^*(n) = p[\alpha(\log\alpha + \log p - \log\lambda) + \beta \log H - (\alpha + \beta) - \beta \log n] \qquad \text{(A9.5)}$$

Equilibrium value of n ($\Pi^* = 0$):

$$\log n^* = \frac{1}{\beta}\left\{ \alpha \log\left(\frac{\alpha p}{\lambda}\right) - \log(e^{\alpha + \beta}/H^\beta) \right\} \qquad \text{(A9.6)}$$

In this case we have clear equivalence of the market equilibrium to the social optimum. Compare equation (A9.6) with equation (9.44) in which $g = \mu = 0$.

2. *Economy–diseconomy case*

(i) Social optimum for a given n

$$W = pn^{1+g}\left(\alpha \log z + \beta \log\frac{H}{n}\right) - \lambda (nz)^{1+\mu} \qquad \text{(A9.7)}$$

$$\frac{\partial W}{\partial z} = 0 \rightarrow z(n) = \left\{\frac{\alpha p}{\lambda(1+\mu)}\right\}^{\frac{1}{1+\mu}} n^{-\frac{\mu - g}{1+\mu}} \qquad \text{(A9.8)}$$

$$W^*(n) = \frac{pn^{1+g}}{1+\mu}\left[\alpha \log\left\{\frac{\alpha p}{\lambda(1+\mu)}\right\} + \beta(1+\mu)\log H - \alpha - \Omega \log n\right] \qquad \text{(A9.9)}$$

$$\Omega = (\alpha + \beta)\mu + (\beta - \alpha g)$$

From equation (A9.9), we can deduce the optimizing value of n:

$$\log n^* = \frac{1}{\Omega}\left[\alpha \log\left(\frac{\alpha p}{\lambda\,(1+\mu)}\right) - (1+\mu)\log\left\{ e^{\left(\frac{\alpha+\beta}{1+g}\right)} / H^{\beta} \right\}\right] \qquad \text{(A9.10)}\langle(9.44)\rangle$$

(ii) Numerical example for the social optimum

Parameter values: (9.55)

$$W^*(n) = \frac{1000}{18}\, n^{1.2}\,(8.570895 - 1.92 \log n) \qquad \text{(A9.11)}$$

$$n^* \cong 38, \qquad W^* \cong 6934 \qquad \text{(A9.12)}$$

See Figure 9.1.

(iii) Market equilibrium for a given n with a special business tax s.

From equation (9.47) and $nh = H$, we have

$$\log r = \log\{\beta p(1-s)\} - \log H + (1+g)\log n \qquad \text{(A9.13)}$$

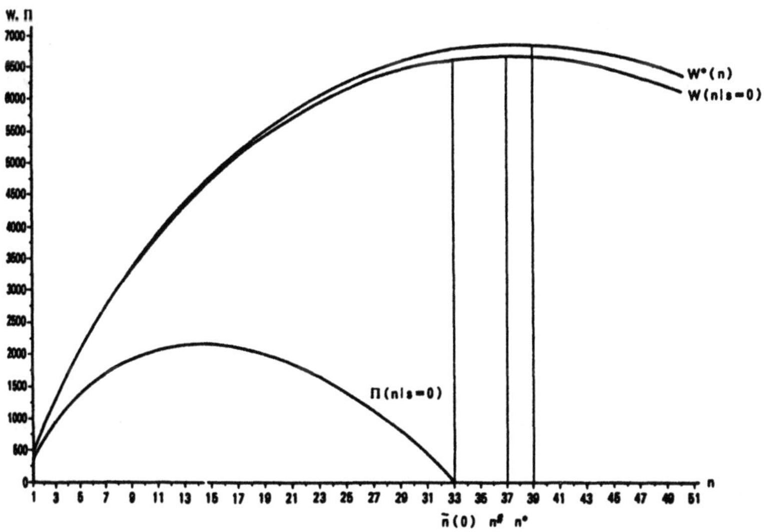

Figure 9.1 Social optimum and no-intervention market equilibrium

Equation (A9.13) and equation (9.46) give us the following:

$$\Pi(n) = \frac{p(1-s)n^{1+\varepsilon}}{1+\mu}\left[\alpha \log\left\{\frac{\alpha p(1-s)}{\lambda}\right\} + \beta(1+\mu)\log H - (1+\mu)(\alpha+\beta) - \Omega \log n\right] \quad \text{(A9.14)}$$

The corresponding value of the social welfare is calculated as:

$$W(n) = \frac{pn^{1+\varepsilon}}{1+\mu}\left[\alpha \log\left\{\frac{\alpha p(1-s)}{\lambda}\right\} + \beta(1+\mu)\log H - (1+\mu)\alpha(1-s) - \Omega \log n\right] \quad \text{(A9.15)}$$

It is obvious that $W(n) < W^*(n)$ for any value of n if $s = 0$.

(iv) Numerical example for the no-intervention market equilibrium

Parameter values: (9.55) and $s = 0$

$$\Pi(n \mid s = 0) = \frac{1000}{18} n^{1.2}(6.728452 - 1.92 \log n) \quad \text{(A9.16)}$$

$$W(n \mid s = 0) = \frac{1000}{18} n^{1.2}(8.528452 - 1.92 \log n) \quad \text{(A9.17)}$$

Equilibrium values

$$\tilde{\Pi} = 0, \quad \tilde{n} \cong 33, \quad \tilde{W} \cong 6704 \quad \text{(A9.18)}$$

Welfare maximizing value of n for (A9.17):

$$n^* \cong 37, \quad W(n^*) = 6751$$

See Figure 9.1.

(v) Second-best optimization with respect to s

By equation (9.51).

$$\tilde{n}(s) = \left\{\frac{\alpha p(1-s)}{\lambda}\right\}^{\frac{\alpha}{\Omega}} H^{\frac{(1+\mu)\beta}{\Omega}} e^{-\frac{(1+\mu)(\alpha+\beta)}{\Omega}} \quad \text{(A9.19)}$$

Putting equation (A9.19) into (A9.15) gives us the following:

$$\tilde{W}\{\tilde{n}(s), s\} = p\{\tilde{n}(s)\}^{1+\varepsilon}(\beta + \alpha s) \quad \text{(A9.20)}$$

188

Using equation (9.53), we have

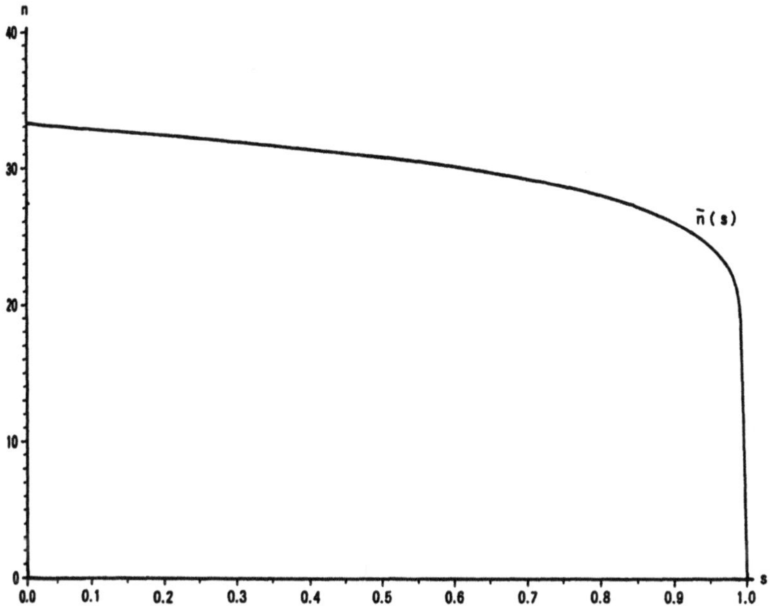

Figure 9.2 Market equilibrium with special business tax (I)

$$\frac{d\widetilde{W}}{ds} = \frac{\alpha(\alpha + \beta)p\widetilde{n}^{1+g}}{\Omega(1-s)}\{(\mu - g) - (1 + \mu)s\} \tag{A9.21}$$

and (second-best) optimizing value of s is calculated as:

$$\bar{s} = \frac{\mu - g}{1 + \mu} \tag{A9.22}$$

(vi) Numerical example for the second-best social optimum

Parameter values: (9.55)

$$\widetilde{n}(s) = 33.261548(1-s)^{0.104167} \tag{A9.23}$$

$$W\{\widetilde{n}(s), s\} = 3724.418222(1-s)^{0.125}(1.8 + 0.36s) \tag{A9.24}$$

See Figures 9.2 and 9.3.
For $\bar{s} = 1/3$, we have

$$\overline{\Pi}\left(n \mid s = \frac{1}{3}\right) = \left(\frac{1000}{18} \times \frac{2}{3}\right)n^{1.2}(6.647359 - 1.92 \log n) \tag{A9.25}$$

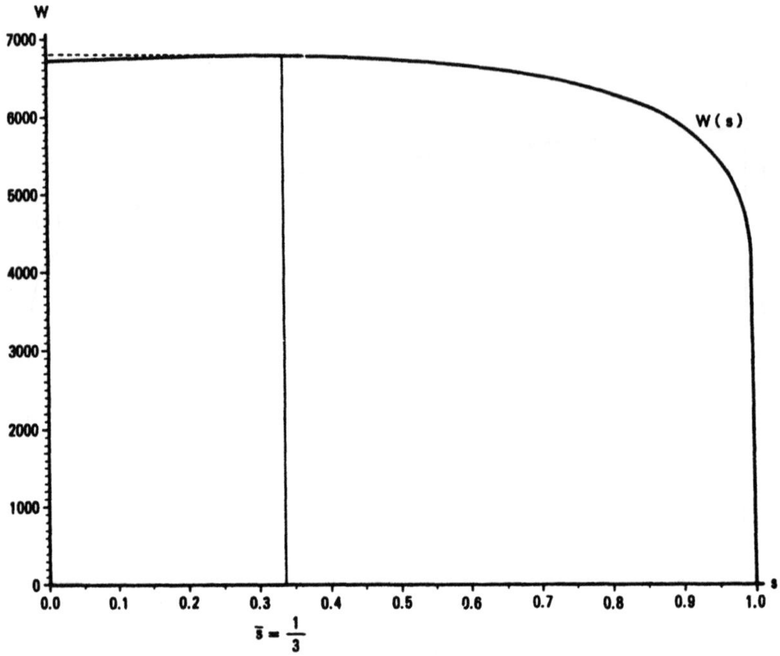

Figure 9.3 Market equilibrium with special business tax (II)

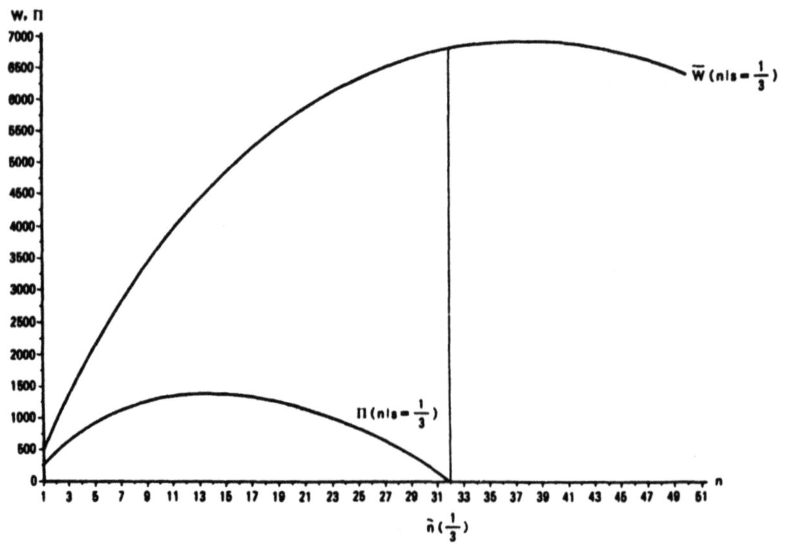

Figure 9.4 Second best social optimum

Table 9.1 Comparison of different systems

Systems	*Variables*		
	n	*s*	*W*
Social optimum	38	–	6934
Market equilibrium	33	0	6704
Suboptimal number of firms	37	0	6751
Second-best social optimum with tax	32	⅓	6797

$$\overline{W}\left(n \mid s = \frac{1}{3}\right) = \frac{1000}{18} n^{1.2}(8.567359 - 1.92 \log n) \quad \text{(A9.26)}$$

(Second best) optimizing values are, therefore,

$$\bar{s} = \frac{1}{3}, \quad \bar{n} \cong 32, \quad \overline{W} = 6797 \quad \text{(A9.27)}$$

See Figure 9.4. For a comparison of different systems, see also Table 9.1.

Notes

1. More rigorously speaking, $f(\cdot)$ is of increasing return to scale initially (for small values of output), is of constant return at some level of output, and is of decreasing return for larger values of output.
2. Equation (9.48) implies that scale elasticity of the production function is unity at this market equilibrium.
3. Actually the (second-best) optimal level of s and the values of related variables are:

$$\bar{s} = \frac{1}{3}, \; n(\bar{s}) = 32 \text{ and } W(\bar{s}) = 6797, \text{ in which } \bar{s} = \frac{\mu - g}{1 + \mu}$$

See appendix.

References

Hatta, T. and T. Ohkawara (1991) 'Commuting and Land Price in the Tokyo Metropolitan Area', in Y. Noguchi and J. Poterba (eds), *Economics of Housing in Japan and the United States* (Chicago: University of Chicago Press).

National Land Agency, Japanese Government (1987) *The Fourth Nationwide Comprehensive Regional Development Plan* (*Yonzensoh* in Japanese).
Rhodes, J. and A. Kan (1971) *Office Dispersal and Regional Policy* (Cambridge: Cambridge University Press).
Sakashita, N. (1987) 'A Critique of the Fourth Nation-wide Comprehensive Regional Development Plan', *Kosokudoro-to-Jidosha* (*Expressways and Automobiles*), vol. 30, no. 9, pp. 7–11 (in Japanese).
Sakashita, N. (1991) 'Optimal Utilization of the Central Business District: Congestion Charge, Land Tax, or Special Business Tax', ISEP Discussion Paper, No. 473, University of Tsukuba.

[14]

Infrastructure and the Space Economy, ed. by K. Peschel, Heidelberg (1990) 53–67

Economics of Multi-Habitation

by

Noboru Sakashita

1. Introduction

In the Fourth Nation-wide Comprehensive Regional Development Plan worked out by the Japanese government in 1987, there were a concept and policy recommendation of "multi-habitation".[1] People were encouraged to possess the second residence apart from their original residence partly because it may activate local areas which were losing their population as a consequence of reconcentration of population and economic activities to the Tokyo Metropolitan Area in 1980s. The aim of the present paper is to explore rationale of this multi-habitation policy from the viewpoint of regional economic theory.

A clue to the matter is the optimal allocation of living time for each household or individual. The allocation of living time decides the weighted average level of utility for each household as well as productive capacities of different regions. Maximizing the average utility under the constraints of regional productive capacities yields certain optimizing conditions in the setting of multi-habitation. It is important to know that the average utility maximized in the multi-habitation model is higher than the utility at the social optimum of single habitation with free mobility because the former does not have the equal utility constraint which is indispensable in the latter.

In section 2 which follows, a social optimum model of single habitation is formulated as a reference model. Introduction of a Benthamite social welfare function changes some of optimizing conditions which give us a hint to for–

mulate multi-habitation models. In section 3, the simplest model of multihabitation is introduced and the results of optimization are compared with those obtained in section 2. Section 4 explores a market mechanism model with policy intervention which can attain the equivalent conditions to the social optium. In section 5, the existence of incentives for individuals to switch from single habitation behaviour to multi-habitation behaviour is discussed as well as the possibility and desirability of "initial" subsidization to promote multi-habitation behaviour. Concluding remarks are given in section 6.

2. Social Optimum with Single Habitation

We utilize an extremely simplified version of David WILDASIN's general model (WILDASIN, 1987) as a starting point of discussion. Consider a two-region economy in which free migration between the two regions is assured. In region i (i=1,2), a resident enjoys his(her) utility U_i by the consumption of a private good C_i and a public good G_i, i.e. $U_i=U_i(C_i,G_i)$. Region i's productive capacity is expressed by its specific production function F_i the sole input of which is the residents' labour L_i. The total population of the two-region economy is fixed as $\bar{L}$, i.e. $\bar{L}=L_1+L_2$. U_i, F_i and $\bar{L}$ complete the description of socio-economic environment in which this two-region economy operates.

Let us consider the optimizing problem for a social planner who wishes to maximize the level of people's utility under the constraint of free migration, i.e. equal utility between the two regions. The problem is formulated as follows:

$$\begin{aligned} &\text{Maximize} \quad U_1(C_1,G_1) \\ &\text{w.r.t.} \quad C_i,G_i,L_i(i=1,2) \\ &\text{subject to} \quad U_2(C_2,G_2) - U_1(C_1,G_1) = 0 && (1) \\ &\qquad F_1(L_1) + F_2(L_2) - C_1L_1 - C_2L_2 - G_1 - G_2 = 0 && (2) \\ &\qquad \bar{L} - L_1 - L_2 = 0 && (3) \end{aligned}$$

The optimizing conditions for the above problem are:

$$\frac{\partial U_i}{\partial C_i} = \frac{\partial U_i}{\partial G_i} L_i, \quad i = 1, 2 \tag{4}$$

$$F_1' - C_1 = F_2' - C_2 \tag{5}$$

Equation (4) implies a famous Samuelsonian condition for the supply of (local) public good in each region, and equation (5) is sometimes called 'social net benefit condition of migration'.[2]

As HARTWICK pointed out, the constraint of equal utility embodies the philosophy of Rawlsian social welfare.[3] If we introduce the concept of a Benthamite social welfare without equal utility constraint instead, we have the following different problem:

$$\text{Maximize} \quad L_1 \cdot U_1(C_1, G_1) + L_2 \cdot U_2(C_2, G_2)$$
$$\text{w.r.t.} \quad C_i, G_i, L_i (i=1,2)$$
$$\text{subject to (2) and (3)}$$

In this case we have a little different set of the optimizing conditions:

$$\frac{\partial U_i}{\partial C_i} = \frac{\partial U_i}{\partial G_i} L_i, \quad i = 1, 2 \tag{4}$$

$$\frac{\partial U_1}{\partial C_1} = \frac{\partial U_2}{\partial C_2} \tag{6}$$

$$U_1 + \frac{\partial U_i}{\partial C_i}(F_1' - C_1) = U_2 + \frac{\partial U_i}{\partial C_i}(F_2' - C_2) \tag{7}$$

We have Samuelsonian conditions again (equation (4)), and there is a stronger condition of equal marginal utilities of private good between regions (equation (6)) which implies equal amount of consumption of the same if the utility function is separable in C_i and G_i. Equation (7) replaces equation (5) of the previous case. Later the same equation will be interpreted as "social net benefit condition of multi-habitation" in a different context.

If we add the equal utility constraint (equation (1)) to the Benthamite problem, it becomes completely equivalent to the previous Rawlsian problem so that it is clear that the average utility $(L_1U_1 + L_2U_2/\bar{L})$ in the Benthamite optimum is higher than the utility $(U_1 = U_2)$ in the Rawlsian optimum. This fact gives us a strong hint to consider an economy where multihabitation is encouraged.

In reality, however, it is almost impossible for us to dispense with equal utility constraint even in a planned economy, because it will cause a great social strain if the utility levels of different regions are kept unequal for long time. We must have, therefore, some device to realize a Benthamite-like social optimum *without* strain and this is the background of our multi-habitation model. Finally we wish to make it clear that the Rawlsian social optimum can be achieved by a market economy with modest intervention by the goverment. What is needed is a combination of interregional income transfer by the central goverment and optimal supply of local public good by the local government in each region.

3. Social Optimum with Multi-Habitation

Let us consider that each household in the economy spends 100p percent of time in region 1 and 100(1−p) percent in region 2 every year. We assume further that movement cost between two regions is negligible. If the total population L is large enough, region 1 can maintain labour input of approximately (pL) always and region 2 can do that of ((1−p)L). Per capita consumption of the private good is p-and-(1−p)-weighted average of C_1 and C_2, but local public good must be supplied constantly at the levels of G_1 and G_2.

Social planner's problem in this case is:

$$\text{Maximize} \quad \{pU_1(C_1, G_1) + (1-p)U_2(C_2, G_2)\} \qquad (8)$$

w.r.t. $C_i, G_i, (i=1,2), p$

$$\text{subject to} \quad F_1(p\bar{L}) + F_2\{(1-p)\bar{L}\} - \{pC_1 + (1-p)C_2\}\bar{L} - G_1 - G_2 = 0 \qquad (9)$$

In mathematical sense this problem is perfectly equivalent to the problem of Benthamite optimization in the previous section so that we have the following four optimizing conditions two of which are exactly the same as those in the Benthamite optimization, i.e.[5]

$$\frac{\partial U_1}{\partial C_1} = \frac{\partial U_1}{\partial G_1} (p\bar{L}) \qquad (10)$$

$$\frac{\partial U_2}{\partial C_2} = \frac{\partial U_2}{\partial G_2} ((1-p)\bar{L}) \qquad (11)$$

$$\frac{\partial U_1}{\partial C_1} = \frac{\partial U_2}{\partial C_2} \qquad (6)$$

$$U_1 + \frac{\partial U_1}{\partial C_1} (F_1{'}-C_1) = U_2 + \frac{\partial U_2}{\partial C_2} (F_2{'}-C_2) \qquad (7)$$

Equations (10) and (11) are variants of the Samuelsonian condition in the multi-habitation model, and equation (6) means the equality of marginal utilities of private good with the same interpretation as in the Benthamite model. Equation (7) means the following. If an individual (or household) shifts marginal length of time from the living in region 1 to that in region 2, region 1 loses one person's utility and the gap between his(her) marginal productivity and consumption of private good which is his(her) contribution to the regional economy. All values are evaluated by the dimension of utility and are calculated in annual term. To the contrary, region 2 gains the same set of values as region 1 loses. At the optimum, therefore, the loss in region 1 is equal to the gain in region 2, and there is no *social* incentive for an individual to shift the marginal time. We call this condition "social net benefit condition of multi-habitation" which is a generalization of the "social net benefit condition of migration" (equation (5)) in the Rawlsian optimum (RO).

Although mathematically equivalent, the multi-habitation optimum (MHO) has quite different implication when it is compared with the Benthamite optimum (BO). In BO the total population $\bar{L}$ is divided into region 1 (L_1) and region 2 (L_2) as *different* groups of the residents so that U_1 and U_2 are utilities of different people. In MHO, however, the same individual divides his(her) living time into the two regions by the ratio of p vs (1-p) so that $(pU_1 + (1-p)U_2)$ is the total utility of *one* specific individual. Therefore, there is no risk of social strain between regions in spite of the difference between U_1 and U_2. This is a very peculiar characteristic of MHO. Since MHO is mathematically equivalent to BO, its utility level is of course higher than that in RO.

It is important to know that we may be able to have an MHO even if one of two regions does not have productive capacity. If there is no production activity in region 2, $F_2{'}$ in equation (7) vanishes. Even so we can have an MHO if U_2 is intrinsically much higher than U_1. The two utility functions, U_1

and U_2, are basically the same function of C_i and G_i and comparable with each other. If, however, there is the third argument in each utility function which is region-specific, the two will become different functions on the surface but will be still comparable with each other. More concretely, we make comparison between $U(C_1, G_1, R_1)$ and $U(C_2, G_2, R_2)$ where R_1 and R_2 are region-specific factors (regional amenity for instance). If R_i's have positive effect on U_i and if R_2 is much larger than R_1, we may have an MHO in which people do not make productive activities in R_2. Region 2 is nothing other than a pure resort area. (Perhaps, however, one may do some business activities, for instance, writing articles or composing music, even in resort areas.)

It might be appropriate to say something more concerning equation (6). If the variable C_i is separable from other arguments in utility function and if its marginal utility is monotonically decreasing, equation (6) implies the same amount of consumption (in annual term) by an individual in different living places. It is a very natural conclusion. Usually, however, C_i is *not* separable from, say, region-specific factors which enter the utility function. People drink cold beverages more in hotter region and prefer hot dishes in colder region. In that case, equation (6) does not imply equal consumption in different regions.

4. Multi-Habitation Market Equilibrium

The next question for us is to explore some system of the market economy with government intervention by which the equivalent situation to MHO can be realized. First we analyze a market system supported by the central government. Secondly we consider another system in which local governments perform certain rôle in the working of the system.

4.1 Market Equilibrium Supported by the Central Government

In this system an individual (household) maximizes his(her) weighted-average utility subject to budget constraint. His(her) income consists of wage in region 1(w_1) and the same in region 2 (w_2) plus an additional income which does not depend on his(her) residential location (Y). All variables are expressed in annual term.

$$\underset{\text{w.r.t. } C_1, C_2, p}{\text{Maximize}} \quad \{pU_1(C_1,G_1) + (1-p)U_2(C_2,G_2)\}$$

$$\text{subject to} \quad \{pw_1+(1-p)w_2 + Y\} - pC_1 - (1-p)C_2 = 0 \tag{12}$$

The following optimizing conditions are derived.

$$\frac{\partial U_1}{\partial C_1} = \frac{\partial U_2}{\partial C_2} \tag{6}$$

$$U_1 + \frac{\partial U_i}{\partial C_i}(w_1-C_1) = U_2 + \frac{\partial U_i}{\partial C_i}(w_2-C_2) \tag{13}$$

Equation (13) resembles "social net benefit condition of multi-habitation" (equation (7)) but we need an additional condition in order to state complete equivalence of these two equations.

Next we assume that a representative firm with a production function $F_i(L_i)$ maximizes its profit in each region under potentially competitive situation.

$$\underset{\text{w.r.t. } L_i}{\text{Maximize}} \quad \{ F_i(L_i) - w_iL_i \} \quad , i = 1,2$$

The optimizing condition is:

$$F_i'(L_i) - w_i = 0 \;, \quad i = 1,2 \tag{14}$$

The labour market in each region is cleared by the following equation.

$$L_i = p_i\bar{L} \;, \quad i = 1,2 \tag{15}$$

Combining equations (13), (14), and (15), we can have the exactly same relation as equation (7) here.

Behaviour of the central government is formulated as follows. If it takes p as given, it can indirectly determine the volume of total consumption of private good Q by deciding the levels of G_1 and G_2, i.e.

$$Q = F_1(p\bar{L}) + F_2\{(1-p)\bar{L}\} - G_1 - G_2 \tag{16}$$

With an *arbitary* conjecture concerning the pattern of allocation of Q between the two regions, α vs $(1-\alpha)$, the central government can formulate its optimization problem as follows:

$$\underset{\text{w.r.t. } G_1, G_2}{\text{Maximize}} \left[pU_1\left\{ \frac{\alpha(F_1 + F_2 - G_1 - G_2)}{p\bar{L}}, G_1 \right\} + (1-p)U_2 \left\{ \frac{(1-\alpha)(F_1 + F_2 - G_1 - G_2)}{(1-p)\bar{L}}, G_2 \right\} \right]$$

Then the following condition is derived.

$$\alpha \frac{\partial U_1}{\partial C_1} + (1-\alpha)\frac{\partial U_2}{\partial C_2} = \frac{\partial U_1}{\partial G_1}(p\bar{L}) = \frac{\partial U_2}{\partial G_2}\{(1-p)\bar{L}\} \tag{17}$$

Since $\frac{\partial U_1}{\partial C_1}$ and $\frac{\partial U_2}{\partial C_2}$ are always equalized with each other owing to the behaviour of (homogeneous) individuals (equation (6)), equation (17) becomes equivalent to equations (10) and (11) at MHO.

Finally the residence-free non-wage income of an individual can be defined as follows if there is an adequate reimbursement system.[6]

$$Y \stackrel{\text{def}}{=} \frac{F_1 + F_2 - (G_1 + G_2) - \{pw_1 + (1-p)w_2\}\bar{L}}{\bar{L}} \tag{18}$$

Combining equation (12) and equation (19) we can derive the basic supply and demand relation in MHO (equation (9)).

Accordingly we could derive all conditions which characterize MHO for this market equilibrium under the general supervision of the central government. In this scheme the supply level of local public good in each region is determined in a synchronized manner by the central goverment. To some extent this is not an imagination but a reality in Japan. The Japanese governments eager to subsidize resort development in local areas selectively probably guided by some different principle from MHO. We cannot, however, find the rôle of local government in the scheme of this subsection, and it is unrealistic to disregared local autonomy in the world of multi-habitation. In the next subsection we proceed to the model with local governments.

4.2 Introduction of Local Governments - A Try and Error Process

Let us assume that the level of G_i is tentatively determined by the local government of region i as $\bar{G}_i$, i=1,2. An individual determines his(her) time allocation which maximizes his(her) utility under the supply of $\bar{G}_1$ and $\bar{G}_2$ and related budget constraint knowing that all individuals will take the same behaviour. Then similar conditions as equations (6) and (13) are derived.[7] By these conditions and the budget constraint, the "optimal" p^0 is determined as a function of $\bar{G}_1$ and $\bar{G}_2$ i.e. $p^0(\bar{G}_1, \bar{G}_2)$. Next, a local government, say that of region 1, determines the new optimal level of G_1 taking $(p^0\bar{L})$ and $((1-p^0)\bar{L})$ given and under a subjective presumption of autarky. Then there will be the new level of $\bar{G}_1(p_0)$ and the level of $\bar{C}_1(p_0)$ presumed by the local government with a Samuelsonian condition between $\bar{G}_1$ and $\bar{C}_1$. Similarly there will be $\bar{G}_2(p_0)$ and $\bar{C}_2(p_0)$ determined by the local government of region 2. Now there will be another process of adjustment by individuals and the new level of p, i.e. p^1, will be determined as follows:

$$p^1\{\bar{G}(p_0),\ \bar{G}_2(p^0)\} = \varnothing(p^0) \tag{19}$$

Therefore we observe a repeated process of $p^{t+1} = \varnothing(p^t)$ which may result in a stationary equilibrium.

There are, however, two difficulties in this try and error process. The first difficulty is that it is not clear whether the above process is stable or not. A sufficient condition for the stability is combination of $\varnothing > 0$ and $\varnothing'(p)<1$ for all possible p, but the function $\varnothing$ may be too complicated to be checked for these properties. The second difficulty is that C_1^* and C_2^* which are actually determined by consumers at the equilibrium (p^*) are generally different from $\bar{C}_1(p^*)$ and $\bar{C}_2(p^*)$ which are fictitiously determined by the local government at the same equilibrium. Therefore, there is no guarantee that we can have Samuelsonian conditions at the equilibrium.

One possibility to overcome these difficulties is an adequate intervention by the central government to break autarky presumtion by the local governments. It imposes positive and negative subsidy S on both of the local governments, i.e.

$$F_1(p\bar{L}) - pC_1\bar{L} - G_1 + S = 0 \tag{20}$$

$$F_2\{(1-p)\bar{L}\} - (1-p)C_2\bar{L} - G_2 - S = 0 \tag{21}$$

The resultant equilibrium values $p^*(S)$, $C_1^*(S)$, $C_2^*(S)$, $\bar{C}_1(p^*(S))$, and $\bar{C}_2(p^*(S))$ can be induced to make $C_1^* = \bar{C}_1$ and $C_2^* = \bar{C}_2$ and to realize Samuelsonian conditions by selecting appropriate S.

Is it possible to conceptualize a system of this sort in which local autonomy is reestablished? Considering the existence of fiscal externality and inefficiency of free migration in the single habitation system, we think, the possibility is not so promising.[8]

5. Incentive to Switch from Single Habitation System to Multi-Habitation System

People are usually living in a single habitation system in which equal utility between regions is realized. Is there strong enough incentive for them to switch from the current system to that of the multi-habitation autonomously? Let us begin with RO in the two-region single habitation economy in which $U_1(C_1^*, G_1^*) = U_2(C_2^*, G_2^*)$. Each individual supposes that he(she) can obtain disposable incomes of C_1^* and C_2^* in each region. The problem to be solved is:

$$\underset{\text{w.r.t. } C_1, C_2, p}{\text{Maximize}} \quad \{p_1U_1(C_1, G_1^*) + (1-p)U_2(C_2, G_2^*)\}$$

$$\text{subject to } pC_1^* + (1-p)C_2^* - pC_1 - (1-p)C_2 = 0 \tag{22}$$

This problem can be approached by a step-wise manner. We first maximize the objective function with a fixed p, then the following optimizing condition is obtained:

$$\frac{\partial U}{\partial C_1} = \frac{\partial U}{\partial C_2} = \lambda \tag{23}$$

where λ is a Lagrangean multiplier for the constraint (22).

Next we maximize the maximized objective function with respect to p. By the envelope theorem we have:

$$\frac{d\Phi}{dp} = \frac{\partial\Phi}{\partial p} = U_1 - U_2 + \lambda\{(C_1^*-C_2^*) - (C_1-C_2)\} \tag{24}$$

where Φ is the related Lagrangean form. The second-order derivative is:

$$\frac{d^2\Phi}{dp^2} = \frac{\partial U_1}{\partial C_1}\frac{dC_1}{dp} - \frac{\partial U_2}{\partial C_2}\frac{dC_2}{dp} + \frac{d\lambda}{dp}\{(C_1^*-C_2^*) - (C_1-C_2)\}$$

$$+ \lambda\left(\frac{dC_2}{dp} - \frac{dC_1}{dp}\right)$$

$$= \frac{d\lambda}{dp}\{(C_1^*-C_2^*) - (C_1-C_2)\} \tag{25}$$

by equation (23). We can calculate $\frac{d\lambda}{dp}$ by comparative static solution to the first stage optimization problem, i.e.

$$\frac{d\lambda}{dp} = \frac{1}{Q}\{(C_1^*-C_2^*) - (C_1-C_2)\}\left(\frac{\partial^2 U_1}{\partial C_1^2}\right)\left(\frac{\partial^2 U_2}{\partial C_2^2}\right) \tag{26}$$

where $Q = p\,\frac{\partial^2 U_2}{\partial C_2^2} + (1-p)\,\frac{\partial^2 U_1}{\partial C_1^2}$ (<0). From equations (25) and (26) we can conclude that:

$$\frac{d^2\Phi}{dp^2} < 0 \tag{27}$$

It has become clear that the objective function is concave with respect to p. However, continuity of $C_1(p)$ and $C_2(p)$ at $p = 0$ or $p = 1$ is unclear because we have switches of the phase there. If the utility function is separable between C_i and G_i, we can say that:

$$\lim_{p\to 0} C_i(p) = C_2^*\ , \quad \lim_{p\to 1} C_i(p) = C_1^* \tag{28}$$

by equations (22) and (23) and the continuity is established.

In the continuity case we can safely say that there is enough incentive for individuals to switch from single habitation behaviour to multi-habitation behaviour (see figure 1). An individual adopts a time allocation of $\hat{p}$ and $(1-\hat{p})$ with given G_1^* and G_2^*. Then local or central governments start to change G_is in response to $\hat{p}$ and the whole adjustment process described in the previous section begins.

Figure 1: Switch from Single Habitation to Multi-habitation

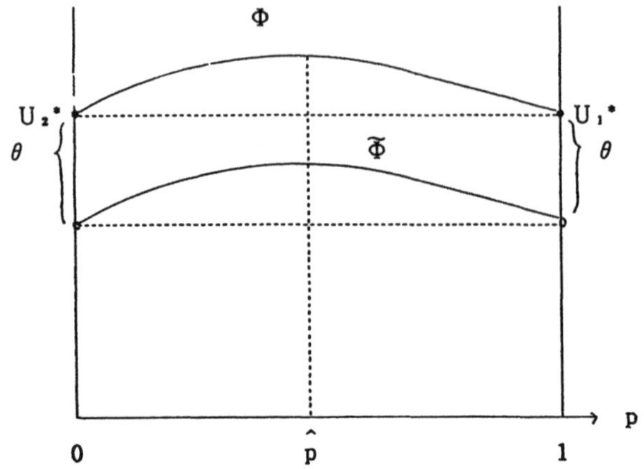

If there exists some "set-up" cost or movement cost θ in order to shift from single habitation to multi-habitation such as construction cost of the second house for instance, the maximized $\tilde{\Phi}(\hat{p})$ net of the set-up cost could be lower than $U_1{}^*(U_2{}^*)$ in single habitation. In this case the switch process does not start (see figure 1). Even if $\tilde{\Phi}(\hat{p})$ net of the set-up cost is higher than $U_1{}^*(U_2{}^*)$, an individual needs some "finance" to start multi-habitation behaviour so that it does not begin automatically when the financial market is not perfect. In the latter case there is a necessity for the government to give a subsidy to individuals to initiate switches from single habitation to multi-habitation.

6. Concluding Remarks

There are several things to be discussed more concerning multi-habitation behaviour. First, rise in labour productivity in the form of upward shift of production functions may give different impacts on the maximized utility levels in RO and MHO. Therefore, a switch from single habitation to multihabitation may start at the certain level of technical progress in production, i.e. people become affordable to begin multi-habitation behaviour at certain stage of economic growth.

Second, the local or central governments may attempt to improve the amenity of the regions by certain investment in natural environment etc. to attract people there. This action changes the position of region-specific utility functions. Some benefit-cost analysis can be in order for the public activities of this sort utilizing the model developed here.

Introduction of heterogeneity among individuals will be another important generalization particularly to make comparison of the present model with a Tiebout type model of separation. On the other hand, introduction of private capital etc. will not change the conclusion obtained here essentially.

Appendix: Numerical Example of Rawlsian Optimum and Multi-habitation Optimum

A numerical calculation has been done to deduce the values of several variables at RO and at MHO. The specification of related functions is given below table 1. In this example, RO gives smaller C and larger G in rgion 1 compared to them in region 2 and assures the same utility level between the two regions. On the other hand, the level of C is equalized for the two regions, but G_1 is bigger than G_2 implying higher U in region 1 than region 2 at MHO. Therefore, p is much bigger than (1-p) and it is also bigger than $(L_1/\bar{L})$ at RO. The gap (U_1-U_2) at MHO is offset by the same in $(\frac{\partial U_i}{\partial C_i} F_i')$ because of equation (7), i.e. $F_2'>F_1'$.

Table 1: Numerical Examples of RO and MHO

	(i) Rawlsian Optimum	(i) Multi-habitation Optimum
U_1	0.83	0.90
U_2	0.83	0.57
p	—	0.83
AVERAGE U	—	0.84
C_1	0.17	0.18
G_1	3.37	3.75
C_2	0.22	0.18
G_2	1.18	0.74
L_1	78.8	—
L_2	21.2	—

Specification of Functions

$$\begin{cases} U_i = 2 + 0.8 \log C_i + 0.2 \log G_i , \ i=1,2 \\ F_1 = 1.2 L_1^{0.6} , \ F_2 = L_2^{0.6} \\ \bar{L} = L_1 + L_2 = 100 \end{cases}$$

Although the difference between U_1 at RO and $(U = pU_1 + (1-p)U_2)$ at MHO is very small, the two optima give quite different allocation of local public goods between the two regions.

FOOTNOTES

[1] National Land Agency (3, p. 57).

[2] See Wildasin (6, Chapter 2).

[3] See Hartwick (2).

[4] See Sakashita (4).

[5] The secondary condition for the maximum is not so easy to be worked out. One possibility is to make a two-step approach. First solve the problem with a fixed p, then show that the maximized objective function, say $\hat{\Phi}$, is concave with respect to p. In this case, if the derivative $\frac{d\hat{\Phi}}{dp}$ becomes zero for some $p \varepsilon (0,1)$, then we can have an interior maximum. Calculation of $\frac{d^2\hat{\Phi}}{dp^2}$ may be messy, but it becomes much easier with an assumption of separable utility.

[6] Notice, however, that the value of Y could be negative which means a lump-sum charge to finance the supply of local public goods.

[7] A consumer's problem is as follows:

$$\underset{\text{w.r.t. } p, C_1, C_2}{\text{Maximize}} \ \{pU_1(C_1, \bar{G}_1) + (1-p)U_2(C_2, \bar{G}_2)\}$$

$$\text{subject to } F_1(p\bar{L}) + F_2\{(1-p)\bar{L}\} - (\bar{G}_1 + \bar{G}_2) - \{pC_1 + (1-p)C_2\}\bar{L} = 0 \qquad (F.1)$$

The optimizing conditions are:

$$\frac{\partial U_1}{\partial C_1} = \frac{\partial U_2}{\partial C_2} = \lambda \bar{L} \qquad (F.2)$$

$$U_1 + \lambda \bar{L}(F_1' - C_1) = U_2 + \lambda \bar{L}(F_2' - C_2) \qquad (F.3)$$

[8] See the following literatures: Boadway and Flatters (1), Sakashita (4), and Sakashita (5).

LITERATURE

Boadway, R.; Flatters, F., 1982: Efficiency and Equalization Payments in a Federal System of Government: a Synthesis and Extensions of Recent Results, Canadian Journal of Economies, Vol. 15, pp.613-633.

Hartwick, J.M., 1980: The Henry George Rule, Optimal Population, and Interregional Equity, Canadian Journal of Economics, Vol. 13, pp.695-700.

National Land Agency, 1987: The Fourth Nation-wide Comprehensive Regional Development Plan, Ministry of Finance (Japan) Press, (in Japanese).

Sakashita, N., 1988: Spatial Interdependence and Externalities, ISEP Discussion Paper Series (University of Tsukuba), No. 391, (Presidential Address, The 35th North American Meetings of Regional Science Association, 11th Nov.

Sakashita, N., 1989: Market Equilibrium and Optimum Social Welfare in a Two Region Economy, R. Sato and T. Negishi ed.: Developments in Japanese Economics, Tokyo, Harcourt Brace Jovonovich Japan, Chapter 3.

Wildasin, D.E., 1987: Urban Public Finance, Fundamentals of Pure and Applied Economics, Vol. 10, Chur: Harwood Academic Publishers.

Regional Science and Urban Economics, Amsterdam, Vol. 25 (1995) 427–434

An economic theory of urban growth control

Noboru Sakashita

Institute of Socio-Economic Planning, University of Tsukuba, Tsukuba Ibaraki 305, Japan

Received September 1993; final version received October 1994

Abstract

Economic theory of urban growth controls by Engle et al. (*Journal of Urban Economics*, 1992, 32, 269–283) is extended to the direction of endogenous residents' utility in a closed two-city economy. It is shown that the growth control policy is justified strictly only in the case in which there exist some size-related externalities in the process of urban growth. It is also shown that if the growth control policy is needed anyway, it is necessary to have an intervening policy concerning the population allocation among cities even before growth.

Keywords: Endogenous utility; Size-related externalities; Optimum allocation of population

JEL classification: R11; R52

1. Introduction

A comparison between the equilibrium path of urban population growth without control and that with efficient growth control under the presence of (population) size-related externality was studied by Brueckner (1990). Engle, Navarro and Carson (ENC, henceforth) dealt with the same problem using a comparative static analysis instead of the dynamic modelling of Brueckner (ENC, 1992). Although these authors obtained interesting and clear-cut results, both of their models are based on exogenous residents' utility. They are forced, therefore, to use the total value of land rents absorbed by the absentee landlords as the criterion of efficiency which is, to say the least of it, not so appealing.

The purpose of this paper is to generalize the theory of growth controls by

SSDI 0166-0462(95)02094-2

ENC into the direction of endogenous residents' utility. Firstly, the paper will again show that the growth control policy is justified only in the case where some size-related externalities exist in the process of urban growth. Secondly, it will be shown that if the growth control policy is needed in any sense, it would have been necessary to have an intervening policy concerning the population allocation among cities at the initial stage before growth.

Discussions in the past about growth control policies were generally separated from those about the optimal population size. However, the essence of both problems is the existence of (population) size-related externalities, so these two problems must be dealt with from the same viewpoint of the optimum allocation of population among cities (see, for example, Henderson, 1987).

2. The basic model and comparative statics

We start with the following set of assumptions. These assumptions are basically the same as those made by ENC, but there is some generalization.

(i) There are two cities in the economy: say, Tokyo (suffix t) and Sendai (suffix s).[1] People (households) can freely migrate between the two cities. Each household, however, must reside in one of the two cities. Therefore, the total population of the economy ($\bar{N}$) is divided into the population of Tokyo (N_t) and that of Sendai (N_s) exactly.

(ii) Every household consumes one unit of housing service wherever it locates within a city. The unit is produced by one unit of land and one unit of physical capital. The utility of a household is dependent on housing service h and composite good c, which it consumes, i.e. $U = U(h, c)$.

(iii) When an equilibrium is reached, every household must enjoy the same utility level within a city, as well as between cities, because of free relocation and free migration.

(iv) Each household must commute to the CBD of its residing city.

(v) Unit commuting cost in each city is expressed by k_t and k_s. k_t could be dependent on the population size N_t (congestion externality); on the other hand, k_s is supposed to be constant.[2]

(vi) City i can accommodate $Q_i(s_i)$ households in which s_i is the border of city i. Q_i may be called the accommodation function.

From Assumption (iii) of equal utility, we have the following equation:

[1] In Japan, Sendai is considered as the back-up city in the event of Tokyo meeting with some disaster.

[2] This asymmetry is assumed only for the purpose of reducing the complication of calculation.

$$U^* = U(1, Y_t - R_t(x_t) - k_t(N_t)x_t - P)$$
$$= U(1Y_s - R_s(x_s) - k_s x_s - P),$$
$$x_t \in [0, s_t], \quad x_s \in [0, s_s], \tag{1}$$

in which Y_i is the per capita income in city i ($i = \mathrm{t, s}$), $R_i(x_i)$ is the rent in city i at x_i, which is the distance from the CBD of city i ($i = \mathrm{t, s}$), s_i is the border of city i ($i = \mathrm{t, s}$), and P is the price of physical capital. The rent profile in city i ($i = \mathrm{t, s}$) is expressed as follows by Assumptions (iv) and (v):

$$R_t(x_t) = R_t(0) - k_t(N_t) \cdot x_t, \tag{2}$$

$$R_s(x_s) = R_s(0) - k_s \cdot x_s. \tag{3}$$

If we can assume that the opportunity cost of land at the city border is zero, we have the following relations:

$$s_t = R_t(0)/k_t(N_t), \tag{4}$$

$$s_s = R_s(0)/k_s. \tag{5}$$

By the definition of the accommodation function in Assumption (vi), we have the following equations:

$$N_t = Q_t(s_t), \tag{6}$$

$$N_s = Q_s(s_s). \tag{7}$$

Finally, by Assumption (i), population allocation is described as

$$N_t + N_s = \bar{N}. \tag{8}$$

By rearranging Eqs. (1)–(7), the system is condensed into the following two equations if k_t is independent from N_t:

$$Q_t\left\{\frac{R_{0t}}{k_t}\right\} + Q_s\left\{\frac{R_{0s}}{k_s}\right\} = \bar{N}, \tag{9}$$

$$Y_t - R_{0t} = Y_s - R_{0s}, \tag{10}$$

in which $R_{0i} = R_i(0)$ is the rent of city i ($i = \mathrm{t, s}$) at its center. By Eqs. (9) and (10), R_{0t} and R_{0s} and the corresponding level of utility (U^*) are determined (see Eq. (1)).

For the system of Eqs. (9) and (10) we can apply a comparative static analysis to see the impact of an increase in Y_t. First, we analyze the case of no externality, i.e. $k_t'(N_t) = 0$. For simplicity, we assume that $k_t = k_s = k$ for a while. Differentiating Eqs. (9) and (10) by Y_t (assuming $k_t = k_s = k$ in addition) and solving for dR_{0i}/dY_t ($i = \mathrm{t, s}$) and dU^*/dY_t, we have

$$\frac{dR_{0t}}{dY_t} = \frac{Q'_s}{Q'_t + Q'_s} > 0, \qquad \frac{dR_{0s}}{dY_t} = -\frac{Q'_t}{Q'_t + Q'_s} < 0, \tag{11}$$

$$\frac{dU^*}{dY_t} = U_x\left(1 - \frac{dR_{0t}}{dY_t}\right) = U_x \frac{Q'_t}{Q'_t + Q'_s} > 0, \qquad U_x \equiv \frac{\partial U}{\partial x}. \tag{12}$$

Eq. (11) shows that the impact of an increase in $Y_t(\Delta Y_t)$ is divided into an increase and a decrease of central rents in the two cities. Eq. (12) shows the final welfare impact of ΔY_t.

Secondly, if there is a commuting cost externality, we have the following equations instead of Eqs. (9) and (10):

$$Q_t\{R_{0t}/k_s(N_t)\} = N_t, \tag{13}$$

$$N_t + Q_s\{R_{0s}/k_s\} = \bar{N}, \tag{14}$$

$$Y_t - R_{0t} = Y_s - R_{0s}. \tag{15}$$

Differentiating these equations by Y_t, we have the following results:

$$\begin{pmatrix} Q'_t k_t & 0 & -(Q'_t R_{0t} k'_t + k_t^2) \\ 0 & Q_s k_s & k_s^2 \\ -1 & 1 & 0 \end{pmatrix} \begin{pmatrix} \frac{dR_{0t}}{dY_t} \\ \frac{dR_{0s}}{dY_t} \\ \frac{dN_t}{dY_t} \end{pmatrix} = \begin{pmatrix} 0 \\ 0 \\ -1 \end{pmatrix} \tag{15a}$$

$$\frac{dN_t}{dY_t} = \frac{1}{D} \cdot \frac{k_t}{k_s} \cdot Q'_s > 0, \tag{16}$$

$$\frac{dR_{0t}}{dY_t} = \frac{1}{D}\left\{\left(R_{0t}k'_t + \frac{k_t^2}{Q'_t}\right)\frac{Q'_s}{k_s}\right\} \quad \left(0 < \frac{dR_{0t}}{dY_t} < 1\right), \tag{17}$$

$$\frac{dR_{0s}}{dY_t} = -\frac{1}{D} k_t < 0, \tag{18}$$

$$\begin{aligned} \frac{dU^*}{dY_t} &= U_x\left(1 - \frac{D - k_t}{D}\right) = U_x \frac{k_t}{D} \\ &= U_x \frac{Q'_t}{Q'_t + \frac{k_t}{k_s} Q'_s + R_{0t} \cdot \frac{k'_t}{k_t} \cdot \frac{Q'_s Q'_t}{k_s}} > 0, \end{aligned} \tag{19}$$

$$D = \left\{R_{0t} \cdot k'_t + \frac{k_t^2}{Q'_t}\right\} \frac{Q'_s}{k_s} + k_t > 0. \tag{20}$$

By comparing Eq. (19) with Eq. (12), we can conclude that the existence of a commuting cost externality mitigates the welfare impact of ΔY_t if $k_t(N_t)$ is approximately equal to k_s.[3]

3. Policy analysis of urban population allocation

As policy measures for controlling urban population allocation, we adopt a tax (additional rent) r on land use in city t as well as a subsidy (negative additional rent) s on the same in city s, and self-financing of this tax-subsidy policy. The reason why we prefer these measures to a physical zoning policy is that the former policy can avoid the arbitrariness under physical zoning in selecting permitted developers.[4] Assuming $Y_t = Y_s$ $(=Y)$ additionally, for the sake of simplicity, we have the following system:

$$R_0 = r + k_t(N_t) \cdot q_t(N_t) = -s + k_s q_s(N_s)\,, \quad r, s > 0\,, \tag{21}$$

$$rN_t = sN_s\,, \tag{22}$$

$$N_t + N_s = \bar{N}\,. \tag{23}$$

Here $q_i(N_i)$ is the inverse function of $Q_i(s_i)$, the accommodation function, $i =$ t, s. This system can be solved for r, s, and N_s when N_t is given.

From the viewpoint of the society as a whole, the criterion of efficiency should be the minimization of the total transportation cost in the above case of equal income endowment among people. The latter problem can be formulated as

$$\min_{\langle N_t \rangle} \left[\int_0^{N_t} k_t(N_t) \cdot q_t(x)\, \mathrm{d}x + \int_0^{\bar{N}-N_t} k_s \cdot q_s(x)\, \mathrm{d}x \right]. \tag{24}$$

The optimizing condition is

$$k_t(N_t) \cdot q_t(N_t) + k_t'(N_t) \int_0^{N_t} q_t(x)\, \mathrm{d}x - k_s \cdot q_s(\bar{N} - N_t) = 0\,. \tag{25}$$

If there is no externality (i.e. $k_t' = 0$), combining Eq. (21) with Eq. (25) we have

$$r + s = 0\,. \tag{26}$$

[3] The denominator of Eq. (19) is bigger than that of Eq. (12).

[4] A similar argument was made by Brueckner concerning a development fee policy. See Breuckner (1990, p. 245). Also see Richardson and Gordon (1994).

Eq. (26) means the conventional wisdom that a market equilibrium without intervention ($r = s = 0$) is optimal under the absence of externality.

Even if the criterion of efficiency is switched to the minimization of each city's central rent, R_0 (equivalent to the maximization of residents' utility), we can obtain the same result ($r = s = 0$) in this model. Let us discuss this assertion in the following.

By Eqs. (21), (22), and (23), we can deduce the single equation for r and N_s as follows:

$$r\bar{N} = \{k_s q_s(N_s) - k_t(\bar{N} - N_s) \cdot q_t(\bar{N} - N_s)\}N_s \,. \tag{27}$$

From this equation we can calculate dN_s/dr and then dR_0/dr as follows:

$$\frac{dR_0}{dr} = \frac{\{k_s q_s' N_s - k_t q_t' N_t + (k_s q_s - k_t q_t)\} - k_t' q_t N_t}{(k_s q_s' + k_t' q_t + k_t q_t')N_s + (r + s)} \,. \tag{28}$$

First, we examine the case of no externality (i.e. $k_t' = 0$). We assume that the efficiency condition, $r + s = k_s q_s - k_t q_t = 0$, is holding in the beginning. In addition, for a linear or circular city for which we can have a well-behaved $q(\cdot)$ function (i.e. $q = \alpha N$ or $q = \beta N^{1/2}$), we can show that the expression in curly brackets in the numerator of Eq. (28) becomes zero and then $dR_0/dr = 0$.[5] Therefore, a policy of no intervention is also desirable from the viewpoint of the residents' utility.

The reason for this equivalence is that, for these well-behaved accommodation functions, there is a fixed relation between the total transportation cost and the total land rents (see Arnott and Stiglitz, 1980). Since the total gross income ($TGI = \bar{N}Y$) of the residents in our model is divided into total consumption, total transportation cost (TTC), total capital expenditure ($\bar{N}P$, fixed), and total land rents (TR), maximization of the per capita consumption of a private good ($(TGI - TTC - TR - \bar{N}P)/\bar{N}$) is equivalent to the minimization of TTC if TR is a given increasing function of TTC. Under the circumstances, the residents' utility maximization, which may induce some endogenous growth control policy, is not contrary to social efficiency.[6]

Secondly, if $k_t' > 0$, starting from the situation of a market equilibrium with a well-shaped $q_i(N_i)$, $i = $ t, s, in which $r = s = 0$ and the expression in curly brackets $= 0$, an increase in r induces a decrease in R_0 ($dR_0/dr < 0$) by Eq. (28), (i.e. an increase in the residents' utility). Under this situation the growth control policy is justified from the viewpoint of the residents' utility.

[5] In the case of a linear city, for example, $q_i = \alpha N_i$ ($i =$ t, s). Therefore, $k_s q_s - k_t q_t = 0$ implies $N_t = [k_s/(k_s + k_t)]\bar{N}$ and $N_s = [k_t/(k_s + k_t)]\bar{N}$ as well as $k_t q_t' N_t = k_s q_s' N_s$.

[6] A detailed analysis of endogenous growth control policy is given in Epple et al. (1988).

4. Population control policy in the growth process

In this section we only consider a linear city case and we give a concrete expression to the function $k_t(N_t)$, i.e.

$$k_t(N_t) = k_t + \theta N_t . \tag{29}$$

In addition, we assume that, as a result of economic growth in Tokyo, there will now be a gap g between Y_t and Y_s. Then in the right-hand side of Eq. (21), there will be an additional constant, g. In this case, instead of the system of Eqs. (21), (22) and (23), we have the system

$$R_0 = r + (k_t + \theta N_t)N_t = g - s + k_s N_s , \tag{30}$$

$$rN_t = sN_s . \tag{31}$$

By these equations we can solve r in the form

$$r = \frac{(\bar{N} - N_t)\{g - (k_t + k_s)N_t - \theta N_t^2 + k_s \bar{N}\}}{\bar{N}} . \tag{32}$$

Then putting (32) into (30) we have

$$\begin{aligned} R_0 &= \frac{1}{\bar{N}}[(\bar{N} - N_t)\{g - (k_t + k_s)N_t - \theta N_t^2 + k_s \bar{N}\} + (k_t N_t + \theta N_t^2)\bar{N}] \\ &= \frac{1}{\bar{N}} \psi(N_t) . \end{aligned} \tag{33}$$

Minimizing R with respect to N_t we have

$$\frac{d\psi}{dN_t} = 3\theta N_t^2 + 2(k_t + k_s)N_t - (2K_s \bar{N} + g) = 0 . \tag{34}$$

(Furthermore, we have $d^2\psi/dN_t^2 = 6\theta N_t + 2(k_t + k_s) > 0$ as a sufficient condition of the minimum R.)

From Eq. (34), the optimal value of N_t is deduced as

$$N_t^{\#} = \frac{-(k_t + k_s) + \sqrt{(k_t + k_s)^2 + 3\theta(2k_s \bar{N} + g)}}{3\theta} . \tag{35}$$

On the other hand, the non-intervention solution in this case is the solution of the system of Eqs. (30) and (31) in which $r = s = 0$, and it is

$$\tilde{N}_t = \frac{-(k_t + k_s) + \sqrt{(k_t + k_s)^2 + 4\theta(k_s \bar{N} + g)}}{2\theta} . \tag{36}$$

It is easily shown that $N_t^{\#} < \tilde{N}_t$. This is a direct indication of an endogenous growth control policy.

5. Concluding remarks

In this paper we have shown that (i) from the viewpoint of efficient resource allocation, urban growth control policy is justified when there are (population) sized-related externalities,[7] (ii) if an urban growth control policy is needed at all events, some market intervention has been necessary *before* growth in order to achieve the optimal allocation of population between cities,[8] and (iii) if there is no (per capita) income gap between two cities and if there is no externality in both cities, maximization of the residents' utility results in the social optimum in the sense of the minimization of the total transportation cost. An income gap and/or externality may disturb this equivalence.

Acknowledgements

The author is grateful to two anonymous referees for their valuable comments on an earlier version of this paper. Needless to say, the author is solely responsible for remaining errors.

[7] The relationship between the optimal population and another type of externality, i.e. the provision of the public good, was analyzed by Fischel (1978).

[8] Size-related externalities could be absent at the initial stage of urban growth. If this is so, a growth control policy is not needed at the beginning but will become necessary later. The infrastructure of a city is, however, usually small at the beginning proportionally to the size of the city population so that some intervention policy may be needed even at the early stage of urban growth.

References

Arnott, R. and J.E. Stiglitz, 1980, Aggregate land rents, aggregate transport costs and expenditure on public goods, Quarterly Journal of Economics 97, 471–500.

Brueckner, J.K., 1990, Growth controls and land values in an open city, Land Economics 66, no. 3, 237–248.

Engle, R., P. Navarro and R. Carson, 1992, On the theory of growth controls, Journal of Urban Economics 32, 269–283.

Epple, D., T. Romer and R. Filimon, 1988, Community development with endogenous land use controls, Journal of Public Economics 35, 133–162.

Fischel, W.A., 1978, A property rights approach to municipal zoning, Land Economics 54, no. 1, 64–81.

Henderson, J.V., 1987, Systems of cities and inter-city trade, in: J. Lesourne and H. Sonnenschein, eds., Systems of cities and facility location, Fundamentals of pure and applied economics vol. 22 (Harwood Academic Publishers, Chur, Switzerland).

Richardson, H.W. and P. Gordon, 1994, Market planning: Oxymoron or common sense, Journal of American Planning Association 59, no. 3, 347–352.

MIX
Papier aus verantwortungsvollen Quellen
Paper from responsible sources
FSC® C105338

If you have any concerns about our products,
you can contact us on
ProductSafety@springernature.com

In case Publisher is established outside the EU,
the EU authorized representative is:
Springer Nature Customer Service Center GmbH
Europaplatz 3, 69115 Heidelberg, Germany

Printed by Libri Plureos GmbH
in Hamburg, Germany